Follow Your Heart

Follow Your Heart

Memories of a Hellish Childhood by
Frances Louise Armbrust

ISBN 1-58597-391-2

Library of Congress Control Number: 2006927459

LEATHERS PUBLISHING
4500 College Boulevard
Overland Park, Kansas 66211
888-888-7696
www.leatherspublishing.com

I DEDICATE THIS BOOK to my children, grandchildren and great-grandchildren, especially those who thought I was too hard on them during their growing up years. Sometimes it meant your life for you to mind and mind immediately. I realize you didn't or couldn't understand this at the time. I did what I had to do to keep you safe, fed and clothed. I know our life journey was tough, but for some people it just happens that way. We made it, though, didn't we? You are all grown up, with families of your own – count your blessings. I pray that life's journey will be easier for each of you. I want all of you to know that I am proud of you, and I love you very much. Keep on helping each other, and don't lose track of one another. May Jehovah God bless you and keep you in His heart forever.

I would like to give a special thanks to everyone that helped us along life's rough road. Thanks to you, I didn't cave in, and I will finish my journey in peace. I owe special thanks to Mrs. Bermingham, Mrs. Martin, Uncle Arthur, Wealthy (my mother-in-law) and the man who owned the restaurant on Wells Street in Chicago. Thanks to all of you, I made it. I raised my children to adulthood, and most of them are doing well. I want you to know that I have followed your examples and helped as many people as I could on this rough road of life.

Last, but not least, I thank God for my husband, George, the only man that could have put up with all my faults, my family and my funny ways. I know Jehovah God has a special place in His heart for George.

I Samuel 16:7

God sees not as man sees,
for man looks at the outward appearance,
but God looks at the heart.

INTRODUCTION

THE SIX OLDEST children in my family were born in show tents. Our parents did not register our births when we were born. They did not have the time or money to worry about such "trifling" matters. According to Mother, when they lost a child, they dug a hole and buried the child wherever they were camped. She said, "I have three children buried in this way."

I can only approximate the dates of birth and ages of my siblings and myself. There are no accurate records of some of our births. I have at least 21 siblings from three different women – the woman I call "Mother," the woman I call "Aunt Joe" and my sister, Vesta, who was just a girl. My father, Otis Patten, fathered at least 17 of my siblings.

I know the true mother of only seven of the children. The women, themselves, didn't seem to know which children belonged to them. I believe they just didn't want to accept the responsibility for us. We were physically, emotionally and sexually abused. Father performed abortions on all four of us girls whom he had impregnated. We were kept isolated and didn't go to school. Our parents deliberately kept us children ignorant. We were punished severely for talking to anyone other then our siblings. We were even tied to trees while our siblings threw rocks at us, as a punishment. If Father knew about friends, we could no longer play with them.

My mother and father often talked about a traveling show they had owned. They called it "The Bare Cat Ramblers." Father said, "Kitty walked the tight rope. [Mother was called 'Kitty,' or 'Katie.'] Aunt Joe and I were clowns. We lived in show tents and cooked outside, like the Indians used to do. We traveled all over the United States. I enjoyed this a great deal. That is the best way to live."

I don't remember the traveling show business. My older sister, Vesta, told me she remembered it. She said, "I worried about Mother falling off the tight wire when she walked on it. No matter how Mother felt or how pregnant she was, she walked the tight wire. Father sometimes had me sing for the people while he played the guitar."

I looked at my mother as something that could break if a person wasn't very careful with her. You had to be careful and not make her angry because she might hurt herself, and then you would be in trouble. She was very beautiful. She not only looked beautiful, but she "acted beautiful." Every last hair on her head had to be just so; when she sat, her dress had to lay just right. When speaking with other people, she talked differently than she did when speaking to the family. We children considered her to be a special person. When she gave you any kind of attention, it made you feel special too, for that moment. She was easily irritated, and Aunt Joe usually let her have her way.

Mother didn't do much around the house except for some cooking, especially if we were to have company. She loved to fix my hair in long corkscrew curls that she made by combing my hair around her finger. She liked doing this because people gave her attention over my curly hair. People always told her how pretty my hair was, and this made her smile.

Once, a Salvation Army woman brought clothes to Mother for us to wear. My father didn't like it when Mother accepted them. Mother and Aunt Joe seemed to be afraid of making my father angry. If either of them thought something had happened that might displease him, you could feel the tension.

Father was the only person who could hurt Mother, unless he asked for Aunt Joe's help. Many times he did ask for Aunt Joe's help, I believe, just to intimidate Mother. My mother didn't fight him back very often; she just took her punishment like a child. I believe the times that she fought back are the times that I can remember the reasons they were fighting and what was said. Aunt Joe and Father treated her like she was a "dummy," and Mother resented this.

Grandmother and Grandfather Cahala were the parents of Mother and Aunt Joe. Grandmother Cahala. was a large Indian woman. It appeared to me that she was the "boss" of her house. Grandfather Cahala was a small, quiet, Irish man. He might have been four feet tall. He had a dirty mouth, which made my grandmother angry. Grandfather was also blind. He knew every inch of his farm, though, and could do anything that anyone else could do, but we just had to be careful not to leave sticks or toys lying around that he might trip over.

Aunt Joe was a large woman and very demanding, like her mother in many ways. Mother was small like her father. She did whatever my father and Aunt Joe told her to do. Aunt Lois was a deaf and mute younger sister to Mother and Aunt Joe. She was always a shy, timid person. Uncle Junior, Mother's brother, was older than Aunt Lois by a few years. Aunt Dorothy was Mother's baby sister. There were more uncles and aunts, but these were the ones living in Grandfather's house at the time.

Grandmother and my mother often argued over my age. Mother told me, "Aunt Dorothy is a few months older than you."

Grandmother said, "She is two years and eight months older than Frances is."

It is confusing when your family argues over your age. Who do you listen to? I had more faith in what my grandmother and Aunt Joe said. Many times it seemed as though Mother didn't understand what went on around her, or maybe she just didn't care.

I can't, for the life of me, remember what Father looked like. When I try to remember him, I feel like a bowl of jelly inside, and all the bad things he did to me come rushing into my mind. It is as though I am that scared little child waiting to die any minute again, or praying he wouldn't kill my sister. I don't know if I am afraid to remember, or if I just hate him so much that I can't remember.

What I do remember about him is that almost everyone was afraid of him, as they always did his bidding. When we had company from his work, he played the guitar or violin and sometimes drew beautiful pictures for us children. But that was only when he wanted to impress someone, such as his boss. He was an intelligent man and seemed to be able to do anything he wanted to do.

My grandparents owned property thirty-five miles from Antigo, Wisconsin. Trees surrounded their house. I loved to visit them. I could hide in the trees or behind a bush and my father and mother couldn't find me. I often did this if I thought I was in trouble.

When I couldn't run away and hide, I ran to Grandmother. She never let my parents or Aunt Joe hurt me. Spanking was all right, but beatings were out of the question, as far as Grandmother was concerned. Life at her house was good; I felt she loved and wanted us. We were treated with kindness and allowed to be children.

At this time in my life, I feared my father and Aunt Joe with all my heart. I also looked up to my father and believed he could do anything he wanted to do, and no one could stop him. I feared Aunt Joe, but not to the same degree as I feared Father. She could be kind at times.

I have had a desire to please people all my life, and I feel helpless and afraid when I fail to do so. I have tried to give my children everything I could possibly give them. Most of the time, that wasn't very much. What I had most to give them was love.

When my children became teenagers and rebelled, I became afraid of them. I tried not to let them know this. My husband and I just plain spoiled the last two children, along with my grandson, Christopher, and granddaughter, Audriannia, of whom I have guardianship.

I was able to have some success in life with the help of my foster mother, Mrs. Bermingham, who taught me the importance of getting an education, and how to love and trust a few people.

With the help of my mother-in-law, Wealthy, I was able to learn the skills needed in life to care for my children, and keep my children and myself alive in this world. These skills didn't come easily. I owe Wealthy a lot and didn't even know enough to realize it or to say thank you.

Now that I am getting older, I would like to play with my grandchildren and great-grandchildren, without having to take responsibility for their care. My ultimate goal is to do some traveling, while I am still physically able to do so. It would be nice to take one of my grandchildren with me from time to time, as I would enjoy this very much.

But first, I need to tell my story...

CHAPTER ONE

WE LIVED ON the third floor of an apartment building on Armitage Street, in Chicago. Mr. and Mrs. Newman, friends of Mother's, lived upstairs, and Aunt Joe lived with us. The Coffman store sat on the corner.

My first memory is of Aunt Joe sitting me on a round table to comb my hair. The table tipped over and some dishes broke. Mother and Aunt Joe fought over the broken dishes. Mother said, "You stupid imbecile! You ornery bitch! How many times do I have to tell you not to sit the kids on the table?"

Aunt Joe retaliated by saying, "At least I have the good sense to care for them. I don't sit on my ass, reading all day."

Mother and Aunt Joe continued to argue until Father came into the dining room and put a stop to it. He told them, "Stop acting like children."

They got busy cleaning up the mess that Aunt Joe and I had made. I was just scratched, but Mother and Aunt Joe's fighting gave me a terrible headache, so I cried.

Mother and Aunt Joe often fought over who was going to sleep with Father. Sometimes they both slept with him. One night Father wanted Mother and Aunt Joe to sleep with us children, and Vesta, my oldest sister, to sleep with him. I will never forget the fight that took place that night. Someone called the police. Mother and Aunt Joe stepped out of the window and stood on the ledge outside, so the policemen couldn't see them. Father said, "All you kids, pretend to be asleep." We obeyed quickly, and not a sound was made by any of us.

Father answered the door. The police looked around our house and found only the mess they had made while fighting. They looked in our closets with flashlights. When they left, Mother and Aunt Joe stepped back in the window. I could see how badly they were beaten. They both slept with us children. Vesta slept with Father, alone. I could hear her crying, and I wondered why she was unhappy. I felt sorry for her, but there was nothing I could do to make her feel better. I got a wet washcloth and wiped away some of the blood from my mother's face as she cried. I lay beside her until she fell asleep, and then I went to my hiding place in the closet and finally fell asleep.

All the children on the block liked to play in front of the Coffman's grocery store. Sometimes Mr. Coffman gave us candy, and he always told me how pretty and cute I was. Mrs. Coffman let me hold the dustpan for her while she cleaned the floor in the store at night. She always bragged about what a good helper I was and rewarded me with a piece of candy. I enjoyed the attention they gave to me.

Sometimes the fire hydrant in front of the Coffman's store would spew out a lot of water. It was as if someone had turned on a big faucet. All the children liked to play in the water during the summer.

Mr. Coffman didn't like it when we drew hopscotch on the sidewalk in front of his store. In the winter when we had snowball fights in front of his store, he would be unhappy with us. That was the only time he yelled at us kids.

Mostly, it was the bigger kids that did that kind of thing. The smaller children sat on the curb and played in the mud a lot, and we made ourselves awfully dirty. This made Mother and Aunt Joe angry. They had to get us cleaned up before Father got home. Father didn't want us playing outside. He didn't want us to have any friends, or talk to anyone other than the family. He said, "One of you will say the wrong thing and get me into a lot of trouble. What happens in this house is no one's business, but mine. Do all of you understand this?"

Mother and Aunt Joe worked as nurses' aids on different shifts. Mother was also taking an L.P.N. course through the American School of Home Nursing. Mother said, "Father was a lawyer and he graduated from a law school in Terre Haute, Indiana. He was also a member of the Bar Association." Mother told all of our neighbors that my father was a lawyer. This must have been important to her. I sensed that this made her feel like she, too, was important and not as dumb as Father and Aunt Joe claimed she was. Mother proved this by getting her nursing degree.

Mother was also proud when Father played the violin and guitar, while Vesta sang. We would all gather around and listen to them. I loved it when the family could sit in the same room and not fight. Sometimes, my father would draw pretty pictures for us kids. This didn't happen often, unless we had company that our father was trying to impress. It was, indeed, a rare treat. I could tell how happy this made Mother; she seemed to glow all over. I wanted to sing also when I got older, like my sister, if only Father would let me take lessons. I love music and wanted to play the guitar too.

When Father was at work, Mother and Aunt Joe locked any child that could walk, outside. I remember begging Mother to let me in the apartment to use the bathroom, but she refused. I went in the alley behind Mr. Coffman's store. Mr. Coffman caught me and bawled me out. I cried and he gave me a donut. He said, "Never do that again; it is very dangerous." From that day on, he let me go to the bathroom in his store. I learned to love this old couple.

I remember a time when everyone was looking for my sister, Delores. She was found in the basement, hiding in the coal bin with coal all over her. Delores was crying and had blood on her dress. Mother became very upset when she noticed that Father had coal dust all over him too. She told him, "You have molested Delores."

She seemed to be accusing my father of hurting my older sister, Delores. Delores acted like she was very afraid to stay in the same room with Father.

Aunt Joe said, "You rotten, cock-sucking, mother-fucking son-of-a-bitch! Don't you think the three of us are enough for you?" (Aunt Joe was talking about herself, Mother and my sister, Vesta.)

Mother said, "You rotten, dirty scoundrel; she is just a baby."

They fought for a long time. Father was mean, but this time I felt sorry for him. What had he done that made them treat him so badly? I didn't understand what all the fuss was about. Someone in the building called the police. When they knocked on the door, Mother opened the door and said, "Everything is okay." Mother picked Delores up off the floor and held her in her arms, covering her bloody dress with her apron.

The police asked a few questions, wrote on some paper and left. As they left, they said, "Keep the noise down. We are tired of answering the complaints coming from this apartment."

Mother wanted to take Delores to the doctor. Father said, "No fucking way. She is my daughter; I have certain rights. I can do what I want with her. Josephine, what the hell were you doing in the basement anyway?"

Aunt Joe said, "I was looking for your daughter and I found her, you son-of-a-bitch. Surely you can find someone a little older than this child."

Mother didn't take my sister to the doctor. She did, however, try to comfort her and bathed her. Mother didn't do this often, and even though I couldn't see anything wrong, this must have been something really bad. Delores slept with our mother and Aunt Joe that night.

I didn't blame Father for hurting them this time. Father ran from the apartment and didn't come back that night. Mother and Aunt Joe fed us supper and put us to bed. For a change, things were quiet. I couldn't sleep, so I crawled in the closet and dreamt about being at Grandmother Cahala's, my favorite place. The closet is where I always went when I was upset.

Father came home from work the next evening, and Aunt Joe had supper ready. Things seemed to be normal, just the usual fussing over who was sleeping with whom.

A few months went by and some kind of a problem came up over a woman at Father's office. Mother and Father fought. Father had what Mother called a suspension from work. Mother and Aunt Joe were not happy about this; it meant Father couldn't go to work for a while. I wondered if Father was happy.

The next day we rode a train to Grandmother Cahala's house in Pelican Lake, Wisconsin. I can still see the smoke from that train in my mind. I was afraid of the train, and this made Father angry. He was not in a good mood; he was still angry with Mother and Aunt Joe. He yelled at me and said, "I am going to beat your goddamn ass if you don't shut up!"

Mother said, "Shut up yourself; you are embarrassing me and everyone boarding this train. Not to mention the fact that you are making us look like white trash." Father backhanded Mother, and she said no more. Mother had her hands full with eight children at this time. Five of us were very small.

After we boarded the train, it was fun to watch things go flying past us and to watch the different ways that people dressed and acted. My parents were quiet, not speaking to anyone.

When we got to Grandmother's, she gave all of us a big hug, as she always did when we visited her. While we were at Grandmother's, Father took a belt to me. I was small enough to run under the kitchen table and hide under Grandmother's dress without bumping my head on the table. Grandmother took a broom and hit my father with it. She chased him out in the yard. When she came back into the kitchen, one of her eyes was red. She said, "No one will take a belt to a baby in my house. I wonder how he treats these children at home? Well, he won't do it here!"

We stayed at Grandmother's until Father's suspension was over, and then we went back home where Aunt Joe was. She had stayed behind to work, and was able to keep the rent and utilities paid, so we would have a place to come back to.

Sometimes, when we were at Grandmother's house, we sat in the yard and listened to the adults talk. One evening, as we were sitting in the yard while the grownups talked, Father said, "You kids might want to gather around and listen to this too. Those of you old enough to understand might want to know something about your heritage some day."

He went on to say, "My mother was an Indian girl. Her Indian name was Blossom. Father called her Mary. When my father married my mother, he was disinherited from the family. No one in his family would let my father or me in their homes. He was physically kicked out of the family for marrying an Indian girl. My father was very unhappy. He was under a lot of pressure, and he started drinking moonshine. My mother didn't seem to mind the abuse that Father dished out. I remember asking her if she hurt after Father beat her during one of his drinking bouts. She said, 'It is a wife's duty to make her husband happy. If I can't do that, I need to be punished. I will always love your father.'

"While my father was drunk, he went with other women. Father's brother, Uncle Jerry, encouraged this. He had hoped Father would leave my mother and marry a white woman. He felt this would fix Father's relationship with the rest of the family. I guess my Uncle Jerry loved my father and was trying to help him. His intentions were good, but this made things worse. I can't blame him; I must put the blame where it belongs – on Father and me.

"When Mother found out about Father's unfaithfulness, Father hid all the knives in the house. He knew about the Indian traditions. He did everything he could under Indian law to keep Mother from hurting herself. He was only allowed to do so much without disgracing her more than he already had. Mother said, 'Son, find Mother a big kitchen knife and bring it to me.' I went and got a large knife where I had watched my father hide it and gave it to her. She stabbed herself in the stomach with it several times before she fell to the floor. My mother died before Father could get help for her. Mother committed suicide while her whole family watched because I gave her a knife my father had hidden. I had been taught to always mind my mother.

"She is buried in an unmarked grave somewhere near Guthrie, Oklahoma. I have always felt responsible for my mother's death. I can't even find her gravesite to put flowers on, or to tell her how sorry I am."

He spoke very softly, and I thought he was crying. "I was very young and had been taught to mind my parents. That is why I got the knife for my mother. I just didn't know any better; I thought I was being a good son. I was about three years old at the time. There are many Indians buried in unmarked graves.

"My father's family made fun of me and called me a half-breed. I wasn't very comfortable around them. You might say I grew up alone, and I learned to enjoy being alone. I just told the whole world to go to hell, and lived my life the way I wanted to. No one cared to try and stop me."

I thought this was a very sad story.

Vesta said, "Father, why didn't a grown person stop you from giving your mother the knife? If they were standing there, just watching and doing nothing, someone should have stopped you."

Father said, "It is Indian tradition: when a man is unfaithful to an Indian woman, the Indian woman kills herself to show how much she and her family were shamed. No one had the right to interfere with her actions. My father broke the law when he hid the knives from my mother. It was for that reason the tribe rejected me. Indian people have laws too. They are different from the white man's laws. The Indian people are a very proud people. She made the choice to protect her family's honor. She did what she thought she had to do, but I wish she had thought about me. I had to grow up without a mother. Her people refused to accept me as a part of them."

Delores and I whispered to each other, and wondered if this was what had made Father so mean.

La Verne asked, "Why didn't your father get a beautiful grave stone to mark her grave with?"

Father said, "It was against white man's law to mark an Indian's grave. You see, in those days, an Indian did not have the status of a white person's pet pig. White men chased the Indian people off their land, and then tried to annihilate them.

"The Indians could no longer provide food and shelter for their families. Indians were tortured, made fun of and allowed to die for lack of food. White men only gave them the lowest kinds of jobs. The United States government offered them handouts instead of allowing them to live and work on their own land. Many of the Indians refused the handouts. They were ashamed to accept welfare. The Indians only wanted the right to live on their land and be allowed to take care of their own families. Many Indian children died from the lack of food.

"White people are wasteful and greedy; they think only of what they want. They don't understand nature, or how to preserve wild life or the land. The Indians outsmarted the white people's government; the Indian people are smarter than white people. Today, the government of the United States pays the Indian people a monthly check for the suffering they caused them. The white people won the physical battle, but the Indian people won the moral battle.

"Today, most Indian people don't even know about their heritage. Only a few tribes have tried to preserve some heritage for their youth. They hold yearly celebrations, hoping this will help teach them the customs and beliefs of their ancestors. Many still live on reservations and still use their laws."

Another time while we were visiting Grandmother Cahala, Mother told us what her life had been like when she was a girl. She said, "Father lost his eyesight while he was still quite young. He had an eye disease that caused him to go blind."

Aunt Joe said, "A fire destroying their house and all of their belongings didn't help matters much. Grandmother was trying to save some of their belongings and wouldn't leave the house. Grandfather burned his eyes trying to get all the children and Grandmother out of the house."

Mother continued, "Before Father lost his eyesight, he had been a logger. He worked with several hundred men. They worked for long hours. Some of the men slept in tents; others slept in Father's barn. They had a very large tent they used as a kitchen and dining room. We were in good shape financially. We had everything we needed and almost everything we wanted; we were spoiled.

"When Father started to lose his eyesight, he still had to work. He even tried to work after he couldn't see at all. He nearly cut his leg off sawing down a tree. He had to quit working; things changed for my family at this time. We had no way to support ourselves; it was a rough time for us.

"I was the oldest child and was thirteen years old at the time. It was up to me to provide food to put on the table. To help keep my family from starving, it was necessary for me to work. I started cooking for the loggers. I cooked for at least two hundred men a day. It was long hours and hard work. I tried to serve breakfast at 6:00 a.m. I had to start breakfast at 4:00 a.m. to accomplish this.

I served supper around 6:00 p.m. After the men had eaten, it was my responsibility to wash all the dishes and clean things up. I was lucky if I finished by 10:00 p.m. I got so tired and my legs hurt at night. There were times when I didn't think I could make it through the day. My brothers kept us in firewood, and sometimes helped me clean up at night. This helped me a lot more than they realized; it gave me more time to sleep.

"The only transportation we had was a horse and wagon in the summer, and a horse and sled in the winter. It wasn't easy for people to move around. We walked almost everywhere we went. My sister, Fern, fell in a snowdrift and almost froze to death. The whole county looked for her.

"The winter my little brother died, the snow was so deep the horses couldn't get through. We couldn't go anywhere. Father couldn't take my little brother to the doctor. My parents might have been able to save him if the roads had not been impassable. When my brother died, my parents put him in the back room where it was cold. I often sneaked into the room at night after work. I stood by his bed and looked at my tiny little brother lying there, unable to move. When Mother found me standing beside my brother, she scolded me and made me leave the room.

"After the snow melted, we held a funeral in the town church, and buried him in Antigo. I went often to visit my little brother. I missed my baby brother; I prayed for God to give him back to us. I knew how much Mother missed him." By the tone of my mother's voice, I knew she missed her brother too.

Another time, I remember Father started to tell us about General George S. Patton. He said, "You are third cousins to General Patton." Father was very proud of his heritage. He told us that his father had changed the spelling of our name from "Patton" to "Patten" after he had been thrown out of the family for marrying Father's mother, an Indian woman.

Mother interrupted Father's story. She said, "You kids, don't believe a word of it! Don't believe your history books either. History books paint General Patton to be a great man. This is not true. Family rumors are that he was a very bad man. When he and his men captured a village, they killed all the men and boys. They took turns raping the young girls and women. They even raped the very young baby girls. They shot the girls and women that were still alive after they were through with them. The babies, they threw up in the air and caught them on the end of their bayonets. They sat in the camps and drank, having sex with the bodies of the women. They bragged about all the things they had done. And what they intended to do to the next village they captured."

Father said nothing; I could tell he was very angry. I think Father was afraid of Grandmother Cahala. Father would never have let Mother get away with this, otherwise. Mother really had her nerve to be brave enough to interrupt Father while he was talking. I wondered what Father would do to Mother when no one was looking. Mother didn't seem to be worried about it.

I was not happy about going to bed, but it was that time. I thought about the stories my parents had told us. I thought, perhaps, my father had never had the chance to learn how to love people. Maybe he did not understand how mean he really was. I worried about my mother because she had interrupted Father. I could still hear the adults talking when I fell asleep.

We left my grandparents' house when my uncle, Junior, heard Aunt Lois scream and went to check on her. He found my father in my Aunt Lois' bedroom. Aunt Lois had her pants off. Uncle Junior accused Father of doing something wrong to his sister, Lois. Father said, "I have done nothing wrong; I have not touched the little bitch."

There was a lot of confusion. This was a big issue between my grandparents, my parents and Aunt Joe. Grandfather ran and got his long gun. I was very frightened. I crawled under Aunt Lois' bed, and the other children ran downstairs. We were all very frightened. Grandfather had never done this before. He could not even see. He could have shot anyone; he could go only by our voices.

My grandparents wanted Aunt Joe to stay home with them, but Aunt Joe refused saying, "Otis is my man too and, in fact, he would rather have me than Kitty [my mother]. I am going with my man."

Grandmother said, "Is this what you want, Kitty?"

Mother said, "I need her to help care for these kids."

Grandmother said, "You are my daughters; I love you. This man is no good. You are both playing the role of a wife to this man. Now he wants Lois! What is happening to this world? You are no better than he is. May God have mercy on your children!"

Grandfather pointed his gun at Father and said, "Get out before I shoot all of you in the ass! Don't ever come back."

I crawled out from under Aunt Lois' bed, where I had crawled when all the fuss had begun. Grandmother said, "Get out, all of you. I don't want to see any of you again." I felt like our grandmother hated us because of something Father had done.

We rode the train back to Chicago. It wasn't pleasant; I could feel the tension between the adults. They were cranky and short with us children. We were told not to talk to Mr. and Mrs. Coffman or Mr. and Mrs. Newman about what had happened at our grandparents' house. No one had to remind us not to talk out of school. We already knew better. Vesta slept with my father until Mother and Aunt Joe were no longer angry with my father.

When we misbehaved, Mother said, "If you children don't behave, I will put all of you in an orphanage. An orphanage isn't a good place to be. Children are treated very badly. They have no food or clothes. They get very cold in the winter; they have no blankets to keep them warm. No one to care how uncomfortable they are; no one loves them. The children are made to do all the work." We believed she would really do this, and we feared it with all our hearts.

One night as mother was telling us this story, my sister, Vesta, mumbled under her breath. She said, "There are eight of us children in this room. You guys are fighting like fools in the other room. And you have the audacity to yell at me to go to sleep. What a joke! Do you really expect me to be able to sleep? Grow up, why don't you? Go ahead, put me in an orphanage; see if I care. It has to be better then living in this hellhole. Why can't we live like other people? Other kids can talk to each other in school. I would at least like to be able to talk to the other kids."

My parents' fighting upset me and it made my head hurt. It

hurt so badly, I felt like I was going to vomit. It felt like my head was hanging off the bed. I thought, "Why couldn't they just stop fighting?" In my head I was screaming, "Stop! Stop! Please stop fighting and making so much noise. I can't stand it any more."

I vomited all over the bed, and Aunt Joe was mad. She slapped me in the face as she cleaned up the mess. She had to get all the children out of bed and change the sheets. Everyone was crying, and this made my head hurt more.

When she was finished making the bed, she said, "Be quiet and listen. I will tell you a story." She told us this story often. Aunt Joe told us the story of Raw Hide and Bloody Bones. That was her favorite story to tell us. It was a very frightening story and scared us half to death.

She said, "There are two wild men that roam the streets and alleys at night, listening for the children that are not asleep. Their names are Raw Hide and Bloody Bones. They have special powers, and can climb any building and walk through any wall. As they roam the streets and alleys at night, if they hear a child making any noise at all, they walk through the walls and eat the child. Raw Hide will eat the flesh off your bones. Raw Hide gives your bloody bones to Bloody Bones, who eats all your bones, even the very small ones. Not one piece of bone is left. When the parents come to wake the children in the morning for breakfast, they find a note pinned to the pillow saying, 'Raw Hide and Bloody Bones have been here. Keep your children quiet or we will eat them. We are still hungry; we must find more naughty kids. Keep your children quiet. We get hungry when they wake us. Good night and good luck. Let us sleep in peace tomorrow, and you will keep your children.'"

Aunt Joe said, "Go to sleep if you want to be here in the morning." We were very quiet.

One night while we were sleeping, the ceiling fell down. All eight of us children got plaster in our eyes. We were frightened, and we didn't understand what had happened. Mother and Aunt Joe cleaned the plaster out of our eyes. They shook out our bedding and tried to make us go back to bed. We were afraid to do that, so all eight of us were crying.

Father got angry and said to Mother, "Sweep the plaster out from under the bed, and let them sleep under their beds so I can get some sleep."

We slept under the bed that night. Mother said, "I will take them to Mother's tomorrow until the ceiling is fixed."

Father replied, "No, you won't! Your parents will never see any of these kids again. Don't ask me again. Do you understand? Do you? "

After Father went to work, Mother put us on a train and took us to Grandmother Cahala's. Our grandparents tried to refuse to take care of us. Mother told them about the ceiling falling on us. Finally Grandmother said, "Okay, if things are really that bad. We don't want the children to suffer. It isn't their fault what you fools do. Come on, children. You too, Kitty. I'll fix us something to eat. But mind you, you come after them as soon as possible."

We ate and Mother left in the cab she had waiting. She said, "I have to leave now, so I can catch my train. I promise to come after the children as soon as it is possible. Thank you, Mother." I wondered how much trouble Mother would get into for disobeying Father. I prayed he didn't hurt her. We were put to bed, and I went to sleep promptly. I woke fresh and ready to get into mischief the next morning.

I climbed up a tree and couldn't get down. Orlando ran to get Grandfather. Grandfather got a ladder and helped me down. He said to the boys, "The difference between boys and girls is boys have an elephant trunk between their legs, and girls have a slit. That is what makes boys smarter than girls. A girl should never climb a tree; girls are supposed to act like young ladies. They should learn to cook and sew for their families. That is the way it should be."

Too soon, the ceiling was fixed and Aunt Joe came to get us. I cried to be allowed to stay. Many times it was noisy at Grandmother and Grandfather Cahala's, especially when Father and Mother and Aunt Joe weren't there. But it was a pleasant kind of noise, the noise of children playing.

At home there was constant fighting, bickering and cursing, and we were afraid to play and make noise. I could feel the tension ne family. Neighbors were always yelling at the people in our apartment to be quiet. People didn't seem to like us. I felt nervous and afraid most of the time. Just a little peace and quiet would have been good; a hug would have felt really good.

I never knew when someone was going to get mad for who knew what, and come after one of us kids. I felt safer outside, playing in front of the Coffman store, than I did in our apartment with our parents. Sometimes when the neighbors called the police on my parents, I was afraid the police might take us to an orphanage. Mother always threatened to do this to us. Not knowing what might happen next is not an easy way to live. It is very frightening and uncomfortable. Every time there was a problem, we were sent to Grandmother Cahala's.

One night, we spent the night with Aunt Fern and Uncle Guy. They lived in another part of Chicago. Like our house, there was some fighting, cursing and discontent in their home. I didn't feel the presence of love and gentleness. Children needed to stay away from the adults as much as possible.

Uncle Guy wasn't so bad, but it was best to stay out of Aunt Fern's hair. They had two daughters, Gloria and Beverly. Gloria got sick to the stomach during the night. She tried to run to the bathroom, but didn't make it and vomited on the floor. Aunt Fern said, "Shit, you ornery little brat, you didn't have to do that." She spanked Gloria and made her clean up the vomit. When I tried to help Gloria, I got spanked too.

Aunt Fern was a big woman like Aunt Joe, but heavier. She had bushy, red, curly hair, and she looked like a witch to me. I didn't like her, but I loved to play with Gloria and Beverly. They were different than their parents. They were easy to get along with, and were not tattletales like some kids. We got into plenty of mischief together, but we enjoyed it. We didn't get together very often.

My only friend's name was Linda. She lived in the same apartment building as we did. Sometimes when Father wasn't home, Mother and Aunt Joe let me visit her. Her mother bathed me and dressed me up in nice clothes. I went to the zoo with Linda and her mother a few times. I always enjoyed visiting them because their house was so peaceful and quiet. I could feel the difference in their attitudes, and it was a soothing feeling. They hugged us kids once in a while.

When Father learned Mother was allowing me to visit Linda, it made him angry. I wasn't allowed to visit Linda any more. Father went to Linda's apartment and fought with Linda's father. Father told him, "If I catch you even looking at, let alone speaking to, a member of my family you will pay the price. Get the drift? Huh? Do you get the drift? I had better never hear of my daughter being in your apartment again. My daughter is not even allowed to speak to you or anyone else in this building. For your sake, I hope you understand my meaning."

After that day, when I passed Linda or her family in the hall, they wouldn't speak to me or even look at me. They looked down at the floor and walked past me. I was embarrassed by what my father had done, and I missed playing with Linda. I was sad and confused; I thought her parents didn't like me any more. What had I done? Why did Linda act differently toward me? Why had Father been so mean to my friends? I liked to have friends to play with, didn't Father understand that? Why couldn't he understand how I felt; couldn't Mother explain it to him? I didn't understand. I was happier and safer in Linda's apartment than I was on the street.

A few of our neighbors moved from the apartment house. We had never heard that kind of chaos from them. They seemed happy to be leaving the apartment.

I played outside and even though I didn't play with the children in the neighborhood, I was still playing among them when I was locked out of the apartment. I didn't mix well with other children. How could I when I was not allowed to talk to them? I stayed as far away from them as I could, and still played in the mud and fire hydrant when it spewed water. It was fun to get messy. Sometimes it was fun to listen to Mother and Aunt Joe complain about us getting so messy, until they got really angry and whipped us for being so dirty. I often got whipped for talking to people; I just couldn't keep my mouth shut.

Mother always let us in the apartment when it was time for

Father to come home. I wondered if he knew that we were locked out of the apartment every day. If he didn't know, I wasn't going to tell him. Father might go downstairs and hurt Mr. Coffman. I liked playing outside, especially now that Mr. Coffman let me use his bathroom when I needed to. Also, many times Mr. Coffman would feed us. If I couldn't play with Linda any more, I wanted to keep my friendship with the Coffman's. I wasn't supposed to talk to anyone. Father couldn't find out about my friends, Mr. and Mrs. Coffman; that had to be our secret.

One night, Mother got very angry when my father wanted Aunt Joe and Vesta to sleep together with him. Father had already slept alone with Vesta. She didn't like it; I had heard her cry. He wanted Mother to sleep with us girls, and Mother did not like this. Father and Aunt Joe beat Mother very badly, and Mother slept with us girls. Vesta slept with Father and Aunt Joe. My mother seemed mad at Vesta and Aunt Joe. Vesta didn't want to sleep with Father, but he made her do it anyway. My sister was crying and I felt sorry for her.

My mother was crying and bleeding. I rubbed her with lotion. As I tried to comfort my mother, I asked, "What is the big deal about sleeping with Father?"

Mother said, "You can't understand; you will learn soon enough. Go to sleep." I listened to Vesta cry, and I wondered what difference it made where she slept. I hoped Father never wanted to sleep with me.

Another memory I have was of a time when we went to a Christmas party where my father worked. My parents and Aunt Joe stood on a stage and put on a show. They colored their skin black and made fun of the African American people. The only white skin you could see was around their eyes. They looked and acted very silly. The people clapped and clapped, and acted like they enjoyed it.

I was worried about my parents hurting someone's feelings. I sure hoped that there were no black people there. I looked around and didn't see any. I was maybe four years old. I was ashamed of my parents and Aunt Joe that night. It is not nice to make fun of people; God made them who they are. When I played on the street, all the children played together. They made fun of no one. (Except for the Patten children, we were not supposed to play with anyone, so most of us stayed away from the group. This was different; we were told to play with the other children.)

Every child at the party received at least two gifts from Santa Claus. I received a beautiful doll that I loved. By mistake, I also received a green combine that had working parts. I was really fascinated by the way that combine worked, and I thought it was really neat. The boys received toy cars, trucks, trains and airplanes. Every boy seemed to be satisfied except my brother, Orlando. Orlando started making a fuss because he wanted my combine. I called him a brat, so Mother made me give it to him. When she went back to the party, I took my combine away from him. I tore it in as many pieces as I could, and I threw it in the trash with the used wrapping paper. My little brother soon forgot about the combine. I don't think anyone found out I had torn the toy combine up; at least I didn't get in trouble for it.

We stayed up late that night, and we ate and drank until we could not eat or drink any more. Some of the kids fell asleep on the floor. Everyone had a good time.

When we got home things turned into turmoil and every child was crying. Father took the toys away from us. I couldn't figure out why Father wanted to do this. But frankly, it made me mad as hell and I wanted to try my hand at fighting him, but I was afraid to.

Mother and Aunt Joe just stood by and let him do this. How could they do this? I believed he was just drunk and wanted to mistreat us. We were never allowed to play with our new toys. What Father said went; right or wrong, it made no difference.

Mother gave our toys to a Salvation Army lady. I wanted to scream out, "No! No! I want my doll!" I was afraid to cry. My beautiful doll was gone; all the toys were gone. I thought, "Why? Tell me why? I need my doll. I love her. Give her back to me!"

I hated Mother at that moment. She should have taken up for us children when Father took away our toys. I believe that was my first doll. I never had another doll that I can remember.

Not long after the Christmas party, Mother took me to preschool. Mother always combed my hair around her finger and made long curls. My teacher wanted Mother to braid my hair. Every day my teacher remarked on my hair; she called me the "want-to-be-princess." This caused the other children to pick on me. One day Aunt Joe braided my hair, and my teacher had me get up in front of the class and turn around so everyone could see my braids. She said, "Our want-to-be-princess is a peasant, like the rest of us today." I was very embarrassed standing in front of the class.

The next day when Mother fixed my hair, I wanted her to braid it, but she wouldn't. I cried and Mother wanted an explanation. I told her what the teacher was saying about my hair. Mother went to school with me that day. I could hear Mother yelling at the teacher, as I stood out in the hall. I couldn't understand what she was saying. I could tell by the way she was yelling, she was mad. Boy, was she ever mad! That was the only time I remember my mother standing up for me. It made me proud, and I felt important too.

I didn't go to school after that day, until later when we lived on the farm. I played all day on the streets of Chicago, unless Father was home. When Father was home, we had to sit quietly in the apartment. On these days I was miserable, but I was afraid to complain. The only time we were allowed to speak was if it was to make my parents look good. Otherwise, they believed a child should be seen, but never heard. We might say something to cause trouble to the family.

Once a week we went to a church, where the older girls took piano and singing lessons. The teacher, Mrs. Ray, had no patience with us. I didn't enjoy going there. I wanted to play the piano too, but Mrs. Ray refused to teach me, saying, "You are too young."

Mrs. Ray made all the children sit in the pews. She had the whole room full of children. She called the child's name when it was his or her turn to play the piano. This was piano lesson day for all the children in the church. Even the kids who were too young had to sit in the pews. We had to be polite and say, "Yes, Madam; no, Madam; yes, Sir; no, Sir; please; thank-you and excuse me," or we stood in the corner. We did have bathroom breaks; we had to stay there all day.

If we weren't good, Mrs. Ray made it a point to tell our parents.

She was a tattletale. If Mrs. Ray told Mother we had done something bad, Father whipped us with his belt. I would do anything to avoid that, and so would the other children. I truly dreaded piano and singing lesson day. Mostly, it was because I wasn't allowed to participate in the piano playing and singing. I didn't feel that I was too young to take lessons.

My sister, Delores, had a friend named Susan Degman. She played at the Coffman's store with us. She especially liked to play in the fire hydrants and help Delores draw pictures on the sidewalk with chalk. Sometimes children shared their chalk with other children. Mr. Coffman was always getting after them for messing up the sidewalk in front of his store. Susan and Delores were very close. They played together on the streets. This was the only child my sister played with. Susan's father didn't like my father, but he was nice to us children.

One night Susan was kidnapped out of her bedroom and killed. Her body was cut up in little pieces and hidden all over the city of Chicago. It took a long time for people to find her body parts. When I saw Susan's mother she hugged me and cried. Finally, they found all the parts of her body, except one of her hands. She was about five or six years old. My sister, Delores, missed her very much; Susan had been her only friend. Delores was very lonely, now that she didn't have a friend.

We attended Susan's funeral. Mother said, "It is proper." At her funeral, they had a red rose where her hand should have been. She was dressed up in a very pretty pink dress. But she did not look like Susan. Her parents were crying, and everyone else looked very sad. As we walked past her casket, Mother lifted me up so I could see Susan and say good-by to her. I kissed her on the cheek. Her skin did not feel right; it felt hard and cool, not warm like my skin.

I asked my mother why the rose was there and she said, "The police couldn't find that hand. The bad man killed her and cut her up in little pieces."

Susan's mother gave all of Susan's clothes to my sister, Delores. My father wouldn't let Delores wear them. Mother fussed about this and said, "It is wrong to throw such beautiful clothes away."

After Susan's death, Mother and Aunt Joe sometimes told us that if we didn't be quiet, the bad man who took Susan would come and get us, and do the same thing to us that he had done to Susan. I became very afraid of dying, after seeing what had happened to Susan. I was afraid to sleep in the bed. I started sleeping under the bed or in the closet. Of course, I got into trouble when I was caught. My sisters and brothers made fun of me and called me "chicken," "baby," "scaredy-cat" and everything else they could think of to hurt my feelings. My parents couldn't understand why I was so frightened. I started wetting myself at night.

After a while, the police came and talked to Mother, Father and Aunt Joe, as well as everyone in the apartment house, asking questions. They asked Mother questions about my father. They looked around our apartment using flashlights, and then left. I don't know what they were looking for or why they searched our apartment.

My father seemed very nervous. This frightened me even more. Father said, "Don't talk to the police. They are bad people."

Mother took us to Grandmother Cahala's again. Mother and Grandmother argued. While Grandmother tried to refuse, Mother said, "I have to hurry and catch my train." She left, leaving us with Grandmother.

I knew Grandmother did not want us there. You could tell that by the way she treated us. Something was different; she did not show us the same kind of attention. She didn't mistreat us, but the atmosphere was not the same. We still felt loved and wanted, however. I felt safe when I was with Grandmother because she watched us more closely.

One day Grandmother had a picture taken of us. She told us, "This will probably be the last time I will see you children. Please don't take lessons from your parents. Try to remember the things Grandma and Grandpa have taught you. Be good, all of you. If I never see you again, God bless you. I love you all. Never forget about your grandma and grandpa when your parents come to get you."

Aunt Joe came and got us. Aunt Joe didn't even stay to sleep. We rode the train home. On the way, she talked to me about the

Depression. She said, "Things were very hard. The government rationed all the food, supplies and gas. Each family could have only so much food. It didn't matter how big the family was; people couldn't buy food, even if they had money. Some people turned to violence to get food. They stole and killed people for food. It was a very dangerous time to live. It is still a dangerous time. It will take many years for people to recover from the Depression. Some people may never recover, especially all of the polio victims.

"You were born after the Depression was easing up a little, but we were still feeling the effects of it. You had a twin sister, named after Aunt Fern [Mother's and Aunt Joe's sister]. She died from polio and whooping cough at a year old. You were very sick. Your mother and I worked hard to keep you alive. Finally, the doctor said, 'There is nothing more I can do. Just keep her as comfortable as possible. She should not last long.' You are stubborn, and you refused to die. Kitty and I took turns staying up at night watching you. That is why you are so scrawny.

"The doctor brought his milk to you, and you began to get stronger. Without Dr. Brown's help, you would have died. Your mother had no milk in her breasts because we didn't have enough food for her body to produce milk. Dr. Brown saved your life by bringing his milk to you. Some people helped each other. It is never all bad, remember that. If you look hard enough and do not give up, you will find something good somewhere in this world – try to remember that.

"But I believe there is another reason you refused to die. You are different than the other kids. It's hard to explain to you."

My sister, La Verne, spoke up and said, "You can say that again. She is a brat."

Aunt Joe said, "Shut up and go back to sleep." Then she continued talking. She said, "Things are going to get rough for you kids. It will be worse for you than the Depression was for us. If any of you children survive, I believe you will. Otis is a hard man to live with. Never mind, you will find out when the time comes. There is someone 'upstairs' looking out for you – there always has been. You will be okay. You are a survivor."

That was one of the few times Aunt Joe was nice to anyone. I had no idea what she was talking about. It must have been something she thought was important. Maybe she was just trying to be nice to me; that was a rare occasion. I was grateful she was in a good mood, instead of slapping me, and yelling at me and the other kids.

I tried to watch the landscape as the train moved toward home. I understood Aunt Joe thought I was being a good girl. I was very careful not to say anything that would upset her. I didn't want this train ride to end. I wished I could make the train slow down. It would have been nice if I could have just stopped time for a while. I wanted to ask questions about what she was saying. I was afraid to because it might have changed her mood. The other children were asleep.

Sitting beside Aunt Joe on the train, alone, made me realize she was just a person, after all. I felt very grown up. I enjoyed talking to grown-ups when the opportunity presented itself. Aunt Joe was easy to talk to tonight, but I got the feeling she was talking to herself. I was getting bored listening to her, but I tried very hard not to show it because she might have gotten mad. I couldn't stay awake any longer, and I fell asleep with the other children. All of us kids awoke when the train stopped.

Then we were in Chicago, and Aunt Joe said, "Stand quietly against this building." Aunt Joe hailed down a taxi, and she got one. We all climbed into the taxi and went home. We were tired and hungry. Aunt Joe looked worried, and she said, "When we get home, you children be quiet going up the stairs. Don't make a sound. We don't want to wake anyone, now do we, children?" Sometimes I thought Aunt Joe was a strange person, and other times I loved her.

When we got home, we were not allowed to go to bed. There were no beds or any other furniture in the house. Susan's clothes were lying in a corner of the living room. Mother had peanut butter and jelly sandwiches ready for us.

I got the feeling something was terribly wrong. My mother was crying. She tried to hide it, but I could see her tears. Mother and

Aunt Joe got angry when we tried to ask questions. We were told to shut up and eat as fast as we could. We wondered where all our stuff had gone.

Father had a car with a trailer behind it, packed with all our stuff in it. We hadn't yet figured out that our stuff was in the trailer behind the car. I saw Father in the alley as I looked out the window. He was walking back and forth. I thought that maybe he was looking for something. He checked the trailer several times. He talked to some man for a while, and then the man left. He walked down the alley a ways and put something in someone else's trashcan. I wondered why; this was unusual for my father to do something so stupid when we had trashcans behind our apartment.

I could feel the fear my mother was feeling. I just didn't know why she was afraid. What was going on? Why were we leaving all of a sudden with no explanation? Did Raw Hide and Bloody Bones get another one of our friends? But something was happening; I could feel it. All of us children could feel it. The younger ones were crying, and no one could make them be quiet.

Someone yelled out his or her window, "Shut up, so we can sleep! Don't you people ever sleep?"

Father yelled back, "Fuck you, you nosy son-of-a-bitch, get your nose out of my ass! You could sleep if you would just mind your own business." For a minute, it looked like he was going to fight another one of our neighbors.

Father seemed to be mad, and Mother was nervous, maybe even afraid. Aunt Joe seemed to be worried. All of the grown-ups seemed very upset. Of course, this upset all of us kids. Most of us were too afraid to let anyone know we were upset; it could make things worse.

Father came back up the stairs and made a last inspection of our apartment to make sure we had not forgotten anything. It was getting dark now. I could hardly see out of the windows any more. Father said, "We have to get started right away."

I asked, "Where are we going?"

Mother said, "We are leaving."

Mother said good-bye to her friends, Mr. and Mrs. Newman,

while Father stood by impatiently. Did Mr. and Mrs. Coffman know I was leaving? I wanted to tell them good-bye. Mother said very sharply, "NO! Be quiet! Do as you are told or we will leave you kids here alone."

I stopped complaining and did as I was told. Mother and Aunt Joe took us down the back stairs. Aunt Joe said, "Be very quiet now; no one make a sound. We don't want to make that mean man holler at us again, do we?"

We were on our way to somewhere; our parents refused to tell us where we were going. All we knew was that the grown-ups were in a hurry to get started going somewhere. Our imaginations ran away with us. Some of us dreamed of a wonderful place, but my sister, Vesta, seemed to be dreaming of something awful. I could see it in her face. I knew she was unhappy about having to leave her school. I knew she had some friends in school that my parents didn't know about. She wasn't supposed to talk to anyone, not even the kids, which she told me was an impossible order. Vesta liked school and did well in school. I thought that maybe this was why she was upset. Or maybe she knew, at this point, that we wouldn't be coming back.

Vesta was to be respected and minded by the rest of us children at all times. Father believed everything she said, even if it wasn't true. She got us in trouble sometimes for things we didn't do. Most of us children were very jealous of her and our Father's relationship. I think Mother and Aunt Joe were jealous of Vesta sometimes, too.

Vesta was the oldest living child, as Mother always put it. Mother said, "Vesta was our lucky child. She started the beginning of our living children. Poor little Fern didn't have the fight in her to make it. Frances had enough fight for both of them. She gets sick easy and can't stand the sunrays, but she has a strong constitution. William and Catherine starved to death. I had to bury three children in a hole where they could never be found, and almost four."

None of her talk meant much to any of us children. When she rattled on like this, we were too young to understand. We just understood that Mother was sad and unhappy.

Chapter TWO

IT WAS LATE February or early March when we left Chicago. Somehow they managed to stuff all of us in the car. It was dark outside and we couldn't see out the windows. The bigger children held the smaller children on their laps. The babies soon fell asleep, and everybody else quieted down, not making a sound.

The grown-ups wanted to get out of the city in a hurry. It seemed to take a long time to get out of the city of Chicago. After we were out of Chicago, I could feel them relax a little. It seemed that the tensions were gone and they were more civil to us children.

Father stopped somewhere before morning and put up a couple of tents, so people could get some rest. By that time, none of us children were tired anymore. Our parents made us get in the tent anyway. As soon as our parents were asleep, Vesta; Delores; La Verne; my brother, Orlando; and I sneaked out of the tent to investigate our surroundings.

We were all worried that Vesta would tell on us. She liked to do this sometimes because Father would give her some kind of goodie for doing so. We had a lot of fun that early morning. Since all the other children were sleeping, we didn't get caught.

Vesta brought up a conversation with La Verne, Delores and I about the reason we were leaving Chicago so quickly. Because of everything that had happened recently, we believed that Father might have killed Susan Degman. We knew our father was capable of such a thing, and this made us even more afraid of him.

I felt that my mother and Aunt Joe also believed that this was the case. We didn't know for sure what Father had done, but we did know from Mother's and Aunt Joe's words and actions that he had done something very bad.

This may have just been some little girls' fearful reading of the atmosphere, but if he had done something, he never got caught. There were many things that my father got away with.

We felt like we had accomplished something that night; we had pulled something over on Father. We were pleased with ourselves. That was the bravest thing anyone could ever do. We were proud of our accomplishment. No one woke up and caught us. We were lucky this time; we could have gotten into a lot of trouble.

When our parents and Aunt Joe woke us the next morning, the sun was fairly high in the sky. We were given a peanut butter and jelly sandwich and a cup of water, and told to go to the bathroom. My father said, "I am not going to stop ten minutes after we get on the road. Do what you have to do now; it is now or never."

We each made a trip out into the woods where we felt we couldn't be seen by anyone. Then we piled back in the car and Aunt Joe drove for a while. We still had not been told where we were going.

Father was quiet for a while, even being so crowded. The day was more pleasant than it was the day before. Most of us children were excited about the different landscape we were seeing, and busy wondering what was around the next curve in the road. Except for taxi cabs, I don't think any of us had ridden in a car before.

At first it was different and exciting. It wasn't long before the excitement wore off and everyone became cranky. Our parents got upset because we were making too much noise, and one of us continuously had to go to the bathroom or needed a drink of water. When one child wanted something, all the others joined in and wanted something too. The grown-ups got very irritated with us, even though we were trying the best we could to behave.

Our legs hurt from holding the little ones; the babies got tired of having to sit still. Father, Mother and Aunt Joe started yelling, cursing and threatening us. We were thirsty and hungry. Father stopped and got something in a little bottle to drink, but he didn't get anything for us to eat or drink. We started asking questions like, "When are we going home? Where are we going? We want to go home!" We were told to shut up and be quiet, and that we couldn't ever go back home. Life was about to change for us, but they didn't say how it would change.

This frightened us kids who were old enough to understand. Finally, our father stopped at a store. Mother and Aunt Joe made us some sandwiches, gave us a glass of milk and allowed us to go to the bathroom. We were grateful, for it gave us a chance to stretch our aching legs. We chased each other around and around until we were told to get back in the car. Break-time was over; we knew better than to complain.

After a while, Father decided to teach Vesta how to drive. Mother and Aunt Joe had fits. It did them no good to protest; Father had made up his mind. Vesta was going to learn to drive on this trip. Father said, "By the time we reach the farm, she will be a perfect driver."

We had a few close calls, but by sitting on Father's lap, she truly learned to drive and did a good job of it. Vesta was very proud of herself and Father was proud of her, too. Mother and Aunt Joe were not so happy about it. Vesta drove for a long time. She seemed to be enjoying it. She was no longer afraid of driving. My mother still fussed about it from time to time.

It was time for gas and another bathroom break. We couldn't run around because we were at a gas station. When we got back in the car, Mother changed places with Vesta. Mother rode in the front seat, and Vesta seemed to be pleased about the change. Vesta was no longer driving. Father was doing the driving. He drove with one hand and put his other arm around Mother and asked her to scoot closer to him. This seemed to please Mother and made things more peaceful.

We drove until suppertime. Father was looking for a good place to stop so we could all go to the bathroom and eat supper in the same place. Aunt Joe started complaining that we were going the wrong way. Father wouldn't listen to her. He just said, "Shut up." He kept on going the same way for a while. Then he said, "This is the perfect place." He pulled over by a lot of trees. We went to the bathroom and ate some sandwiches.

Then Vesta and Father went for a walk in the woods, which made Mother angry. We kids played while we waited for them. They were gone quite a while, and Aunt Joe went into the trees to look for them. This created an argument and got everyone off on the wrong foot. Vesta acted very proud of the scene she thought she had caused. Mother and Aunt Joe started pounding Vesta with their fists. Father pulled them off of her and beat on them instead. Mother and Aunt Joe said, "No more of this shit," to Vesta, and said to Father, "We are ready to go."

Father replied, "We will go when I am ready and not before." He made all of us sit on the ground and wait for him to drink his bottle. Even Mother and Aunt Joe had to sit on the ground.

Finally, Father said, "I am ready now to get in the car. All of you children had better be quiet, if you know what's good for you."

We were all as quiet as we could possibly be. Aunt Joe sat in the back with us children for a while because she was so mad at Father. She didn't want to sit in the front seat. My sister, La Verne, sat in the front seat with Father and Mother.

After we were back in the car, we were told our father had bought an 80-acre farm that was 21 miles from Alton, Missouri, and we were moving there. We were told to stay in our seats and keep our mouths shut. Our parents had seemed to be in a hurry to get out of the city, but now that we were out of Chicago, they seemed to be taking their time. We had a lot of car trouble along the way. Mother, Father and Aunt Joe fought a lot. There was constant bickering and cursing between them. We were crowded – we had eight children and three adults in a 1939 or 1940 Ford sedan, I believe.

Vesta whispered, "I don't believe there is such a place as Alton, Missouri. Where are they taking us, and what are they going to do to us? I am very frightened."

It seemed like we traveled for many days, and we camped a lot. As much as I liked watching the beautiful world fly by, I began to worry about things too. We were all tired of being crunched up in this small car. We needed a bus for this many people. The trap kept blowing off the trailer, and my father had to stop and fix it.

Father drank constantly from a little bottle. When the bottle got empty, he found a store that sold that kind of stuff and bought another bottle. He seemed to need a lot of those little bottles. Father was yelling louder, and started to snap at Mother and Aunt Joe.

We were stuffed in the car like sardines and terribly miserable. At one point, my mother even cried. I don't remember what the issue was. It appeared to me that Mother and Aunt Joe didn't like leaving Chicago. They said, "We like being around people and stores. We don't want to live in the sticks where there is no excitement at all. We will get too bored.

My parents decided to take a detour to see Yellowstone Park and the Grand Canyon. Aunt Joe said, "You are just killing time, Otis. You are not even going toward Missouri. Now you want to go to Yellowstone Park? What are you up to?"

Father said, "We are not expected for a while, yet we left because we had to. Remember, I had to leave."

It was miserable getting to the park, but great after we got there. It was truly beautiful. I was seeing a part of the world that was too beautiful to exist, or so I thought. It was even better than Grandfather Cahala's house.

There were beautiful green mountains you could stand on. You could look right down into the center of the Earth. Aunt Joe said they were called canyons. To me, it was looking at the middle of the earth. The waterfalls were awesome. It looked like God had turned on his faucets. I had never seen anything so beautiful. This was a place I would always remember.

Once in a while, I could see a small animal running away, trying to hide from us. When I tried to catch them, someone always called me back – of all the rotten luck. I might have caught some animals if they would leave me alone. I had a lot of fun chasing after anything that moved.

My parents were relaxing, talking and smiling; they were truly being nice to each other. Aunt Joe was pleasant to be with. I had never seen my family like this. It was a good feeling, and I tried to be very good. I didn't want this to end.

There were not many people in this place. Mother and Aunt

Joe got some food and blankets out of the trailer. We had a picnic on top of the world, where I could watch that wonderful waterfall. I watched my father pat my mother's behind, and they began holding hands. What was happening was a wonderful thing; I hoped the feeling of togetherness would never end. Aunt Joe and Vesta walked ahead of my parents. They didn't even seem to mind. In fact, they were enjoying themselves.

We stayed in Yellowstone Park for several days. Because we couldn't camp in the park, we camped along the side of the road.

Too soon it was time to go. Oh, how I wanted to stay! Father yelled, "Everyone in the car; we have to go." I settled down to watch out the window. I was learning a lot about places I hadn't known existed.

Dennis started fussing and people got cranky. Father threatened to throw all of us out along the side of the highway and leave us there. Aunt Joe said, "Shut up! It is your fault we are in this situation. Make the best of it, man."

That started an argument. I got a headache and wished they would all shut up. When I fell asleep, they were still arguing. Aunt Joe took over the driving while I was sleeping. We camped somewhere where there were a lot of big mountains made of rocks. My head still hurt and I was sick to my stomach.

We were back on the road early the next morning. Father didn't give us time to eat breakfast. Aunt Joe asked, "What is the big hurry?"

Father didn't answer her question. He just said, "Get in the back seat with the children. Kitty and Vesta will sit up here with me."

Father had a car accident. No one was hurt, but the trailer wheel was bent very badly. Father was at fault because he was drinking too much. Father had to unload the trailer along the side of the road to fix it. It was at night and all of us were bawling because we wanted to sleep. Father fixed the trailer, but then a police officer gave him a ticket for drunk driving. The officer made my father follow him.

The police officer went to the judge's house and woke up the judge, who made my father pay the ticket right then. The judge then said, "You are drunk. You can't drive in this condition." Speaking to the police officer, the judge said, "You see to it that he gets a room for these children tonight. Let the bastard go in the morning. Having so many children is enough to make him drink. He is probably going crazy with so many kids in that car."

Father rented a motel room, but he was not happy about it. I slept very well in the motel room, even with the turmoil that was going on between our parents. A bed felt good.

We had car trouble again, and Father said, "We are close to Hot Springs Park. I will see if I can get us towed there." Father disappeared for a long time. He came back with help. We were towed to Hot Springs Park and camped for several days, while Father fixed the car.

We were allowed to play if we stayed within the eyesight of our parents and stayed out of Father's way. I enjoyed this stop; we had a good rest. Aunt Joe took advantage of this time to rest, so we had to play quietly. Mother also did a lot of studying in her nursing books. She got upset if we made too much noise, saying, "I can't concentrate if you kids refuse to keep your mouths shut."

As long as Father was busy, we could do pretty much as we pleased. When he missed us, we were in a lot of trouble. We had been told to stay close to camp. My Aunt Joe was supposed to watch us, but she wanted to sleep. All of us kids didn't mind her sleeping.

When we got too close to Father, he cursed and yelled at us, saying, "You stupid little bastards, get out of my way." He yelled at Aunt Joe and Mother, saying, "You stupid, mother-fucking, lazy women, can't you even watch these kids?"

Mother was studying her nursing books, and she didn't like to be bothered. She yelled for Aunt Joe, saying, "You stupid bitch, watch after these children. You aren't doing anything."

Father worked on the car for several days while we played in the park. Finally the car was fixed, and we were on our way once more. Father was sober that day. Maybe the day would pass pleasantly with less noise; I sure hoped so. For some reason, the adults behaved themselves that day.

We camped at least once after we stayed at Hot Springs in the big park. Delores and La Verne passed the time by trying to teach me how to count the trees and cars that flew past us as we drove down the road. A turn here and a turn there; then our father made the wrong turn. He was lost; this made him quite frustrated. He stopped to look at the map, and we kids were allowed to get out and stretch our legs, as long as we stayed out of the road. Then Father was through studying the map, and we were back on our way. He found the right road and turned on it.

Mother and Aunt Joe were talking decently to each other. I think they were more excited than us kids were. It sounded like they might have been making plans for our new life. I couldn't hear much of what they said over the other children, but they looked and sounded happy for a change. They, too, seemed to be enjoying the scenery. Aunt Joe admired the lovely trees we passed by.

After a while Father said, "Almost there; it won't be long now." I got very excited and began wondering what our new home looked like. I glued my eyes to the window. The closer we got, the more excited I became. Would I be able to find a friend in our new apartment house? The only single-dwelling house I had ever seen was Grandfather and Grandmother Cahala's. I hadn't quite understood that we were to be the only people living in the house. The only way of life we kids knew was living in an apartment house. Having a house all to ourselves would be new to us.

The other children seemed to get ants in their pants too. We couldn't sit still and we were all talking at once. The grown-ups were a little more tolerant of our behavior, it seemed. Everyone was anticipating getting this horrible trip over with. Every house we passed was a disappointment. At this time, we wanted it to be our new home.

Father turned down a dirt road and said, "Okay! Don't burst at the seams. It will be around a couple more bends in the road yet."

To us it seemed to take a long time to go around those couple of bends. Someone asked, "Will we be allowed to associate with other people in this new place?"

The question was ignored, as were many more of the questions that we children asked our parents. Maybe they didn't know the answers to our questions and couldn't answer them.

There were trees along the road on both sides, just like when we went to see Grandmother Cahala. There had been very few houses for some time now. The houses we passed were all one-family houses. This seemed strange to us. We had seen a lot of one-family houses since we left Chicago. We believed only rich people lived in one-family houses. That's the way it was where we came from, so we thought.

Chapter THREE

SUDDENLY FATHER SAID, "Here we are." He pulled up into a large driveway. Everyone got out of the car and looked around. Father seemed satisfied with what he saw. He was very excited and said, "I will plant fruit trees over here; I will plant a garden there. The kids can learn to milk the cow. We have all kinds of privacy, no more neighbors sticking their noses up my ass. I can do anything I want here, and no one will complain about it or even know about it. This is great. Think about it, Kitty! All this land is mine. We can run around nude if we want to. No one can tell us what we can't do. I can do as I please. Hear that, kids? I will do as I please. I am finally free to do anything it is possible to do. I would like to see the man that can stop me."

When we were all out of the car, an old man and an old lady came out of a little house. They came out to greet us and ask whom we might be. They introduced themselves as Mr. and Mrs. Sam. Father introduced himself and Mother. Mother went into the little house to look around.

When she came out of the house, she was angry. She said, "This house is nothing but a shack. I can't live like this. There is no place to store food or clothes; there is no refrigerator. The cook-stove uses wood. Who will cut the wood? There isn't even any covering over the floors. Babies will have slivers in their knees. It will be hot in the summer and cold in the winter. This house is too small. My God, where are we all going to sleep?"

Aunt Joe said, "What were you thinking, when you bought this stupid place? This place is not good enough for dogs. Are you sick?" She felt his forehead. She said, "No fever, how about a stomachache?"

Father knocked her hand off his stomach and said, "Leave me alone unless you want your cock-sucking ass kicked." Aunt Joe quickly stepped away and began to pretend to look at some piles of wood in the driveway. Then she walked down the road a little way and back. She didn't appear to be so mad when she came back, but she was pouting.

The elderly Mr. and Mrs. Sam just stood there quietly. Mother got really mad when she learned there was no bathroom. The hole under the outhouse was full. You couldn't use the outhouse anymore. Mr. and Mrs. Sam told her, "We use the barnyard for a toilet."

Mother asked, "How do you wipe your ass? Do you carry a roll of paper with you, or is there a place you can store paper out there?"

Mrs. Sam said, "The barn leaks; you won't be able to store anything out there. We use old catalogs or leaves from the trees to wipe our butts on. They work just fine; a little rough sometimes, but that won't hurt anyone."

Aunt Joe complained, "You really don't expect me to be able to keep this place clean, do you? Otis! You are crazy to bring us all the way out here to live in something like this. I just won't do it. Leave it to you and you will buy trash every time. You should have let the women pick out the house."

Mother and Aunt Joe were both very upset over the condition of this new home Father had bought. Mother complained, "Even our parents have a bathroom in their house and a pump outside in the yard. I will accept nothing less. Where are we going to get our water?"

Father laughed at them and said, "You will get accustomed to things around here. Just don't nag me about what you don't have or how tired you are. You will get very tired. There is a lot of work to be done. I expect all of you to work your asses off without complaining. I didn't promise that things would be easy, now did I? At least we won't have the neighbors' noses stuck up our asses constantly. You women don't like it, I will put you both on the next bus out of here. The children are going to stay here and work their asses off. Go! Go! Go ahead and leave, if that is what you want to do. When you leave, you don't come back." Mother and Aunt Joe shut up and did not complain any more. They just pouted like mad children.

Mother asked Mrs. Sam, "When can we move into the house?" Mrs. Sam replied, "We were not expecting you for a few more months. We are not ready to move out yet. Our daughter won't come after us for a few more months. You people came a lot earlier then you were supposed to come. That is not our fault. We will try to hurry her up if we can."

The old man asked if Father wanted him to show us around the land. Father accepted, and we followed the man all around the 80 acres. It seemed to take hours. Father and the old man would stop every now and then to talk. Mr. Sam pointed this way and that way. Father asked a lot of questions which Mr. Sam tried to answer as best as he could. At times, he couldn't satisfy Father with his answers. Father yelled at the poor man and demanded the price be lowered. I don't know if that happened or not.

I got so tired that I decided I was going back to the little house. I slipped away from the group, hoping I wouldn't be missed. Mother, Aunt Joe and the rest of the children followed Mr. Sam around the 80-acre farm like a bunch of little chicks.

As I wandered around trying to find my way back to that little house, I thought that this was an awfully pretty place. I thought I might like it. I could get away from all the fighting and noise. My head wouldn't hurt so badly all the time. There were a lot of trees, and the sun was not shining under them. I could stay out of the sun; this was good.

Finally I saw the little house. As I got closer, I could see Mrs. Sam in the yard. When I reached the house, I approached her. She was a nice woman. We talked about all the flowers that grew in the springtime. She showed me some little baby pigs and little chickens. She gave me cookies and milk and said, "Milk comes from a live cow." She showed me eggs in a little house and said, "My chickens laid these eggs. Soon they will belong to your father and mother, and you will have fresh eggs to eat."

She explained to me about the things she grew in her garden, and I was interested. Grandmother Cahala had a garden, but we were not allowed to go into it. Grandmother also grew rhubarb; I loved to eat her rhubarb pies. So I asked Mrs. Sam if we could grow rhubarb and she said, "Goodness child, you can plant anything you want. If you water them and take care of the plants, they will grow."

Mrs. Sam showed me the most beautiful red flowers I had ever seen. She called them poppies. She also showed me some hollyhocks; they were taller then she was. She showed me the cow and explained that that was where our milk came from. She squeezed the cow's tit to show me how the milk got out of the cow. Then she showed me a horse and sat me on his back. The horse started running and I fell off. That made me afraid of the horse.

I was sorry that Mother and Aunt Joe were not pleased with the place. They had so many complaints, but I thought that we could fix just about anything we wanted to. I wasn't sure how we would fix the bathroom problem or the well, so that we wouldn't have to carry water from the Wheeler's place, over 40 acres away, like Mr. and Mrs. Sam had to do. Surely we could figure out a way. After all, we had a bathroom and water in the house in the city.

So I believed we could do it. Father could put some stuff on the floor so the babies wouldn't get slivers in their knees. He could make a toilet in the house and put water in the well. Father could do anything he wanted to. He could fix everything and make my mother and Aunt Joe happy, if only he wanted to.

The house was small; that was one thing I wasn't sure if we could fix. But I sure hoped we would figure out a way to fix that too. I would be glad to sleep in the barn. Maybe some of the other kids would like that too. It was a big barn, and we would have plenty of room. The horse and cow wouldn't take up much room. They couldn't possibly make as much noise as my parents and Aunt Joe did when they fought. Everything seemed perfect to me, except that we needed a bathroom. I wished that Mother and Aunt Joe could see things as I did.

It was a long time before Mr. Sam and the rest of the family returned. They hadn't even missed me. I was glad; I thought about how peaceful it would be here. I could stay away from Father, Mother and Aunt Joe most of the time. I could hide for weeks in this place. I wished it had worked out that way.

The house sat in the middle of the 80 acres. Mrs. Sam said,

"There are lots of beautiful flowers in the spring and summer around this old house. I like to have a lot of flowers, but it is getting to be too much work for me to keep them up."

I loved to look at the flowers in Lincoln Park, but I couldn't touch the flowers in the park. So I asked, "Can I touch the flowers?"

Mrs. Sam said, "Touch them? Baby, you can pick them, or cut them with scissors if you want to."

I skipped off as happy as a lark. I enjoyed the wide-open space, the fresh air and the wonderful birds. I was thankful I didn't get caught talking to Mrs. Sam. Father would have been mad, but I didn't care. That woman was very nice to me.

I didn't care about the house very much. But I thought that it was a good thing we were the only family to live in the house. It was very small, and we would be lucky if all of us could fit into it.

Father broke into my thoughts and said, "I found an excellent place to pitch tents. We can live in tents until Mr. and Mrs. Sam move out."

That flustered both Mother and Aunt Joe. They said to Father, "We are not going to live in tents very long."

Father shouted, "You will live in them as long as it takes; we lived in tents before. You have been there and done that before, so quit complaining. Start acting like grown women, instead of babies."

He kissed Mother and she said. "Okay, I will try, but you must fix this place up a little."

I thought of a lot of good ideas. We could put some tents behind the house, and then we wouldn't have to worry about making the little house any bigger. I would like that too, if all of us kids didn't have to sleep in the same tent. I thought I had everything figured out; I was pleased with myself. We could make a big long pipe to carry water from the Wheeler's well to our well. We could fill the well up so that we would not have to carry water every day.

We pitched tents at the very end of the property, close to the Wheeler's residence. They were our closest neighbors. They lived at the west end of our 80 acres.

There was no dispute over the next several months, and these were the best times of my life. We children were allowed to roam the

80 acres at will. The only restriction was to stay away from the house. I never got caught there, but some of the other kids did and they got beaten with a switch. We were camped in a place where we could see no people. We were isolated. Father could do anything he wanted.

We played all day long; even my oldest sister, Vesta, played with us. I found a giant pine tree that I liked to spend my quiet time in. Its branches were so thick that you couldn't see me sitting up there from the ground. We climbed trees. Since we didn't know where our land began or ended, we roamed around and got acquainted with our surroundings. We had a good time. We sat in our castle in a tree and played many imaginary games. We caught fireflies in fruit jars that Mrs. Sam gave to us. I had never seen fireflies before; bugs with lights were fascinating to me.

At some time during that summer, Mr. and Mrs. Newman (Mother's friends from Chicago) bought a farm about three miles down the road from us. They didn't like the country and did not stay long. They sometimes argued with Mother over the way we children were treated. They tried to get Mother to take us children and go back to Chicago with them. They said, "We are worried about you and the children. We don't want to leave you here alone, without any help."

Mother refused saying, "I'm going to give it a try. Anyhow, don't worry about the children and me. We will be all right." The Newmans went back to Chicago alone. They looked sad.

Finally, the people moved out of the little house. It had a small kitchen with a wide doorway that had no door on it that led into a large living room. Off the living room, was a door leading to a very large bedroom. In the corner of the bedroom, was a big wood-burning heater. The floors were made of wood and they had big cracks in them. I could see the ground through some of the cracks. I now understood why my mother was so upset with the house. Rats and snakes could come into the house and they did sometimes. We shook out our bedding before we went to bed.

We had no electricity or gas, and the well on our property was dry. We carried water from the Wheeler's well, over 40 acres away, to take baths in, cook with and wash our clothes in. We bathed every two weeks in round washtubs. We all used the same water, starting from the youngest up to oldest. Father, Mother and Aunt Joe had their own clean water to bathe in.

The water was very hard to carry. We used five-gallon buckets. I got very tired and I needed help to carry a bucket. La Verne carried two buckets and I helped carry the first bucket, trading sides from time to time so my arms wouldn't get too tired. It didn't take long for us to forget about the good life in Chicago. We were busy trying to survive from day to day. We were not even allowed to think.

We wore nothing but farmers' jeans with the bibs. The girls wore no panties or shorts or bras. Father was right; we worked our butts off carrying water. I was so tired when we were through carrying water, especially on bath day or wash day, that I laid down and slept on the porch.

I didn't know it then, but my work had not yet begun. It was only the children who worked. We were not allowed to sleep in the barn or put tents in the back of the house. If I could only get Father to listen to my ideas, then all of us kids would sleep better. He was just too stubborn.

Mr. and Mrs. Sam left behind the cow, the horse, some chickens and some pigs. We moved in. Fun time was over; hell began for us children. We learned how to milk the cow, and take care of the horse, chickens and pigs. Father plowed up a lot of land, and we children took all the rocks out of the plowed area and put the seed in the ground. We made a large garden where we planted corn and other things. We learned how to can the food we had grown. We also planted 100 fruit trees.

We children did all the chores. We worked until late at night carrying water to water the garden and trees when it did not rain. If Father felt we weren't working fast enough, he used a belt on us. Sometimes Aunt Joe would help us carry water. Sometimes Aunt Joe helped us carry water. Aunt Joe could do many things that Mother couldn't do. She was much larger and stronger. And she didn't cry like Mother did to get her way. It didn't matter who dug the well. It was on the Wheeler's property and we still had to carry water over 40 acres of land.

Father made a big bed and put it in the living room. He also made a table that he stored in the smokehouse. Later, he put all of our dresses in the smokehouse and no longer let us wear them. The only one who could wear a dress was Vesta.

Father killed the cute little chickens and the muddy pigs, and made us eat them. This broke my heart. You are not supposed to hurt critters; you should take care of them. The first few times Father made me eat chicken or pig, I got horribly sick. I vomited all night. Father told me, "Stop this nonsense! You are making yourself sick so you won't have to eat. You are too skinny. Eat or I will beat your ass." I felt sorry for the poor little critters that Father was killing for food.

When my father put an ax in my hands and tried to make me cut off a chicken's head, I was horrified. I didn't want to hurt the chickens; I wanted to love and play with them. He almost beat me to death, but he couldn't make me hurt that poor little chicken. He cursed at me something awful and said, "You are too sensitive; this has got to stop. There is no God. There is no help for you. I am your god and you will do as I tell you, with no questions asked. The day you think your mother-fucking, stupid heart is bigger than I am, come and let me know. Your heart is a cunt, that's all it is and all I will allow it to be, you little fucking bitch." He could not make me cut the chicken's head off, so he made me watch him cut its little head off.

Father, Mother, Aunt Joe and, sometimes, Vesta slept in the large bed that Father had made. Again, there was a lot of fighting over who was going to sleep in the living room with Father. Sometimes two of them would sleep with him. And sometimes all three of them would sleep with him. This was old stuff to us.

Oh, how many times I wanted to sleep in that barn and I was not allowed to, until one of my brothers pulled a piece off a log the barn was made of, and found a snake hiding under there. I no longer wanted to sleep in the barn; that was a bad idea.

The children slept in one large bedroom, all in the same bed. We slept crossway on the full-sized bed, so we could all fit more comfortably. Each child had somebody's feet in his face. I would get awful leg cramps, and many times Delores and La Verne rubbed my legs so that I would stop crying and disturbing the others. If we woke the adults, we would all get whipped. My sisters would have me lay on the floor while they rubbed my legs. The heat from their hands made my legs feel better. When I went to sleep, they left me on the floor and covered me with the other kids' extra clothes. The small bed was reserved for the women who did not sleep with Father. Vesta was considered a woman.

I often liked to hide behind the wood stove that was in the corner of the bedroom. Most of the time I slept there. I felt alone and safe behind the stove.

None of us children went to school the first year we were on the farm. We picked up all the rocks off the farm and made what Father called "tarries." We cut wood and cleared land. If Father thought we did not work hard enough, he beat us until we smelled like fish. The only child who did not have to work in the fields was my sister, Vesta. She stayed in the house with Mother and Aunt Joe. This made the rest of us jealous of her. We felt it wasn't fair for her to get out of working all the time, while the rest of us worked our butts off. She should have been helping us.

I had an allergy to the ultra-violet rays of the sun. My body started swelling, and Mother reminded Father that I had the allergy to the sun. He said, "She can't be treated any differently than the other children."

Most of the time my father was not around, but sometimes he checked to see if we were working hard enough. My sister, Delores, insisted I stay under the trees and throw the rocks out in the field so the younger children could see them, and the other children could make the tarries. When we saw Father coming, I ran out and joined the other children.

One day Father stayed with us a while, and I passed out from the sun. He carried me to the little house. It seemed like I was sick for a long time. My eyes turned black, my body swelled up, I couldn't eat and I felt like I could not breathe.

Mother said, "She will not work in the sun any more. If this child dies from exposure to the sun, you are going to be the one to answer for it."

When there was no way to get out of the sun, I stayed at the house. This put me back in the middle of the fighting. I constantly had a headache, which made me vomit. My parents were concerned about my weight loss because of my vomiting so much, and I was getting thinner and thinner. Father made me eat fish eggs and wouldn't let the other kids have any. The other children felt cheated and took it out on me. They felt about me as we all felt about Vesta; we believed she was treated more nicely.

I helped with the babies and did the dishes. We did the laundry on the rub board. We didn't fix the water problem. We had to carry water across 40 acres from the Wheeler's well. Vesta didn't have to carry water very often. All of us children felt as though Vesta was being treated like a princess. She didn't have to work, and we resented her for that.

Mother did nothing but cook and pout. Aunt Joe sometimes helped her. Aunt Joe liked to herd us around like we were sheep, and all of us children resented that. If one of us stepped on a crack on the porch, she knocked us in the head with her knuckles and made us throw salt over our shoulders so we wouldn't bring bad luck to the family. She was afraid if a black cat ran in front of her. She refused to walk under a ladder, if at all possible. Sometimes Father made her do it, just to be mean to her. All of that seemed very silly to me. What I feared most were the two-legged animals – mainly my father and Aunt Joe.

One day Mother and Aunt Joe were in the kitchen, and Father was lying on his big bed without any clothes on. He said to me, "Come here, Squirt. Since you aren't able to work in the fields, I have invented a special job for you to do. I am going to teach you how to pet my winnie." (He was speaking about his penis.)

Father taught me how to pet his penis. I petted his penis until something sticky came out of it and got all over my hands. I hated doing this. Mother and Aunt Joe stood in the kitchen and watched. When I was through, Aunt Joe put a little water in a basin so I could wash my hands. It was never enough water to keep my hands from feeling sticky. We conserved our water so we didn't have to carry it as often.

When Vesta slept with us girls, she wet the bed. One morning Father said, "Delores, you are getting up during the night and squatting over Vesta and peeing on her. Are you trying to get me to whip the hell out of her? Get your ass out here; I am going to show you who is going to get whipped."

Father took Delores out on the porch and made her lie face down. He put his foot on the back of her neck and beat her until her back, butt and legs bled. Father began beating Delores daily. Delores stunk like dead fish all the time.

When he was through, I helped Delores get to her feet. I took her to the back yard and tried to wash her off with cool rainwater from the washtub that was in the back yard. Father caught me doing this and beat me in the same manner he had beaten Delores, but not as severely.

He cursed at me with all kinds of dirty words and said, "You sympathized with Delores. Your kind gentle heart is going to have to go. I can't stand a weak and sympathetic person, and won't have one in my home. I will beat this out of you, or kill you if I have too. You are going to get over all this sympathy you feel for others. I am the only one you sympathize with."

Delores began withdrawing form the rest of us kids even more. When I tried to talk to her, she reluctantly talked back to me, warning me I was going to get myself in trouble if I insisted on hanging out with her when the opportunity presented itself. I said to her, "That is a chance I have to take. You are a person, too. A person can't survive all this crap alone."

It seemed Father watched and waited for me to try and help Delores or one of the other kids when they reaped his rage. I was told not to have anything to do with Delores because she was ornery and wicked. When I got caught speaking with her, sitting next to her or helping her in any way, I got punished. Our father was relentless; he seemed to know everything.

Father said Delores was his mother-in-law in another life. He hated her then, and he hated her now. He said to me, "You stay away from her; she is not fit company for you. I have something special in mind for you, and that ornery bitch is not going to ruin you for me." I believed him to be somewhat crazy and wondered why my mother couldn't see this.

I couldn't help myself; I had to help her. I couldn't control how I felt. I hurt when she hurt, I cried when she cried, and we became very close. I was the only child that defied Father and had anything to do with Delores. Believe me, I paid the price for it. He said, "You are too small and sickly. I can't beat you as hard as I do Delores."

He made everyone call me "Skitter Legs." The other children couldn't have anything to do with me, unless I was looking after them. Father said, "You are an ornery lover." I was afraid to ask what an ornery lover was; it might set Father off. He might have got madder than he already was.

I got very lonesome. No one talked to me because they were afraid they would be punished too. Delores and I had kind of a secret language. One of us stomped our foot and scratched our head to tell the other one to go to the bathroom. When we got into the woods, we climbed a tree and sat on a branch and talked to each other. We were careful not to be gone too long, especially if Father was present. This was the only verbal communication we had. Around other people, even our brothers and sisters, we didn't talk to each other at all. We had to hide in order to have a conversation, or we would be punished. If Father caught on to our game, he never said anything. We felt like we were putting something over on him, and this pleased us very much.

Delores told me once that she was ashamed of the way she smelled and tired of people making fun of her for it. She said, "I feel better staying away from everyone. But you, you just refuse to give up, don't you? That's okay, I guess I would miss you if you had the same attitude the rest of them do. Really, I am glad you care about me; no one else does. Maybe we are meant to suffer the same kind of fate. Be careful, Father will kill you if he wants to."

These little trips to the woods meant a lot to us. Our brothers and sisters didn't seem to notice if we were gone a little longer then we should have been. One of us went into the woods first, and then a few minutes later, the other one followed in hopes we wouldn't get caught in our deceit.

Chapter FOUR

AUNT FERN AND Uncle Guy came to visit us on their way to Arizona where they had bought some land. (Aunt Fern was Mother and Aunt Joe's sister.) The first thing Aunt Fern wanted to do was to use the bathroom. By now, Mother had found her favorite spot to use the bathroom. Mother escorted Aunt Fern to her toilet spot. We had no paper of any kind.

Mother took Aunt Fern into the woods and showed her how we went to the bathroom. Mother found a log for her to sit on. Aunt Fern had trouble sitting on the log because of her weight. She slipped backwards and fell off the log into the pile of excrement she and Mother had made.

When they came back to the house, Mother was laughing. Aunt Fern complained, "You dumb hillbillies don't even have a working outhouse. How do you expect a fat lady like me to sit on a damn log and take a shit? After I finally got squatted on the log, I fell off the fucking thing into my own shit." Father and Uncle Guy thought that was funny.

Aunt Joe, Vesta, La Verne and Delores walked across the 40 acres to the Wheeler's well and each carried back two five-gallon buckets of water, one bucket in each hand. Mother heated the water so Aunt Fern could take a bath in the washtub. She complained about the lack of privacy.

Aunt Fern wouldn't let her girls go into the woods to go to the bathroom. She dug around in their stuff until she found a large bucket. Aunt Fern made her girls go in the bucket. One of us had to empty and clean it so that the bucket could be used again and not smell. I resented having to do this; it wasn't my place. I felt like it was Aunt Fern's or her children's place to empty their own shit pail, if they were going to use one.

They only stayed for four days. On the fourth day, Aunt Fern said, "We will be leaving in the morning. We are going to see if we can find civilization somewhere before nightfall. I am not accustomed to squatting in a barnyard or sitting across a log to take a shit. To top that off, I had to pick leaves from a tree to wipe my ass with, then take a bath in a washtub in the backyard, after someone carried the water over 40 acres by foot. That is ridiculous, as far as I am concerned. Wait until the family hears about the story of me falling in my own shit! Guy will see to it that they do." Everyone laughed hysterically at her. The way she said it was funny.

The next morning we ate breakfast and helped them pack. We said our goodbyes to each other. They were on their way to find civilization, whatever that meant. Aunt Fern acted happy about it, so it must have been something good. We were not mistreated when Aunt Fern was visiting. We didn't have to work, except to milk the cow and feed the livestock. For this reason, we kids hated to see her go. When she left, life went back to the way it had been.

Aunt Fern and Uncle Guy made it to Arizona where they had bought their land. They moved into their new house and put their daughters in school. Aunt Fern bragged about having running water, a bathroom in the house, a real bathtub and electricity every time she wrote to Mother. This made Mother fuss about the conditions we lived in.

A few months later, Mother got a letter telling her that Uncle Guy had been leaning backward in a kitchen chair, sitting on only two legs of the chair. He had fallen backwards and broken his neck. He was paralyzed from the neck down. Uncle Guy had always sat on the two back legs of his chair. Whenever he came over to visit, Mother complained about that. She would say, "Guy, you are destroying my chair. Please sit on all four legs of the chair."

Uncle Guy died not long after he had broken his neck. We went to his funeral, and that was the last time I saw Aunt Fern. She was very sad and was crying, like Susan's mother had.

Mother said, "Poor Fern, what is she going to do now? She has no formal education; there is no way she can make a living. She has two children to support. She can't run that business they bought by herself; she will need help."

But Mother and Father didn't try to help her at all. Mother talked about how sorry she was for Uncle Guy's unfortunate accident, but no one tried to help Aunt Fern out at all. This was puzzling to me. Didn't anyone care if they had food or clothes? Were they really in need of things? If so, what did they need and couldn't we help her a little bit? Mother and Aunt Joe were her sisters; they should be willing to help her. I wondered if Grandmother and Grandfather would help Fern, or if they were mad at her too. I worried about my cousins, Gloria and Beverly. I felt sorry for Aunt Fern, not having anyone to help her when she had so many people that could help if they only would.

We could make the house bigger, or build another house on another part of our land. When I mentioned this, Mother told me that this was not possible; we needed to take care of ourselves first. I wondered if something like that happened to our family, would Mother feel the same way?

I had a lot of ideas, and no one wanted to hear what I had to say. I was always thinking in those days. I was maybe five years old, and after a few months on the farm, I soon became aware that I didn't have the right to talk or think for myself; it wasn't permitted in our family. If you were brave enough to think, you had better keep your mouth shut about it. That was a hard lesson for me to learn. I sometimes forgot I wasn't supposed to talk unless Father spoke to me first. I had a big mouth that was hard for me to control.

I have always been a thinker and, for me, this was not good. Sometimes Father could see that you were thinking just by looking at you, and then you got into a lot of trouble. You had better not ever deny doing something that Father accused you of doing, even when you were innocent. In our family, you kept your mouth shut and took whatever punishment Father deemed appropriate. We couldn't expect any help from our mother or Aunt Joe. They just watched and said nothing. They were afraid that they might invoke Father's rage, too. Father put the fear of God in everyone he met; most people were afraid of him.

Nothing was done to improve the condition of the house or our living conditions at all, except that, after a while, Father did have us kids dig a new hole to put the outhouse over. We filled the old hole with the dirt we had dug out of the new hole. By the time he had us dig this new hole for the outhouse, the barnyard was filled with human waste. A person couldn't walk through the barnyard without stepping in a pile of waste.

The biggest problem for us children was that we couldn't use the outhouse after we had worked so hard on it. We had to go to the barnyard at night, and into the woods during the day. We resented this because we felt like we had done all the work. If someone had to go to the barnyard, it should have been the adults.

Father was right. He could do what he wanted to out here, and know one knew or cared what he was up to. We longed for the days in Chicago and at Grandmother Cahala's. We lived from day to day and tried hard not to displease anyone. We didn't have the right to complain, so Father said. We were treated worse than the animals, and we began to feel and act like animals – labor animals, that is.

Mother and Aunt Joe were getting more and more unhappy. They talked about leaving a lot, and argued over who would stay with Father and us kids.

Aunt Joe said to my mother, "You should stay because you can cook well. You can make a meal out of nothing. I don't know how to cook well." And this was true. Mother could make the best yeast bread anyone ever tasted. Grandmother had taught her to do this.

Mother replied, "You should stay because you are stronger than I am. You can saw wood and cut it up into firewood. You can carry water and never break a sweat. You know how to work on cars. You can help him more than I can."

Finally Aunt Joe said, The facts of life are that you are the wife, and all these children legally belong to you. They are your responsibility; accept that. That's what you get for claiming my children. Are you going to claim Vesta's, too?"

Chapter FIVE

ONE NIGHT, I got up to go to the barnyard. The only door in the house was in Father's bedroom. Mother was eating jelly and bread in the kitchen. I could see her because of the wide doorway.

The next morning, Father said, "Someone got up during the night and stole a jar of jelly and some bread. I am going to whip all of you until the guilty party admits to it." He lined all of us children up, including the babies. He got his leather strap and started whipping us with it.

Mother said nothing. She and Aunt Joe just watched Father whip us. I was hurt and confused that Mother would let us be beaten for something she knew she had done. I wondered if Father would have beaten her. I was afraid to tell him that Mother had eaten the jelly. He beat us for some time while Mother and Aunt Joe watched. I felt she didn't love us. I felt like she believed we kids were worthless, and that is why she enjoyed watching us get whipped.

Finally, Delores said, "I ate the jelly. I was hungry." I knew Delores was lying, but I still couldn't tell Father that Mother had eaten the jelly. Father took Delores out on the front porch again and made her lay face down. He put his foot on her neck and beat her till she couldn't get up. I helped her up again, and then I got whipped. Mother never did own up to eating the jelly.

Later, I asked Delores why she had lied. She told me that she had to stop the whipping of the babies. They were just too young to be treated that way. I told her I had seen Mother eating the jelly. Delores told me to tell no one else what I had seen. We made a promise to always look after each other. We used blood from the cuts made by the strap Father had whipped us with to seal our oath to always look after each other. No matter what happened, we had to take care of each other. Our father tried to make that goal impossible for us, but he did not succeed.

When my brother, Glenn, was born, Father and Aunt Joe beat Mother up. Delores and I tried to doctor Mother's wounds. Mother set the dishpan on a chair so I could reach it and taught me how to wash dishes, which became one of my jobs.

When Glenn was two weeks old, Mother left and went to Chicago to work. What I didn't understand then, and still don't, was that Aunt Joe was the one in bed. This made nine of us.

It upset me because Mother left us alone with Father. Why I was upset I couldn't figure out. She had never tried to protect us from Father or Aunt Joe in any way. She never tried to comfort us at any time. I told myself I hated her. She shouldn't go away and leave us children with Father and Aunt Joe. They were both very mean to us. What could she be thinking? Delores and I both felt that now we were truly alone; there was no help for us.

It was blackberry-picking time. We got in the car and drove for several hours until we came to a large blackberry field. We picked blackberries until dark, and then we went home and canned them. We also made jelly; we did this many times that summer. Sometimes I went along and watched the younger children under the shade trees, and other times I stayed at home and watched them.

Mother had taught me how to make yeast bread and to cook a little. I washed the canning jars, canned the berries and made jelly. Father said, "You are not to answer the door when we aren't here. When someone knocks, you take the children in the bedroom and keep them quiet. Stay in the house unless you are doing chores. If you are outside when you see or hear someone coming, you hide and keep the young ones close to you. I had better not get word that anyone knew you were here. If I do, you will be damn sorry. I will whip you until you have no ass left." I tried hard to keep the younger ones out of sight of the road.

We did a lot of canning that summer. Father built a stand out of rocks to set a washtub on. The boys gathered the wood and the girls put the food in the jars, and then put the jars in the washtub. We built a fire under it and canned food by the washtub-full. We worked into the night.

After Father thought I had learned enough about canning, he took Aunt Joe, Vesta, La Verne, Delores, Orlaff and Orlando to work in the fields. I was left at the farm with Cathy, Dennis and Glenn. I was told to carry the water before the sun came up and after it went down. I was given some long-sleeved shirts, long pants, a hat and gloves. Father said to me, "Wear these clothes when you are outside in the fields for any reason. Put a long gown on Glenn when you leave the house and set the table on the end of his gown. Take Dennis and Cathy with you."

It seemed to me that Father was gone a long time, and I worried about who would help Delores when Father beat her. Who would share their food with her when Father refused to feed her for some reason?

One night they came home late, but I would rather Father had stayed away forever. Father brought home some green beans. Delores and I were to can them. Father was angry because we were not working fast enough. Instead of waiting until the water-cooled, we tried to lift the tub off the fire so it would cool faster. Delores was able to lift her end a little bit, but I could not lift my end. The tub tipped over on me, and I fell in the hot water.

Father yelled at Delores and said, "Strip her clothes off! Strip them off now! Get her out of that water now!"

I was stripped of my clothes and put to bed with sheets covering me. Father had Vesta cover my whole body with baking soda and water; she had made a paste out of it. It seemed like weeks before I could wear clothes without them hurting my skin. Even before my burns were completely healed, if Father decided I needed it, or if I did something I shouldn't have, I still got my beating.

Once, while walking across the porch, Delores was bitten by a rattlesnake. Father said, "At least it was the expendable one that got bit."

Father cut her leg and sucked out some blood. Many times he said, "Too bad I didn't just let her die from that snake bite. I couldn't have gone to prison for that."

Delores would say under her breath, "I wish you would have let me die, too."

Father bought a new car and painted a picture of a naked girl on each door, covering her private parts with a ribbon. He was proud of his work and took his car into town one day, where some of the women in the area saw his pictures. They had conniption fits and raised a big stink.

When Father told us about the women's dislike for his painting, I agreed with them. Father said that he had told the women they were nothing but "hillbilly, nosy, old biddy-bodies," and that they should mind their own business.

I wondered what their reaction would be if they knew what their husbands did when they came to visit my father. I wondered if they cared how their husbands embarrassed and touched us girls. My mother and Aunt Joe didn't care. The other women didn't care. I felt that if they cared about their families, they had to know what they did over here. I felt they were no better than their husbands or my father.

Chapter SIX

FATHER SOMETIMES BROUGHT as many as a dozen men home to play cards. He got out the round table he kept in the smokehouse. Father, Aunt Joe and the men played cards and drank whiskey. Vesta cooked for them. It was the girls' job to serve the food and keep the whiskey glasses full. As we did, these men would feel our breasts and private parts.

One night, Vesta and La Verne put some kind of hot sauce in their drinks. Father took the mattress off the bed and tied them to it. He whipped them with the leather strap until their flesh was bleeding and they smelled like fish. (Their flesh smelled like fish to me. I don't know any other way to explain the smell of human flesh that has been raw and infected for a few days. I guess it was rotting flesh.)

After the men were through playing cards, they were always drunk. Father would lock us in a chicken wire fence he had made. The fence was about four feet by eight feet. We were made to undress. The men stared at us and made comments about our bodies. We wanted to be invisible. They called one girl at a time over to the fence so they could feel her. It seemed like we were in that fence a long time.

One of the men had bulging eyes – I called him "Bug Eyes." Oh, how I wanted to poke his eyes out with my fingers! But I didn't dare try. As we stood behind the wire fence one night, "Bug Eyes" called me over to him.

Father said, "Take it easy on her, she is not quite ready yet. I have other plans for her, providing she cooperates with me."

All the men laughed, as if my father had said something funny. I did not feel like laughing with them. Instead, I felt ashamed and very small.

When they were through looking at us and touching us, the men went home. Father unlocked the gate and we were allowed to go to bed. At least every weekend they played cards, and most of the time it was more often.

I can't describe how I felt at this time. But I couldn't cry. I was afraid I might get whipped for crying. I really wanted to scream as loudly as I could. I learned to go into a dream-like state where I did not feel what was happening to me. My mind was doing something I enjoyed doing (sometimes I was pretending to pick flowers), while my body was wherever Father wanted it to be. I couldn't see them, feel them or hear them until they screamed at me. This was the only escape I had; mentally, I really wasn't there. Sometimes, in my mind, I was sitting in my big pine tree. I expect the other children did a lot of that too.

Once in a while during the daytime, one of the women would come by looking for her husband, and bring us discarded clothing or something from their garden, which Father wouldn't let us have. They never stayed long and never even asked how we were doing. We were just dirty, worthless kids to them. None of them asked us if we needed any help. They didn't care; it wasn't their problem. I wanted to tell them that Father wasn't the only dirty low-down snake in this part of the land. Their husbands and sons were just as bad. These people were low-down snakes, and I hated them.

For people not to see and understand what Father was doing to us kids had to be because they did not care. What kind of people don't care about children, especially the little ones? We had sores all over our bodies where we had been beaten. We could not hide these sores, especially when Father put us in the chicken fence for the men to look at. Surely one of them told their wife about us? If their wives had paid attention, they would have seen the sores on our arms and legs. They would also have seen how dirty we were, how tired we looked and even how hungry we were, if they had wanted to see. People are blind when they want to be.

Father had found hell when he found this place; he liked it because he was the devil. Mother and Aunt Joe were his helpers, along with the other men who lived around us. I guessed that God was not allowed to go into hell to help kids. When Father turned his hell toward Mother and Aunt Joe, they left and went back to the city, leaving us kids to deal with the hell by ourselves. Sometimes Delores and I even pretended that Father had horns, a tail and carried a pitchfork. The biggest problem presented itself when our pretending seemed to be real.

When Mother left, Father started teaching my brothers to be his helpers. They became sort of Father's demons. He gave them better food, and sometimes candy, when they snitched on us girls for talking to each other or not working hard enough when he wasn't present. Orlaff especially took great pride in this. Orlando and Dennis, even though he was quite young, had some sympathy. But they agreed with Orlaff when he told on us because they thought they had to.

It seemed there was no way out for us. We realized this, and this caused us to take no interest in anything, except trying to please the ones that had the authority to abuse us, as they desired. Many times we acted like a bunch of zombies with no minds of our own. That was the best way to stay out of trouble and to stay alive. We did anything they told us to do so that we would avoid getting abused or shamed in front of those men.

One day Mr. Lawrence, who was to be our schoolteacher, came to our house. He told my father that the church was being opened to use as a schoolhouse. There were now sixteen children of school age in the area. "Your children had better be in school on Monday morning," he said.

We four older children went to school. I started first grade, as best as I can remember, because there was no kindergarten class. I had no shoes to wear, so I went barefoot. We wore our bib jeans to school. We stunk so badly that all the kids made fun of us, so we stayed mostly to ourselves.

The schoolhouse was one room with a closet. We kept our lunches and coats in the closet. We never had enough to eat; we were always hungry, especially Delores. Father gave her less food than the rest of us, and sometimes none at all. Many times I shared my food with her.

The teacher, Mr. Lawrence, caught Delores stealing another child's food. Delores got into a lot of trouble for this. She got her usual beating on the front porch, and was an outcast at school from then on. I wanted so badly to help my sister, but I just didn't know how. I continued to help her when she was beaten. The best I could do was to try to give her more of my food. I got to the point where I couldn't feel the whippings.

Vesta excelled in school; she was Father's pride and joy. He taught the rest of us children that she was special, had special talents and was much more beautiful and smart than any of the rest of us could ever be. This made me feel very small.

One day it snowed really hard, but Vesta insisted on taking the long way around. She wanted to visit with the Wheeler girl. It was shorter to walk through the lane and pastures than to walk along the roads. We walked three and a half miles to school, the short way. How far it was going the long way, I don't know. Delores and La Verne tried to carry me. I was too heavy for them. Vesta was showing off for the Wheeler children and refused to help carry me. My feet were cold, and I was crying. Delores and La Verne did the best they could for me. Vesta seemed to be heartless. She, too, seemed to believe she was special. She acted like my mother – very special.

We had to listen to Vesta because Father had said, "All of you kids, listen to Vesta from the time you leave this house until you get back into this yard. I will beat the child's ass until they can't stand up that gives her any trouble." We had to go the way Vesta wanted to or get in big trouble.

Aunt Joe, realizing I wasn't wearing shoes, grabbed a blanket and ran through the lane and pastures, hoping to get to me before school let out. When she got to the school, she knew she had missed us because she hadn't met us on the way. Aunt Joe figured we must have taken the long way home. She ran down the road until she caught up with us when we were within a mile of home. My feet were frozen; I couldn't go to school for a while.

Vesta got into trouble for not using common sense. Father said, "I expect you to be smarter than the rest of these kids. They are only workers. You are better than they are; use your brains."

A neighbor gave me a pair of shoes. The shoes hurt my feet, but I had to wear them, and I had better not complain to anyone.

Delores and I missed a lot of school because of the beatings we got. We stayed home and did what work we were able to do without being seen by anyone driving down the road. Sometimes I had to make Father's winnie (that is what he called his penis to me) happy. This wasn't very pleasant for me. I always went out in the yard and washed my hands with dirt over and over. After I rubbed dirt all over my hands, I curled up behind the stove in our bedroom.

We taught Orlando and Orlaff how to help us milk the cow, and feed the chickens and horse. We did all the chores before and after school. We worked late at night carrying water to water the garden and trees when it did not rain. The abuse continued if Father felt we were not working fast enough.

We had no ice box, so we put the milk outside in gallon jars at night, and put them under shade trees during the day. The bubbling spring was now too far away for us to use as a refrigerator. When milk sours, it makes whey. When there was whey on top of the jars, Father accused Delores of sneaking into the milk at night and peeing in the milk jar to fill it up, to keep him from noticing that the jar had been touched.

Father tied Delores to a tree and said, "The child that hits her with the biggest rock, I will buy a candy bar for the next time I am in town. Don't hit her with one big enough to kill her. Make sure she feels it, though." I cried and refused to hit her with rocks. Father called me a crybaby. Delores begged me to throw rocks at her, but I refused. I couldn't hurt my sister. My father couldn't force me to throw rocks at my sister.

Father tied me to another tree. He said, "Throw rocks at her, too. Throw smaller rocks at her. She has to learn to get rid of that mother-fucking, soft heart she has. Don't put any scars on her face or body if you can possibly help it. I have other plans for her when she gets old enough. I have to beat these soft, sympathetic, godly, right and wrong feelings she has out of her."

After Father did this the first time, he always kept candy bars to give to the child who hit Delores with the biggest rock. I never in my life hit Delores with a rock; I always refused to. And I always got tied to a tree with Delores.

Father told me, "You are stupid and stubborn. Your emotions are getting you into a lot of trouble. You are a weak individual. There is no place in this world for people like you. I will break you. I will change your thinking, or I will kill you."

I said, "You can't take away what I feel in my heart; not even I can change that. Believe me, I have tried."

This made him even angrier and he said, "We will see who wins this war."

Then one day, Aunt Joe left home and went to Chicago to work, leaving us with Father. At this point, I was sure I hated everyone, even God.

At times, Father would take Vesta, La Verne, Delores, Orlando and Orlaff, leaving the rest of us at the farm. Sometimes they were gone for several days. I didn't mind; we were safer without Father. We did the work that had to be done. I took care of the younger children.

When the schoolteacher, Mr. Lawrence, or anyone else came to the door, we didn't open it. Instead, we took the little ones to the back of our large bedroom where there were no windows and hid. We tried desperately to keep the little ones quiet. Keeping them quiet was not always easy.

Sometimes Mr. Lawrence came to the back door and tried to open it. We always kept it locked. He yelled, "Is there anybody home? These kids need to be in school. Where is their mother? I need to talk to someone. Is anybody home?" He walked away, mumbling to himself. We knew Mr. Lawrence was angry.

Many times I got scared at night. I hid the younger children and myself behind the old heater. I stacked wood high enough to where we could not be seen. I laid a piece of plywood over the stacks of wood. My brother, Dennis, and I put as much wood as we could on top of the plywood, hoping it would look like one big stack of wood. I thought that by doing this, we would be safe if one of Father's drinking friends broke into the house. I tried to be prepared for everything.

When it stormed, we put wood around the table and got under the table. I hoped nothing would get in our eyes if the ceiling fell in. I thought the table was the heaviest thing in the house. It might catch some of the falling debris and keep us from getting hurt.

If we were outside, I watched and listened for any cars coming down the road, or any unusual noise I couldn't identify. If I thought I heard something, we immediately hid ourselves. During this time, my younger sister and brothers would listen to me without argument. We were children who depended on each other for survival. Everyone seemed to sense this.

At that point, there were nine of us children. Vesta was the oldest, and then came La Verne, Delores, myself (Frances), Orlaff, Orlando, Dennis, Cathy and Glenn. We all believed that Kitty was our mother.

There were many times when I was alone with the younger children on the farm. I was very hurt and angry with Mother for leaving us alone with Father. I didn't understand why I had these feelings. Mother and Aunt Joe did very little, and most of the time nothing, to comfort or protect us. I longed to be back in Chicago. Life was easier there. I could still remember playing outside. I longed for the attention and praise Mr. and Mrs. Coffman gave to me.

Aunt Joe came back for a while and, again, there was much bickering in the house. Nothing else changed. They still had their drinking parties, we still got put in the chicken wire fence, and we still got beaten and rapped on the head with Aunt Joe's knuckles.

I felt ashamed and dirty after a beating. I wondered if Delores felt the same way. I taught Delores my mind game of going somewhere else and leaving my body behind. I hoped this would help her feel better about herself because she believed the things Father said about her not being any good.

Once, she said to me, "I wish I had never been Father's mother-in-law." She wouldn't believe me when I told her she had never been his mother-in-law, that he must be crazy to say things like that.

I truly hated rubbing and petting his winnie. I also felt ashamed and dirty when Father sat me on his lap and rubbed his hands over my nipples. He said, "This will make you develop faster." Sometimes he said, "It won't be long now."

Most of the kids did very little talking; we were afraid to. But when Delores and I thought we were alone, we sometimes talked to each other. Mostly we talked about God, and wondered if there was such a person. I think we gained strength from each other. At least I know I gained strength from her. We helped each other as much as we could. Just complaining to each other about our situation helped a great deal.

Vesta started sleeping with Father and Aunt Joe all the time. She didn't seem to mind it anymore. Vesta still wet the bed, and Delores still got beaten for it. How could Delores straddle Vesta with Father in the bed with her, and wet on top of her without Father knowing it? It puzzled me that he could think that. Even I knew this was not possible. I believed he just felt like being mean.

One day, Father gave La Verne and me a feed sack with something in it. He said, "Don't open this sack. Take it out into the woods, dig as deep a hole as you can and bury it." We looked in the sack. It had bloody sheets, blankets and what looked like a small baby in it.

Father and Aunt Joe had a big fight. Father said, "I never want to see your face again. Go! Go!" Aunt Joe left and went to Chicago to work again.

After that, Father sometimes had La Verne sleep with him. He took Delores out to the barn or in the woods for sex. He said she was too dirty and ornery to use his bed. Delores was treated worse than anybody's dog was ever treated, and our mother knew it.

After Aunt Joe left, Vesta ran away. Father and the men he played cards with tracked her down. Father took the mattress off the bed, tied her to the bare springs and beat her with his belt. I wondered if he was going to kill her. I feared he might. He told the neighbors that Vesta was sneaking around at night with the Wheeler boy. When Father was not there, I cleaned her sores with water. That was one of the times I did not hate Vesta.

Vesta graduated from eighth grade that year. She was very proud of herself. I could see her eyes twinkling and the smile she wore on her face. Mr. Lawrence wanted Vesta to go to high school. She had graduated with some kind of honors. She would have to ride a school bus to Alton, Missouri. That was the closest high school.

Father pretended that she would be in school next year, though he knew he had no intention of sending her. I could hear Father and Vesta arguing, and Father saying, "There is no way I will allow you to ride a bus with other people, nor will I spend that much time away from you."

I knew Vesta wanted to go to high school really badly. She would have given anything if Father would have let her go. She wanted to learn at this time in her life. Vesta cried a lot during this time.

Father just yelled at her and said, "If I turn you loose in a high school, you will be nothing but a slut. And you might start talking out of school to a teacher that you think you like, and then I would have to run and leave you behind to keep from going to prison. Eventually, you will talk to someone. I know you will!"

Father didn't realize it, but Delores and I desperately hoped something like that would happen. We didn't dare voice it, but we defiantly prayed for it to happen. When we had such thoughts, we also prayed he couldn't read our minds and didn't know what we were thinking. Sometimes we thought he did because he would whip us while we were thinking bad things about him or Mother and Aunt Joe. Some people could read your mind and we thought we knew that.

Then Father bought a truck and he fixed the engine. He made a small compartment in the front part of the bed, just wide enough for us children to squeeze into. He put benches on each side and a toilet seat under the back window of the cab. We put mattresses and some clothes with all the canned goods in the back of the truck and covered it with a tarp, tying the tarp down good so the wind could not get underneath it. We left the farm late one night. Father was hoping we would go undetected. It must have worked; no one stopped us. Father could do what he wanted.

We didn't realize it, but this move was designed to keep us out of school. We all knew Vesta was sad because Father wouldn't let her ride a bus to high school. This was one incident we thought was a blessing. We hoped things would be better for us now.

We left the farm and started working the fields. Delores and I thought this might be good. If we left the farm, Father couldn't think of so many reasons to beat us. We were wrong; it made no difference. Even on the road, Father found every excuse to beat Delores or tie her to a tree, when we were isolated enough. It was not hard to find an isolated spot or for Father to imagine one of us had done something wrong. Sometimes he just imagined that one of us had said something bad about him. It didn't take much to get his imagination working or his temper up.

When we were on the road, we slept in the back of the truck. Sometimes Father made everyone get out of the truck, and then took one of the girls in the back of the truck. When it rained, we took turns holding the tarp up with a broom handle so the rain would drain off and we wouldn't get as wet.

When we were traveling and stopped to sleep, we were made to climb trees and run. Father said, "You have to keep your strength built up so you will be able to work, and you can't do that as lazy as you are acting. You have to keep your muscles developed or you will be a bunch of wimps."

Then he left and went into a town, leaving us at camp, and brought other men with him when he came back. They played cards, drank, looked at and felt us girls. I thought that there were a lot of bad people in this world. No one could stop Father; he was the devil. Where were all the good people? Had the bad people killed all the good people?

We worked at any kind of crop Father could find. We had to work hard or we got whipped. I could work early in the morning before the sun got hot and late in the evening when the sun was low. We worked from daylight until dark. We each had to do so much work, which was determined by Father, or get whipped.

When we were picking cotton, I had to pick a hundred pounds. Delores had to pick five hundred pounds. Most of the time, I couldn't pick my quota. I could only work a few hours in the morning and evening, so Delores would help me. When she helped me or the crop was not so good, she couldn't meet her quota. I felt bad when she was beaten because she had helped me. She made me promise I wouldn't tell Father. She said, "It is part of our promise to take care of each other. I am stronger then you are. I can take it, but you are too frail and skinny." The other kids did not tell either. On this point we were lucky.

One day we were picking raspberries somewhere. I don't know what state we were in. We were pretending it was Delores' birthday. I was calling it her lucky day. Since we didn't know when our birthdays were, we sometimes pretended it was one of our birthdays. We had learned about birthdays in school. It was early in the morning and the owner of the field, Mr. Palmer, was surprised to see us up so early. Mr. Palmer came over to us after he heard us talking and fooling around. No one was there but us, so we talked to him for a while as we worked.

That afternoon, Mr. Palmer called it a day about 5:00 p.m. He said he wanted us to come to the wagon. When we got there, he had gallons of ice cream. All the workers sang "Happy Birthday" to Delores. One of the kids went to get Vesta, so she could have ice cream, too. Instead, Father came. Father took Delores out in the woods. When he came back, Delores wasn't with him. Father took the rest of us home.

Mr. Palmer, the man we were working for, had an empty garage that he let us live in. He also had a house trailer that Father had bought. Vesta and Father slept in the trailer, while the rest of us slept in the garage. I looked for Delores in the garage and couldn't find her. I asked Father, "Where is Delores?"

He said, "She is out in the woods. She can lie there until she dies. You are not to help her. You keep your damn right-and-wrong ideas to yourself."

After Father went into his trailer, I went looking for Delores in the woods. I found her lying where he had beaten her until she couldn't get up. Somehow I managed to help her back to the garage. Father never knew I had helped her that time. In any case, I didn't get whipped for it.

Mr. Palmer paid Father a visit very early the next morning, while we kids were in the field. We never knew just what had been said. Delores could not work that day, and she was in the garage. Father came to the field and got us, and we left that place. Father never mentioned the conversation they had. He acted surprised that Delores had made it back to the garage. We went back to the farm.

Sometime that winter, we met Mother and Aunt Joe. Two babies were born, Elijah and La Donna. This made eleven of us. Aunt Joe went back to Chicago, leaving the babies with us.

Mother did not stay long after Aunt Joe had left. Father took Mother to the bus station. He had a car accident on the way. Mother was hurt pretty badly. Later, Mother said, "Otis deliberately turned the wheels of the car into the bridge and jumped out, so he would not be hurt. Your father tried to kill me. He was walking down the road away from me and the car, when someone saw the car and stopped."

When Mother healed enough to travel, Aunt Joe came and got her. Father had a few of his drinking parties. Then we left in the truck. I dreaded getting into that truck.

We worked in the fields again. Life continued as before for quite some time. Then Aunt Joe brought a baby girl to us. Her name was Bonnie. This made twelve of us. Father and Aunt Joe fought. Father said, "This baby is not mine; I don't want it."

Aunt Joe took a walk one morning, leaving Bonnie with us. She did not come back. Father was very angry. He said, "I will kill that bitch for this. She had better never come back crying to me again. I've had enough."

Father took us to the Pettigrews' place somewhere between Horatio and De Queen, Arkansas. We were living in a barn at this time. La Verne shared the trailer with Father. We made fun of Vesta for getting so fat. Suddenly one day, Vesta screamed out in pain and she peed a whole lot. Something was wrong with her. I asked if one of the kids would go to the Pettigrews and get some help, so I could stay with Vesta. They were afraid to go without Father's permission. Father was not home, so I went to the Pettigrews, leaving Vesta in their hands.

When I got there, I said to Mrs. Pettigrew, "Vesta is sick. I don't know what is wrong. She wet all over the floor."

Mrs. Pettigrew replied, "Go back to the barn and stay with her."

After about half an hour, a lady named Elizabeth came to help Vesta. Vesta gave birth to Betty in the barn where we slept. Betty was very small. Vesta said that Betty had come early, and that was the reason she was so small. This made thirteen of us children.

After a while, Vesta rejoined her place with Father. While we were at the Pettigrews', Father not only beat us, but he also allowed the boys to whip us, as they saw fit. He said, "I am teaching my boys how to handle their women. This is something they must know."

I started bleeding down below. I was afraid something was wrong with me. I told no one. I didn't know why I bled down there. I just didn't know what Father would do to me if I were unable to work at all. He wanted people that were able to work hard, not a sickly person. We finished the season and went back to the Pettigrews' place.

A year later, Vesta gave birth to Pearl. Father was home, and he delivered her. This made fourteen of us children. Father ran down to the Pettigrews' to show her off. He acted like a proud papa. I wondered if he had acted like that when I was born, or if he had wished I had not been born at all.

La Verne got sick, and Aunt Joe and Mother came down from Chicago. La Verne was taken to the hospital. There seemed to be some kind of legal trouble. Everyone thought La Verne might die. I didn't know until years later that La Verne had developed an infection from an abortion Father had performed on her.

Mother and Aunt Joe stayed at the hospital with La Verne most of the time. They bragged about having showers when they did come home. We children had no water to bathe in.

While Mother and Aunt Joe were at the hospital, Father decided that it was my turn to become a woman. He said, "I am going to the store. Come along with me." He bought a can of root beer for me. Then we drove to a little forest-like spot. Father said. "Get out of the car. I want to go for a walk."

We walked through the trees for a while. Father started feeling me down below, and touching my breasts. He said, "Today, you become a woman." He gently took off my clothes and laid me on the ground. He kissed me and touched me; then he hurt me. He stuck his penis in me down below. I thought that this hurt me; he didn't care.

I started bleeding down below. I wasn't too worried; I had done that a couple of times before. We went for a walk a few more times and Father did the same thing. The woods were beautiful; Father's purpose for walking in them was not. I didn't want to go on these walks ever again with him, but I had no choice. I had to do as my father said, or get beaten to death.

Father suddenly became very upset about La Verne being in the hospital. He said, "She may talk to someone who is too nosy, or say something she shouldn't." He wanted to bring her home. Mother and Aunt Joe said no.

Father said, "You women have nothing to say about it; she is coming home. Shut your traps and get everything ready for her. She needs special attention and care. Get busy and be ready to leave when I get back. It will be safer to leave now."

Mother and my father fought, and then my mother left. Father took La Verne out of the hospital against the doctor's advice. La Verne couldn't walk, and Father carried her like she was a baby. Aunt Joe was angry with Father for doing this, and they fought. Aunt Joe had no choice but to go with us.

We left Arkansas in a hurry. We camped at a state park somewhere in another state. Vesta and her babies moved into the truck with the rest of us kids. La Verne and Aunt Joe stayed in the trailer. Father and Vesta were not there most of the time. I took care of Vesta's babies while they did whatever it was they did. Father often came back drunk. If Vesta was drunk, I don't really know, but Vesta sure tried to act like a queen while we were there.

One day Aunt Joe said, "I will show that mother-fucking son-of-a-bitch what kind of say I have. If I can get La Verne to Dr. Barton, maybe she will be all right. If I don't do something, she is going to die and he will bury her in some woods, God knows where. No one will even know she was ever born. Dr. Barton probably won't give me any trouble or ask a lot of questions. I am not going to jail because Otis is so horny he has to have all the females in his life."

The next time Father and Vesta went out, Aunt Joe took La Verne and Bonnie, and left. Father was very upset and immediately moved us to another spot. Vesta and her babies moved back in the trailer. She was very happy about being able to sleep in the trailer again.

One day Father said to me, "I want you to come with me today. You will enjoy it." We walked for a long time. We came to a wooded area, and Father turned down a dirt road. After a while he stopped and said, "Let's walk down this way."

He was carrying a small leather case. We came to a large log, and he said, "Sit down." I sat down. Then he said, "I am going to have to give you an abortion. Now here is a nice soft spot. Be a good girl and lie down and take off your overalls."

He did not explain to me what an abortion was. He took some shiny tools out of the bag and gave me some whiskey to drink. Then he stuck the shiny tool in my private parts. It hurt very badly. I screamed and screamed. I did not understand why Father was hurting me with that thing. I was afraid to ask any questions; he might hurt me more.

I had my monthly period. I bled a lot. It lasted a long time, but I thought this was because it had been a while since I had had a period. For several days after he did this to me, I passed large clots of blood. I did not feel well, and my stomach cramped. Father did not make me watch after the little ones for a while. The other kids worked for a while, but Father did not make me do much. I appreciated being a recipient of his kindness. Maybe he wasn't so bad after all.

I told my sister, Delores, what Father had done to me. She explained that Father had taken a sharp instrument and killed a baby that was growing inside of me.

I asked, "How did a baby get inside of me and Vesta?" Even though I knew how babies came out of the womb, I didn't know how babies got in. I didn't make the connection that what Father did to me was making a baby.

Delores asked me, "Have you ever bled down there before?"

I answered, "A few times, before Father took me for a walk and hurt me with his winnie."

My sister tried to explain the birds and the bees to me. She said, "Father said he was saving you for something special. I wondered what it was. He made you just like the rest of us when he screwed you. No more fancy sister, you're just a girl. I've watched how you can act like a zombie when you want to. It's time to stop that; you must face reality."

I tried to explain that when our father beat me or made me do things I knew were wrong, I took my mind to a place I enjoyed because that way I did not feel anything. I just did what I was told. I entered into my dream-like state when I couldn't handle what was going on in my life.

I was ignorant because my father kept me ignorant. We went to school a week or two at a time, only when Father was forced to send us. We were not allowed to talk to anyone but our sisters and brothers. I couldn't read or write. My older sisters could read and write, but they had no time or materials to teach me. No one bothered to teach me anything. All I knew was what Delores had told me. Delores had a Bible and sometimes she read it to me when we could get away from the other children. We knew we would get beaten if we were caught reading it.

I performed the act of sex because my father told me to, and I didn't feel like I had a choice to disobey him. He didn't explain what he was doing to me or what the consequences might be. I knew what the consequences would be if I did not mind him. I wanted to avoid those consequences at all costs, if I could do so without hurting another person.

In my heart something told me what was happening to me was wrong. I didn't like to see my sisters and brothers beaten or made to cry for no reason. I didn't like to be beaten or made to pet Father's penis. I most definitely didn't like it when Father hurt me with his penis and put a baby inside me. Or when he put a shiny instrument in me and killed the little baby. I felt it was my fault that he killed the baby. I had made him angry somehow. I felt responsible for the baby's death.

I was beginning to have the ability to put two and two together, even though I still didn't understand fully about the birds and the bees. Delores and I started talking and planning to run away. We got a few whippings for whispering to each other at night.

Then we went back to the Pettigrews'. We parked the trailer in a different spot this time. Instead of living in the barn, we lived in a one-room shack in a field away from Mr. Pettigrew's house. Father and Mr. Pettigrew seemed to be trying to hide us kids for some reason. Somebody had seen a trailer parked by the shack and came to investigate. They found the children who weren't in school.

Somehow Father was forced to send us to school. We were told not to play or speak to other children. We could speak to the teacher only if it pertained to our schoolwork. If any of the kids said we spoke or played with another child, we got beaten. We were not supposed to answer questions from any person that might ask one of us.

Once, the school took us to a ball game. The noise was so loud and my head hurt so badly, that I felt sick to my stomach. I did not feel like I could sit in that seat another minute. I fainted and someone took me home. Father was so angry. I got whipped for fainting, and Delores got whipped for letting it happen. Father knew I couldn't stand a lot of noise; it always made me sick. What did Father expect Delores to do, carry me home without permission?

Pearl couldn't have been more than a year old when Delores and I decided to run away and find Mother. We were sure if we could make her understand how awful things were, she would keep all of us with her.

It was late April or early May of 1952. I was about 11 years old and Delores was about 13. It was fairly warm, but got cool at night. I was worried about the younger children. Delores assured me that if we took them with us, we would get caught. We vowed we would come back for them, no matter what. Delores was not allowed near the other children.

When La Verne was there she was caught up in her misery and paid no attention to the younger ones' needs. That left only me. Vesta took care of her own children. They lived in the trailer with Father and her. Sometimes she asked me to watch them so she could get some rest or go somewhere with Father.

Vesta ate better and dressed better than the rest of us, and most of the time she was treated better. She never had to work. We believed Vesta was very happy; we thought she had everything. The only times I did not hate Vesta were the few times I saw Father beat her. The other kids had no pity for her, not even Delores.

For some reason, even though I knew I would be punished, I always tried to help the child in trouble. It was something I just had to do. I could not explain this need I had. Father cursed my poor sympathetic heart. I couldn't stand by and watch someone suffer when maybe I could do something to make him or her feel better.

Father was right; I was a very stupid person. I took a lot of punishment I didn't have to just because I felt sorry for people. What could I do to stop myself from being so dumb? I felt good when I could help people. I weighed this thing out in my mind. Was it worth it to get punished for helping someone else? I pondered over these things.

The more I thought, the more confused I got. I was angry with Father for putting a baby in my stomach. I was even angrier because he had killed it. Maybe my poor heart, as Father called it, was a good thing to have, not being mean to people like Father was. Yes, I thought, I liked my heart. Father had lost this war. He had been unable to change the way my heart felt.

I would go with Delores. We would run away and find civilization – that's what Aunt Fern had called it. She had said, "Civilization has to be out there somewhere." Maybe we could find it. Maybe if we could find our mother in Chicago, she would not send us back to Father, and maybe we could all live with Mother. I was sure we couldn't go as far as Grandmother Cahala's. Besides, she had told Mother she didn't want to keep us.

I debated all these things in my mind. It seemed like a vicious circle; there were no answers. I felt there was no place in this world for us. No one wanted us; no one cared about us. Why were we born in the first place? Not even Grandmother and Grandfather Cahala cared what happened to us anymore. This was not fair. It seemed other children had people who cared about them. Why didn't anyone care about us? What was wrong with me and my brothers and sisters?

A lot of things raced through my head. I was tired of living in this terrible turmoil. It would be better to be dead. Then you couldn't hear, feel or know anything. It would be more pleasant. We could kill each other, but how? We decided against this; we did not want to die.

We made a lot of elaborate plans that did not happen. It wasn't as easy to run away as we believed it would be. We knew Father might have a lot of nasty men looking for us. This was a terrible risk for us to take, but we both agreed we had to take this risk. Delores would be the boss. She was the oldest and had more knowledge and brains than I did. We agreed on that point. We knew we had to stay off the roads as much as we possibly could, and we could only trust ourselves.

We wanted to pick a night that it would not be raining, and a night that people, especially our father, would be sleeping late. Father didn't seem to like the rain. When we were working and it rained, we continued to work and Father sat in the car.

We were successful on both of these points. Now we had to figure out a way to stay alive. The best we could come up with was to make sure that we stayed together. And to pray a lot — we both remembered that from Mrs. Ray, the piano teacher in Chicago.

We also knew if we couldn't find food to eat, we would have to try to steal it. We planned to stay in the woods, so we thought we wouldn't have to do that. We would find nuts and some berries and stuff to eat. We hadn't figured out that the berries weren't in yet. We could find some acorns to eat, even though they would taste bad.

Delores said, "We can eat earthworms; they won't hurt us. People have lived a long time just eating bugs. Other people have done worse things."

Most importantly, we couldn't let anything happen to our Bible. We had to keep it from getting wet when it rained or when we had to swim. I wasn't a good swimmer. Delores was, so we decided Delores should carry the Bible. She was also much taller than I was.

We also knew that we had to stay together to survive what we were attempting to do. We both knew it was very dangerous, but we were willing to take our chances. We no longer could continue to live as we had been. The baby killing had to stop.

Delores told me, "They're not babies until they are born." I refused to accept this.

She didn't explain to me that the sticky stuff I got on my fingers was what made babies. Delores got flustered with me and she said, "You are stupid and you really do not understand what has happened to you. Oh well, maybe you are just too young to understand. Let's go before we get caught talking to each other."

CHAPTER SEVEN

WE PACKED A change of clothes and Delores' Bible that she kept hidden from Father. We hid them in a bush behind the outhouse that Mr. Pettigrew had dug for us across the field. We waited until we thought everyone was asleep, and then I quietly went into the trailer and woke Vesta. I asked her for a flashlight. I told her I had to go to the outhouse. Vesta gave me a flashlight.

We stayed off the roads so we would not be seen by anyone. After a while, we came to a wooded area that had a lot of undergrowth in it. We knew that it would be hard going, but it would be the safest way. We walked through woods, waded creeks and swam rivers. We were afraid to sit down and rest. When we did, it was only for a few minutes. We were afraid of wild animals, people and my father finding us.

We found plenty of water to drink, but very little to eat. We were very hungry. I don't know how many days we walked. We made sure to stay away from any roads or houses.

One evening, it was beginning to get dark when we came across some men cutting down trees. We could see lunch buckets sitting near a log. The men were putting saws and other tools in the back of a truck. We had to have those lunch pails. We tried to sneak around and get them. One of the men saw us. The men acted like they were looking for tools, and sneaked around behind the trees and brush near the buckets. When we got to the buckets, the men grabbed us.

We refused to tell them our names or where we were from. The men gave us what was left in their lunch pails. Getting something in our stomachs felt good. After we ate, we couldn't get away from them.

One of the men took us to his home in Winthrop, Arkansas. We became very frightened when we realized he was driving toward De Queen. We begged him to stop the car and let us out. He drove about thirty miles before he stopped.

A woman said we could sleep at their house if we wouldn't try to run away. We promised with our fingers crossed. The man and his wife decided not to clean us up before the authorities saw us. We were fed and allowed to sleep on the floor. They seemed to be very nice people. We were tired, hungry and frightened, and refused to speak. But we were so tired that we fell asleep quickly, and we slept well that night.

They woke us up the next morning and fed us. Delores saw some paper and a pencil lying on a small table. She wrote, "Thank you," gave it to the man and took my hand, and we tried to walk out the door. The man and his wife stopped us. They took us to a police station, where we continued our mute treatment. They tried most of the day to get us to speak, but we refused. We were afraid to trust these people. They might have been Father's friends or taken us home.

Finally, a woman came. She said, "My name is Mrs. Christian. I am your caseworker. I am here to help you if I can." She took us to a church where she got some clothes, shoes, soap and shampoo for us. Some policemen accompanied the caseworker. We allowed no one to touch us.

She then took us to a hotel. The caseworker gave Delores the bottle of shampoo. Delores tried to drink it. The police forcefully took Delores in the bathroom where the caseworker showed her how to use the shampoo. She also showed us how to use the tub, and she combed our hair. I vaguely remembered Mother and Aunt Joe combing our hair. We hadn't thought about or seen a brush or comb since we had left Chicago. We hadn't combed our hair for years. We were too miserable to think about it.

The caseworker took us out to eat three times a day. She made sure we had clean clothes and always tried to get us to talk, but she didn't stay with us all the time. Someone always stood outside our door so we couldn't leave. When we talked to one another in the hotel room, we went into the bathroom, shut the door and whispered, so the person standing outside our door could not hear us. We tried to plan our escape, but couldn't come up with a way. Maybe we could out run them if we just opened the door and bolted down the stairs. We were afraid to try.

I wanted to trust Mrs. Christian. Delores said, "Trust no one; we are alone."

Finally, I told the caseworker we were going to Chicago to find our mother because we hated our father. She was surprised to hear me talk and said, "You can speak."

Delores kept trying to make me shut up by slapping my mouth. The caseworker stood between us, so Delores couldn't hit me. I told her Mother's name and that I did not know where in Chicago she was, but I refused to tell her my name.

After that, Delores was mad at me all the time. The caseworker promised to find our mother. Delores told me not to talk to her anymore, or she would beat the tar out of me. I knew she would do it, too. I tried to stay away from her.

A few nights later, we were in bed when the caseworker knocked on our door. She said, "Your father is waiting for you downstairs."

We quickly pushed the dresser against the door, piled the little table and chair in the room on top of the dresser and locked ourselves in the bathroom. The police got into the hotel room. Through the bathroom door, we told them all about Father. We heard Father cursing and threatening us; then we heard men running and Father yelling.

The caseworker convinced us to open the bathroom door, that we were safe. I asked the caseworker to check on the other children and make sure they were okay. She promised she would check on my sisters and brothers and make sure they were doing all right.

The next morning the caseworker came and took us to breakfast. After breakfast, she said we were going for a ride. She took us to the Pettigrews' place to see the other children. Delores would not get out of the car. Mother was there, but Vesta and Father were not. Mother would not even look at me. Orlaff, Orlando and Dennis kept saying, "You are going to die." Glenn, Cathy, Elijah, La

Donna, Betty and Pearl were glad to see me, and cried when I had to go.

When we left, I asked the caseworker about Vesta, and she said, "Another caseworker is looking after her. She is all right."

The caseworker took us to a foster home in Little Rock, Arkansas. Delores and I were allowed to stay together. There were other children there. A very little girl with long braids was in a wheelchair. I loved to comb her hair, and I spent a great deal of time doing this. Delores started beating me up, and she said, "You are not to talk or play with other people."

We stayed together about a week, when the housemother told us we had to be separated because of the way Delores was treating me. Delores was told that if she quit mistreating me, we could stay together. I don't think she realized she was mistreating me. She thought she was protecting me.

When we were told I was going to be moved, we were unhappy. We continued our walks alone. We found a large bridge that we hung out on. Every day Delores would slap me around and say, "See what you have done now? Why didn't you listen to me? We may never see each other again. Pay attention to where they take you. Remember this bridge; I will be waiting for you here. Do you understand? Will you listen to me this time? Just remember the bridge. I won't be able to wait long. Tell me now if you don't understand."

A woman came to take me to my new foster home. I begged to be allowed to stay with Delores. The foster mother of the house said, "It is for your benefit that we are separating you. It is the best thing for both of you. Be on your way now. Don't worry about your sister; I will take good care of her." Delores refused to say goodbye to me.

I got in the car with a young-looking woman. We drove away, leaving my sister standing in the driveway. Delores yelled, "Remember the bridge; don't forget."

This lady did not like to talk. She didn't even introduce herself. I stared out the window and watched the landscape go by.

I worried about my sisters, especially Delores. What was going to happen now? I had so many questions and no one to answer them.

Would this lady be good to Delores? She seemed to be nice enough to me. Would Delores stay with this woman or would they take her somewhere else, too? I prayed she would be happy wherever they took her. I wondered if I would ever see her again. Would someone be there when she needed help? She had to be better off now than she had been before. No one could be as bad as Father was. Would this lady look the other way if her man was hurting Delores?

Where was Vesta, and why couldn't I see her? Had someone hurt her, and they didn't want me to find out? Did she have her babies with her?

I started worrying about myself. What was going to happen to me, and where were they taking me, anyway? What kind of people would I be living with? Were there other kids where I was going? Why, what, where – too many questions. I fell asleep.

I awoke as we pulled into a driveway and the lady said, "Here we are. Come along now, they are expecting us."

We knocked on a door. A lady and a girl opened it, and the lady told the girl, "Here they are, Nancy." (Nancy was another foster child who lived there.)

The lady at the door introduced herself as Mrs. Martin. She asked, "What is your name?" I told her and she walked away, talking to the lady who had been my driver, whose name I didn't bother to remember.

I stood quietly and stared at Nancy while they talked. When my driver left, Mrs. Martin said, "The lady of the house is not home from work yet. That's okay. I am the one that will be spending the most time with you. Come on, Nancy; let's show Frances her room. Maybe you can go along and help her pick out some new clothes tomorrow. I am told she needs them. You can help her pick out some pretty clothes. Get everything she is going to need for school. It will be fun for you."

They showed me my room, and it was beautiful. They tried to talk to me, but I would not answer them. Nancy asked if I wanted to go outside and play, but I just looked at her. Finally, they gave up and left my room. I locked the door behind them and refused to open it.

That room was a haven to me. The color of the walls was a very light blue, and there was a medium-blue rug on the floor. There were two windows that had curtains with little blue flowers on them. I had never before seen curtains, and I thought they were beautiful. There was a big brown dresser with a large mirror on it. I had never had an indoor bathroom and tub to myself. I had also never had a bed of my own. Everything was so beautiful. Even in this wonderful place, I just couldn't get rid of my fear, though. It was always there, just waiting for a chance to jump out of my body, and so I would hide in the closet.

I felt like a princess at Mrs. Bermingham's house. I felt so wonderful at my new foster home that I would have been happy to stay there for the rest of my life. But I was afraid that I wouldn't be able to stay. At Mrs. Bermingham's, I felt like a person who was worth something for the first time in my life.

A different voice called me for supper that evening, and I pretended not to hear. She kept knocking. I finally said, "I'm not hungry; leave me alone."

The voice said, "Okay, maybe in the morning."

The next morning, the same voice called me to breakfast. Again I said, "I'm not hungry; leave me alone."

She tried several times after that to get me to come out of my room. I refused. After a while she said, "I have to go to work now. I'll see you this evening."

She was gone and everything was quiet, thank God. I felt so very alone. I wanted to cry, but I had learned long ago not to cry. I lay in the bed worrying and crying a little before I dozed off to sleep.

Evening came and the lady of the house wanted me to open the door, but I refused. After a while she said, "It is supper time. Come and get cleaned up."

Again I said, "I am not hungry."

The lady outside my door said, "If you don't open this door now, I will call the police. You have to eat something or you'll get sick."

I opened the door; I did not want to go to jail. I wanted to stay as far away from Father as possible. I didn't want to be with him at any cost. He would kill me if he could. This woman was gentle, but I was scared and not sure I liked her.

The lady said, "I am Mrs. Bermingham. My housekeeper's name is Mrs. Martin. You have already met her. This is Nancy. You will be our guest for a while. Go wash up for supper, and we will talk later."

At supper, she talked and I pretended to listen. In my mind, I retreated to Grandmother's house. When Mrs. Bermingham was through talking, I went back to my wonderful room.

I thought that maybe I could like this lady, but Delores had told me not to talk to her. I knew Delores wanted me to run away and go back to the bridge. But I didn't believe I could find it. We had traveled a long way. I thought about trying to find that bridge. I wondered if she was still standing on the bridge waiting for me. How long would she wait for me there in the cold on that big bridge? I knew she would be angry if I did not show up there. I went to bed and wondered what my life was going to be like from now on. I dreamed Delores was sitting on the bridge, waiting for me. She was very cold.

Mrs. Martin wanted us to wash her feet every evening before Mrs. Bermingham came home from work. The other foster girl, Nancy, hated doing this. To me, this was a simple thing to do. I could wash her feet; I had done worse things than washing someone's feet. I washed Mrs. Martin's feet every evening. I did not like this Mrs. Martin, but I really didn't know why. She was nice, but she was scary-looking to me.

Nancy and I took turns washing the dishes. I had to make my bed every morning. I couldn't make it to please Mrs. Martin. She had to teach me to make a bed. She made it a point to let me know I should already know how to make a bed. She made me feel stupid, and this caused me to shy away from her.

Mrs. Bermingham took me to the store and bought me some fantastic clothes. She asked me to pick out the panties I wanted. I didn't know what panties were. I didn't remember ever wearing such things. (I was sure I did when we were in Chicago, but I didn't remember the small details of that life so long ago.) I was too worried about living from day to day. Mrs. Bermingham showed me where to find the panties. She took me in a dressing room, pulled down my overalls and saw I wasn't wearing any. Mrs. Bermingham showed me how to wear them. She did not criticize me for not knowing how to wear panties, or for not knowing what they were. She was very kind. I tried on almost all the clothes in the store. She was very patient with me.

Mrs. Bermingham put me in school. I wouldn't speak to anyone, not even the teacher. When the teacher asked me to read, I could not. When she asked me a question, I did not know how to answer it.

One morning, Mrs. Bermingham went to school with me. My teacher talked to her, and Mrs. Bermingham took me with her when she left the school. She bought me a hamburger and a drink. We went to the park and she sat down on a bench. Mrs. Bermingham stood me in front of her and said, "What is going on with you at school?"

I did not speak, so she pulled me down in her lap and hugged me. I struggled to get away, but she wouldn't let go of me. The more I struggled to get away, the tighter she held me. She said, "Honey, I can't help you if you do not let me. You must talk to me." She was hugging me, and I was still trying to get away. I trusted no one.

I finally got tired of fighting her. I started to cry and said, "I can't read those books. The teacher asks me a question, and I don't know how to answer. Besides, I'm not supposed to talk to anyone. The other kids make fun of me. I don't care; I'm not supposed to play with them either. I don't want to go to school."

Mrs. Bermingham asked, "Who told you that you are not supposed to talk to other people or play with other children?"

I said, "My father and my sister, Delores. I get a bad whipping when I disobey."

Mrs. Bermingham cried with me. She promised to help me with my reading, and she did. She also said, "You can play with anyone you like. I promise you I won't let anyone whip you for it."

After that, we were friends, but I was not there very long. I didn't have time to learn much. I crammed as much learning in as I could. I enjoyed learning new things with her.

I talked to Mrs. Bermingham about the way Delores and I felt about our sister, Vesta. She said, "I understand why you might feel that you hate your sister, Vesta. But, honey, she is just as much a victim as you and Delores are. You need to understand that. You may not see it or understand it now, but someday you will. Your oldest sister is just as afraid as you are. When you see her in the courtroom, you give her two big hugs – one from you and one from me."

I believe that had she not explained to me that Vesta was hurting, too, I may never have been able to feel any love for her ever in my life. This made me think about the time she tried to run away, and when she put hot sauce in the men's drinks. The time she begged so hard to be allowed to go to school, and Father wouldn't let her go because he was afraid she might talk to someone. Father had accused her of wanting to get away from him. Mrs. Bermingham taught me to love my oldest sister, Vesta, again instead of being jealous of her and resenting her place in the family. Vesta had to do as she was told, just like the rest of us. Mrs. Bermingham changed my way of thinking about Vesta.

Mrs. Bermingham helped with my reading and math for several hours a day. She used blocks to teach me the concepts of addition and subtraction. She started in first grade books and was teaching me to read. I was making great progress. She taught me the joy of learning. I was hungry to learn everything she was willing to teach me because I didn't know what might happen next.

One day I came home from school, and Mrs. Martin was sitting in the armchair. She was sick. Mrs. Bermingham was home, and Nancy quickly went out to play. I got Mrs. Martin a glass of water. I took a pillow from the couch and put it behind her head. Then I got a pan of water and washed her feet.

After supper, Mrs. Bermingham came to my room. She sat me on her lap again and hugged me, but this time I did not fight her. She said, "You are a very special person. Where did you learn to take care of people like that? You washed Mrs. Martin's feet, just like Jesus washed his disciples' feet."

I did not tell her that Mrs. Martin had us wash her feet every-day; it might have gotten Mrs. Martin into trouble. I just said, "I enjoyed doing that for her. She is sick and it made her feel better. Besides, she is the cook and I like to eat what she fixes."

Mrs. Bermingham said, "God has a special job for you to do. You must never get discouraged." We talked about God for a while. Then she said, "The trial is coming up soon. You will have to go for a few days. You can come back when the trial is over."

She tried to explain to me what a trial was. I got upset and did not want to go. Mrs. Bermingham said, "You are needed there." I told her some of the things about the way my father treated us. Mrs. Bermingham said, "You must tell this to the judge in the courtroom."

We cried together, and I told her how terribly afraid I was to see my father again. Mrs. Bermingham told me the story of Jesus as she rocked me, like one would rock a baby.

The next few days we talked a lot about God. She did not laugh at me over the way I felt about God. She did ask me, "Where did you learn about God?"

I said, "I don't know. It was just something I felt inside my mind."

She tried to encourage me to tell the court what my life had been like. She said, "Tell the truth at all times. I know in your heart you know this is the right thing to do. Don't be afraid of making your mother or anyone else mad at you. Above all, don't be afraid of your father. I know he is a bad man, but he can no longer hurt you or your sisters. The judge will see to it that no one can hurt you in the courtroom, you will see. There will be other people present. You will never be alone with your father. Maybe you can sit with your sisters and that will give you the strength you need."

She then said, "When you lay your hand on the Bible and swear to tell the truth, you are really swearing to God. If you tell a lie, you are lying to God. You must tell the truth the best way you can. You must not add anything or leave anything out. This would be wrong."

I promised Mrs. Bermingham I would tell the truth on all things, and I would try not to be afraid. She gave me a really nice necklace. I trusted in what she said. I enjoyed the time I spent with Mrs. Bermingham and Mrs. Martin.

I felt that I had found the good people in this world when I became friends with Mrs. Bermingham. I hoped that Vesta and Delores, especially Delores, had found some good people, too. I learned that there really were good people in the world, even if there were more bad people than good. The good people made the punishment bearable.

I didn't want to go to the trial without Mrs. Bermingham and Mrs. Martin. Mrs. Bermingham had to stay and work because she had no one to take care of her business. Mrs. Martin had to stay and take care of Nancy and Mrs. Bermingham. I had to go alone. They said they would pray to God to keep me safe every morning and night. This made me feel better. They knew how to comfort me when I was frightened.

Someone came to take me to the trial. We drove for several hours. When I got to the courthouse, I was taken to the front of the room and told to sit beside Delores. She was sitting in the front row, with a woman sitting beside her. Mother and Aunt Joe were sitting behind her. Father was sitting on a stage in front of us. The women that were with Delores and me got up and walked away, talking. We hugged each other and tried to talk to each other, but my mother or my Aunt Joe rapped us on the head and told us to shut up.

Father started crying and beckoning with his finger for me to come to him. Mother and Aunt Joe were leaning over and whispering, telling me to go. Delores was telling me not to go. There was a lot of noise. More people were moving around. My head hurt so badly that I thought I was going to vomit. I was so dizzy that it was hard for me to stand up.

Father was saying, "Come to your daddy, little one." I had never heard Father speak so tenderly to me before. I was so confused. My head hurt and I felt very lightheaded and faint. I thought, "Stop! Stop! I just can't stand the noise. Please stop talking!"

I had to mind Father. He might beat me in front of all these people. He was crying. He might be hurt somewhere and need someone to help him. Why was he sitting on the stage by himself anyway? I found myself walking toward him.

I heard Delores scream, "NO! NO!"

But I couldn't stop myself. When I got close to him, he pulled a knife out of his clothes and raised his hand to stick me with it. Someone grabbed me and pulled me back just in time. Delores was standing by the bench crying. A policeman in the room said, "Take these girls to the back of the courtroom. Don't bring them forward until we call their names, and wait for an officer to escort them."

Our caseworkers took us to the last seat in the courtroom. They stepped away from us a little ways and told us to stay put. Someone was putting chains around my Father's feet. His hands were behind his back. More people came in the room. There was more noise. I stood up and screamed, "Stop! Stop! The noise – I can't stand any more noise!" Everyone became very quiet for a while, and then they went back to making noise.

Someone put their hand over my mouth; then someone else put their hands under my armpits. Two men were running down the courthouse steps with me. I could hear Delores screaming. I saw Mr. Chandler, a man who was either a relative or close friend of Father's – I don't know which. He ducked behind some cars. The car the men put me in took off. A police car chased us for a while. The man driving turned down a lot of small roads.

When we did not see the police any more, one of the men said, "We lost the pigs."

They laughed and laughed. They refused to tell me who they were or where they were taking me. I thought about jumping out of the car, but the car was moving too fast. This was really scary for me.

When they got to where they were taking me, the other kids were there, even Vesta's babies. Mr. Chandler dropped me off and went back to De Queen, Arkansas. The people who were watching us at the house were hiding us from the courts for my mother and Aunt Joe. The less evidence that could be produced, the less time my father would get in prison. If the courts couldn't find Vesta's children, then they couldn't prove that they were Father's. The less information the authorities had, the better it was for Father.

It was clear that they didn't want us there. Pearl was the only child allowed in the house. Our food was handed to us outside. They gave us a drink if we knocked on the door and asked for it. I felt that we were not welcome there. They were keeping us there because they thought they had to. Maybe they were afraid of Father. I looked after Betty and tried to keep her from getting sunburned. She was fair-skinned and had white hair. Her skin needed to be protected from the sun.

After a few days, Mr. Chandler brought Mother and Aunt Joe to get us. They were fighting over which children belonged to them. Aunt Joe said, "We have to abide by the way the courts divided them. The court gave me La Verne, Bonnie, Orlando, La Donna and Cathy. That's who I am taking. The courts gave you Delores, Frances, Orlaff, Dennis, Glenn, Elijah, Betty and Pearl. That is who you are taking." Delores refused to go with Mother in the courthouse.

The state kept Vesta. Aunt Joe said, "You are lucky if any of them want to go with you. I threatened you to get you to make the trip to check on them. Do what you have to do and shut up." Mother and Aunt Joe denied that any of us belonged to them.

Father had received a sentence of only 21 years in prison. Mother bragged about how the judge was a relative of my father's and that was why he didn't get more time. She said it wasn't over for us girls, and that we would see our father again. Mother said that we would pay the price for our stupidity.

Mr. Chandler took Aunt Joe to the bus station and Mother back to Mr. Pettigrews' house. Mother packed our clothes; we had a couple pairs of bibbed jeans apiece, and the baby's clothes.

Mother gave Father's violin and guitar to Mr. Chandler. This made me quite angry. I begged her to let me have them. I wanted to learn to sing and play them. Mother gave the house trailer, truck and car to Mr. Pettigrew. Mother had never learned to drive. Mr. Chandler drove us to De Queen to catch a bus.

Mother was very cruel to me. She was angry with Delores and

me for running away and seeking help. She told me, "This is the way life is. You take it the way it is dished out to you." She called me names and said, "You have taken my man away from me. I liked my life the way it was. You and Delores have changed it forever. There is no way I am going to give you your father's prized possessions. You must think I am some kind of a fool."

Chapter EIGHT

―――――◆―――――

WE BOARDED A bus to Grandmother Cahala's house. Grandmother complained that she did not want us. Mother ran back to
the taxi she had waiting, and went back to Chicago. I was very hurt
when Grandmother said that she didn't want us.

I didn't feel welcome at Grandmother's anymore. I felt there
must be something wrong with all of us kids. I tried to stay out
of her sight with the smaller kids. Grandmother put the boys in
school. She told me she needed help to feed the children, that I was
old enough to work and that I was to bring her my money every
week to help feed my siblings.

Grandmother found a job for me out in the country. It was
a little house with a lot of kids in it. The flies were so bad you
couldn't open your mouth without them flying into it. This little
house and all the kids reminded me of Father's farm. I complained
to Grandmother about the flies. So she found me another job halfway between Pelican Lake and her farm. I was to babysit for a
young couple. The man was a truck driver and the woman worked
somewhere.

One Sunday evening, Grandmother was driving me back to
my babysitting job. She had a very old car. We were talking and enjoying the scenery when the body fell off the car, with us in it. We
weren't hurt. The wheels and frame of the car kept traveling down
the road until it was out of sight.

We sat on the side of the road and laughed for a while. Then we
walked down to see how far the frame of the car had rolled, and what
kind of damage it had done. It had crashed when it had come to the
next curve. The wheels just kept going straight and the road curved

around. It had landed in a field. There was no harm done. We walked back home and nursed our bruises and scratches. We both laughed; it was funny watching the wheels of the car going down the road.

Grandmother asked a neighbor to drive me to work the next day. The woman I worked for had three children. Her husband was home only on the weekends. But at this time, he was taking a vacation. I lived with these people. At night, I would wake up and find this man standing by my bed staring at me. I was afraid, so I asked the woman to put a lock on my bedroom door. She saw no reason for such nonsense. One night this man tried to get into bed with me. I screamed and his wife came running and made him get out of my room. I walked all the way to Grandmother's in my nightclothes. Grandmother put me to bed; I was very tired.

The next morning, Grandmother went with me to my baby-sitting job. The woman promised Grandmother it would never happen again. I never saw the man again. A lock was put on the bedroom door, and I no longer shared the room with the boy. I felt a lot safer now, and Grandmother went home. I would see her the next week when I got paid.

Uncle Bill came down to see Grandmother. When he found out Grandmother had me working in other people's houses, he came and got me. He stopped in Chicago and bawled my mother out, saying, "Mother is not able to take care of your children. You should be ashamed to dump them on her every chance you get."

He said much more. I did not understand what all that he said meant. He offered to take me home with him, and Mother agreed. Uncle Bill's wife did not like me. Uncle Bill fought his wife over me going to school, and he lost. I had to wash all the dishes, and feed her children breakfast so she did not have to get up in the mornings. I couldn't cook anything, so Uncle Bill bought cold cereals. His wife complained because I didn't know how to cook anything but beans. I had to do all the ironing. I could never do anything well enough for her.

One morning while fixing her children's breakfast, I broke a gallon of milk. She was so angry she slapped me and said, "Get out! You are just like your mother, always wanting something for nothing. You will never amount to a hill of beans. I can't understand people like you." Uncle Bill apologized to me and took me back to Mother.

This put Mother in a bind. She lived at the hospital where she worked. She worked at night so I had to stay on the street all day while she slept. I stayed mostly in the alleys to stay out of sight. Mother didn't want the truant officers to arrest me for not being in school. I didn't mind so much; I did not like people that much. I did get awfully tired of doing nothing. I also got tired of trying to hide behind people's trashcans when someone came by. At night she sneaked me into her bedroom and fed me, and I slept in her bed. I wondered why Mother was hiding me from the people she knew. Was she really that ashamed of me? Did I look that bad, or was it because she did not love me? I tried hard not to do anything bad and to stay out of sight of other people.

Mother had very nice clothes. At night when she let me in to sleep, I tried them on. I enjoyed this; I daydreamed about how beautiful I was. This was my special time. I had fun when I pretended I was someone else with pride and dignity. I knew no one wanted me. I was a rejected person and felt very stupid. I couldn't expect anyone to want me. Mother said, "You are just a bum. You really don't deserve anything after you interfered with my life."

One night, Dr. Brian came to the hospital and walked into Mother's bedroom, unannounced. He found me playing in Mother's clothes. He said, "Who might you be, young lady?"

I was afraid of him and backed away from him. He kept coming into the room saying, "I'm not going to hurt you, child. I need to know who you are so I can notify your folks." When he realized I had backed into a corner and was scared to death, he screamed, "Kitty, come here now!" He made sure my Mother heard him. My mother came running; I guess he scared her.

Mother explained who I was with a great deal of embarrassment. Dr. Brian said, "Where have you been keeping this young lady during the day? I didn't know your children were in the city."

I opened my big mouth and said, "I've been staying in the alley. Sometimes I hide behind the trashcans."

This didn't go over so well. Dr. Brian said, "Kitty, this is dangerous. You are not to allow her to do that again. She can stay here. Maybe she will be able to help you some. Make a good nurse out of her."

This doctor gave me a little bit of hope; he thought I could help Mother. I worked as hard as I could and did everything any of the nurses told me to do. The nurses liked me. I was proud of the work I did, and it was nice to be accepted by the nurses.

When the doctor left the room, Mother yelled at me saying, "You stupid little wild bitch! You could have cost me my job. I didn't want anyone to know you were here. You haven't been eating out of the trashcans, have you? I have been feeding you supper, haven't I? You make sure you don't let anyone see you eat out of a trashcan. I know most of the people who live around here. It would be embarrassing for someone to see you and recognize you as my child. Take my clothes off and leave them alone from now on. They are expensive and you will ruin them."

I assured Mother I wasn't eating out of the trash. I told her, "I am used to not eating, Mother; you have nothing to worry about. I stay away from people. I can't help it if you're ashamed of me. I hate people. When I see or hear someone coming, I hide behind the trashcans. I don't eat out of them. I know better than that. I am not insane, you know. I want to go back to live with Mrs. Bermingham and Mrs. Martin. Just let me go."

Mother said, "You will stay in the building and help me. You will earn your keep this way. I will need to get you some clothes, so you don't look so much like a bum. Stay in my room until I have a chance to take you to a store. You look like a little tramp. It would be embarrassing for the other help to see you. Stay out of my clothes!"

When my mother wasn't looking, I still played in her clothes. To me, this was my special time. I just couldn't give it up. I thought her clothes were beautiful.

Mother and I went shopping in a second-hand store on the other side of the city. Mother was ashamed and afraid someone she knew would see me with her, so she went to the other side of the city. She bought me some clothes that I liked.

I learned to do many things helping Mother in the hospital. The cook in the hospital fed me three meals a day, and she always made sure I got the best dessert. Everyone in the hospital seemed to like me. I was no longer hungry, cold and bored; I had plenty to do. I felt important and was proud of my accomplishments.

After a while, Grandmother Cahala told my mother, "I can't take care of your children any longer. I am sick."

Mother had to rent an apartment. Mother and I took the train and went after the other kids. I had to take care of them. When I tried to mop the floors in the apartment, my brothers poured flour, sugar or anything they could find in the house to make a mess. I complained to Mother, and she said, "Boys will be boys. You just have to clean up after them. That is your job as a girl. Boys make messes; that is what they are born to do. It is our job as women and girls to take care of them, no matter what they do."

Delores was now living with Aunt Joe, so Mother and Aunt Joe said. I do not know when the state of Arkansas released her. Mother would not speak to Delores. No one seemed to care about her. Instead of living with Aunt Joe, she lived on the streets with a gang of other children. She came home once in a while when Mother was at work so she and the rest of the gang could bathe. They always took the towels they had used to a laundromat, so Mother wouldn't know they had been there. Delores tried to stay away from Mother, so she didn't have to listen to the verbal assaults Mother liked to dish out to us.

Vesta called and said that she had run away from the foster home. She hitchhiked to Chicago. Delores and her friends came home to bathe, and I told her what was happening. When Vesta arrived, Mother sent us to Missouri to work in the fields.

We had no place to go. We hoped we could find work in a field somewhere. We slept in the bus station a few nights before Vesta managed to find a place for us to live. Vesta and I cleaned other people houses during the day.

Vesta was about to deliver a baby. She tried very hard not to let us other kids know how frightened she was, but she couldn't hide it from me. I, too, was frightened. The boys didn't seem to notice much of what was happening. Vesta was seventeen years old and ready to give birth. She had the seven of us children to worry about. She found enough work to keep us from starving to death.

A landowner gave us a house to live in. Vesta had her baby boy, William. I helped her deliver him. We had no beds, so we all slept on the floor. We made a special corner for little William. We loved him very much. It was easy to see that something was wrong with him. He didn't cry like most babies; his cry sounded funny. We didn't have the money to take him to a doctor. We made sure he was breathing – that's all we knew to do. I could tell Vesta was worried about him; in fact, she was frightened.

After William was born, Vesta found some kind of work at night. I took care of the babies at night while Vesta worked. She was gone every night, but she kept us fed.

A man named Fredrick moved in with us. He bought a bed for Vesta and himself, and a table for us to eat off of. He also bought us food. He seemed to be a nice man. He never touched any of us in an inappropriate way. He was good to us, and helped care for and feed the little ones. He had Vesta take the baby to a doctor. The doctor said, "This baby is severely retarded. He will not learn like other babies. How far behind he will be, I don't know yet."

Later, Mother joined us. Mother did not like Fredrick. Mother and Vesta fought, and Vesta tried to tell Mother that she was doing the best she could. Mother just wouldn't listen. Mother took the rest of us kids to Mr. and Mrs. Newman's place, leaving Vesta behind. Vesta asked me to please take care of her babies. Fredrick drove us to the Newmans' place in Alton, Missouri. He gave Mother some money for the babies.

The mother I thought I loved had turned into a witch. Mother was no longer timid or shy. She mistreated Vesta's children every day. She called them "little bastards," "home wreckers" and many more things. She hit and kicked them when one of them got near her.

I had awful dreams; I was afraid all the time. I dreamed of being in the chicken wire fence and of Father beating me and having sex with me. I dreamed about the abortion Father had given me. I believed that he and the men he played cards with were hiding and just waiting for me to leave the house so they could kill me. I dreamed someone had killed Delores out in the woods. I woke up screaming. I guess I was half asleep. I ran through the house looking for her.

One night Betty was crying. I could not quiet her down. Mother got up and threw Betty across the room. Betty screamed and cried the rest of the night. After Mother threw her across the room, one of Betty's shoulders was lower than the other. The next day Mother took Betty to town to see a doctor. She said she walked all the way to Alton and back, but I don't think so. Mother came back late that night in someone's car. I saw the car. Betty had broken her collarbone.

Vesta came to the Newman's place to visit every chance she had. This time, she came with a man named Clyde. Vesta had terrible nightmares, just as bad or worse than I did. She woke up everyone in the house with her screaming. Mother now had two daughters who had bad nightmares. She never tried to comfort me, but she never really mistreated me or said bad things about my dreams, as she did to Vesta. The difference between us was that Mother was mean to Vesta over her nightmares. Mother told her, "If you were not a whore, you wouldn't have nightmares."

I knew the real cause of her nightmares. Our father had aborted at least one of Vesta's babies near where we were. Vesta said she couldn't stand being that close to the farm anymore. Vesta hugged and kissed her babies; then she left.

As she left, Mother said, "Good riddance." I worried about Vesta. She was alone in the world, and Mother was driving her away from her babies.

Several times some people came to the farm. They brought food, clothes and blankets for us. Mother accepted help from the man with the bulging eyes. She was there when he and these men stood outside the chicken wire fence and stared at us. She watched him touch us. Where was her pride? I wanted nothing this man offered us. What was wrong with Mother?

Mother did not seem to realize how much shame she caused me, just knowing those men were in our house. When I tried to tell her how I felt about her accepting their help, she just said, "Beggars can't be choosers. Now quit complaining and show your gratitude."

I didn't feel any gratitude. Was she really that dumb, or did she just not care? I said, "What kind of gratitude should I show? The men around here did all kinds of bad things to us."

I was ashamed of myself for asking this question, but I just couldn't help it. I knew my mother knew what they had done to us. Now they were pretending to care if we were hungry. I began taking the babies and fading into the woods during the day to avoid seeing those men coming to the house.

Mother showed no sympathy toward Vesta, and for a long time she only showed hatred toward Vesta, Delores and me. Mother said that she hated Betty, Pearl and little William. She told them, "You are nothing but fucking little bastards. You should have died at birth. You kids are worthless. Trash, trash is what you are. I ought to take you to the dump and leave you there."

At this point, I wanted to run away again, but I couldn't leave the babies behind and I couldn't take them with me. I needed food, milk and clothes to take care of them. I would have had to carry Pearl and little William. Betty would be unable to walk very far. I was stuck, helpless. I had no choice but to stay with the babies and keep them out of Mother's hair.

I thought about Mrs. Bermingham and wished the babies were with her, instead of my mother. I knew she would give them all the love a baby should have. Mother couldn't teach what she didn't know herself.

Chapter NINE

ONE DAY MOTHER said, "Delores has a mild case of polio. Josephine [my Aunt Joe] will not keep her any longer. She is refusing to pay for her therapy. If Delores stays in Chicago, I could get into trouble with the law. The court made her my responsibility, whether I like it or not."

Delores was coming to live with us. Mother was not happy, and she said, "You and Delores put the only man I will ever love in prison. I hate both of you for that. I know Delores was the ringleader. That part doesn't matter; you went along with her. You have to take the responsibility for your part in putting your father in prison."

I got very excited that my sister was coming to live with me again. Mother couldn't dampen my sprits. I got my room ready for her because I knew we would have to share the room. I was about 12 years old at this time, and Delores was about 14.

Mother got someone to take her to meet Delores' bus. She didn't seek therapy for my sister. Delores' left hand was paralyzed. Her left arm was partially paralyzed, and she was very bitter. At first, she acted like she cared about nothing, not even herself.

Mother often slapped us around or used a switch on us when she was unhappy. Mother wasn't big enough to hurt us like Father had, but she had a very wicked mouth and she knew how to hurt us with it. She didn't mind hurting our feelings with her words, and she often did. Delores and I tried to stay away from Mother, as well as keep the babies away from her. We gave her very little chance to mistreat them.

One evening just after dark, Mother packed all of our things, and someone picked us up in a small truck. We kids rode in the back with our things. Mother and William rode in the cab of the truck. We got on a train and went to Bernie, Missouri. Mother said, "Someone will pick us up at the station. Why do you have to worry and fret about everything? You act like you don't trust me." Well, she hit it right on the nose. I didn't trust her.

Vesta was there and had rented a house for us to live in. There was no furniture, only a cooking stove. Vesta said, "I am working in a tavern and can provide some support for my children."

Mother laughed and said, "You are prostituting yourself."

Mother wouldn't let Vesta live with us. Vesta held her babies and cried. She came often to see them and gave Mother money for them. Then Mother got on welfare. Some church people brought us some furniture and clothes. Mother and Vesta fought.

Vesta said, "I should be allowed to live with my babies. You are drawing welfare to pay for their expenses. What I earn is enough to pay you for babysitting and for my living expenses. I will be here to take care of my own children during the day. This will make it easier for you."

Mother would have none of it. Vesta could not stay with us.

The boys were put in school. I don't remember Delores and I ever going to school in Bernie.

I remember that Mother started going out with a man named Mr. Cook, who had trouble keeping his hands off of me. He spent the night several times. Mother was not timid about her relationship with him. She didn't care if we kids knew that she was sleeping with men at night.

I seldom saw Delores. She was busy running around with boys, drinking and smoking weed. Many times she did not even come home at night. Sometimes she would stay gone for days. Once in a while, I would see her give money to Mother. When I asked her about the money, she said, "It was given to me." I sensed something wasn't right with her, and I knew she was lying.

I sometimes took Vesta's three children to the school playground and played with them on the swings. It gave all of us a well-needed break from Mother and the boys. I enjoyed this and so did the babies. Playing with the babies on the playground was relaxing. It was our only escape. We entered another world when we walked through the playground gate.

One day, a man came to the house in a big truck. Mother told me, "This man's name is Charles. He wants to take you for a ride." I didn't want to go. Mother and Charles insisted; they kind of put me in the truck. Mother said, "What's wrong with you? Don't you trust me?"

The man took me out of town and had sex with me. When I resisted, he said, "Behave yourself. I have your mother's permission." He dropped me off in town. I walked the rest of the way home.

I told Mother what had happened, and she said, "Quit complaining. Charles gave me forty dollars for you."

Never again did I go with any man my mother wanted me to go with. No matter what she did, I refused to go. When I kicked up a big enough fuss, the men would drive away. This made Mother angry. She said, "What is your problem? You are not a virgin. You have to learn that life is not all roses. There are a lot of thorns along the way. You can't get through life without stepping on them."

I finally answered Mother's question. "No, I don't trust you and your ideas. They are wrong," I said.

Vesta introduced Mother to a man named Paul Wilburn. One night Mother and Paul got so drunk that they both fell in the bathtub. Paul did not have any pants on, and Mother was in her slip. Delores and I helped Mother out of the tub. We couldn't get Paul out of the tub. Mother was too drunk to help. I never did find out why they were in the bathroom together, dressed as they were.

I soon began to realize that Mother no longer stood on the sidelines and watched what was happening. She was no longer the timid person she was before. I had never seen Mother drunk. I don't think I ever saw her drunk after that. This was out of character for Mother. Usually, she pouted a lot or took her frustration out on a child, but she never drank before.

I questioned Mother about what had happened the night before. She said, "I am a person, too. I have a right to some happiness."

I said, "Mother, the man is married. His family lives in this town. You have no business doing this."

Mother screamed, "Get out of here! Take those little bastards of Vesta's with you!" I took the babies for a walk and came back home.

Delores and I told Vesta what we had seen. Vesta and Mother fought over Paul. Vesta told her, "Paul is one of my johns. You are making it hard for me to make money."

I didn't understand what she was talking about. I thought they were both crazy. Mother had changed, and it wasn't for the better. She was becoming more like Father every day.

One day Mother was sleeping on the couch. William cried every time I put him down, so I laid him in Mother's arms as she slept. Then William wet his diaper. Mother threw him on the floor and kicked him across the room. I thought that Mother had kicked him harder than usual. I was afraid that she had hurt him.

I grabbed William and ran to find Vesta. I found her in a bar in town. When I told her what had happened, she said, "All this time, I have been prostituting myself to feed my babies, and Mother has been abusing them."

I tried to get Vesta to run away with me and take the babies with us. She refused and discouraged me so I wouldn't try it.

Vesta said, "Honey, that is not the way." She checked William over and said, "He is all right. Take him home and take care of him the best you can. I will take care of this. Thank you for bringing him to me."

Why couldn't Mother see how hard Vesta was trying to do what was right for her children and herself? What made Mother hate Vesta so badly? It was her fault that Vesta had to do the type of work she was doing. I knew by now what Vesta was doing to make a living for her babies. I didn't quite realize the stigma of it. I knew I hated to do the things that Vesta was doing. I knew it was wrong. I also knew that if Mother had treated her like a human being, she wouldn't have to do that kind of thing to help take care of her babies. How could anyone mistreat a helpless little baby?

I blamed Mother for what Vesta was doing and for what I knew Delores was doing. I also knew Mother wasn't doing any better. I wanted very much to love my mother and to be loved by her.

Why couldn't she be nice like Vesta was trying to be? I thought, "Please, Mother, quit hating us. Vesta wants to love you, too. What is so wrong with this family?"

I had met enough people after my father went to prison to realize our family was not normal, like most families. I thought, "Somebody, please tell me what is wrong with us that our own mother can't love me or my sisters. We look like other girls. We try to act like other people who are good people. At least I try to do what is right." I still loved her. She was blind if she couldn't see that.

What was so wrong with my sisters that Mother treated them so badly and only wanted them for the money they brought in by prostitution? The only reason she wanted me around was to take care of Vesta's children and to clean up the house a little bit.

I remembered what Mrs. Bermingham had told me about Vesta. It seemed so long ago, but she was right. My sister was hurting, too; my mother had made sure of that. All I could do was take care of her babies as well as Mother would allow me to. And comfort my sister, Vesta, the best I could.

Delores had become hardened. She used bad language and acted like she cared for no one. Except that when I was with her, no man or boy had better try anything vulgar with me.

Mother tried to force me to date and drink with men. I just had no desire to do this, and she didn't understand why. Vesta was depending on me to take care of her children. I felt helpless and pushed into a corner, unable to do what I knew should be done. I wanted to find a better way to help my sisters because neither of them was happy.

Mother didn't seem to notice or care. Things were just too confusing for me. I just took care of the babies the best way I could. I did not know what else I could do for them. I loved them as if they were my own children. I was young and treated them like dolls.

A few days later, Vesta came to the house and asked me, "Please help me dress up the babies as beautifully as you can." We dressed them in the best we had. We thought they were beautiful.

Vesta told me, "I have given the children up for adoption to some very nice people in St. Louis. They will love them and take good care of them. They won't be mistreated any more. They will be happy, warm and have all the food they need to make them healthy. They will wear nice clothes. This is their only chance to survive and grow up to be decent human beings. They will get an education that I can't give them. I love them more by doing this than I would if I let them stay in this family. This family is rotten. It is no good and not fit to raise my children in."

Then Mother came into the room. She complained that we were making too much laundry for her to do. She said, "All these little brats need to wear is their underpants and a shirt. I have better things to do than to wash clothes."

She attempted to undress the babies, but Vesta wouldn't let her. They scuffled around the living room a few minutes. Betty and Pearl started to cry. I picked up the two girls and took them outside. This made Mother angry. She yelled through the door saying, "Go ahead, and choose those little bastards over your own mother." She then walked out of the room.

After a while, a car drove up with two ladies in it. Vesta and I carried the babies outside and gave them to the ladies. We had to pry little Pearl's arms from around my neck. All three of the babies were crying. The ladies assured us they would be all right, and that Vesta had done the right thing. Vesta and I stood in the front yard holding each other, crying, as we watched the babies being put in the car. The car drove away, and I never saw the babies again. William was little more than a year old.

Mother came running out yelling, "What have you two little bitches done? What did you tell those people?"

Vesta said, "I told them the truth – who their father is, where he is, why he is there, how you and Aunt Joe knew what was happening and sometimes watched us while we were doing it. How Father had sex with you and me together. I told them how Delores and Frances ran away to put a stop to Father killing our babies, and maybe even us. That you knew it was happening, you just went to Chicago so you did not have to be mistreated anymore. How you and Aunt Joe left us behind, knowing what Father was doing to us."

She continued on, "You, Mother, are the bitch, not us. Don't ever call one of us a bitch again. You have no right to do that. What happened to us is your and Father's and Aunt Joe's fault. We have lived through hell because of the three of you. How do you live with yourself?

"We were only kids. Delores and Frances are still kids. You, personally, put my babies through hell, and for what? It's not their fault that you allowed Father to have sex with me. You told him he could do as he pleased to me and the other children.

"You, Mother, are the crazy one, not us. You need help. Frances is the only one who has the guts to stand up to you, and she is a child. Well, I have learned a few things from her! You should be teaching us girls some morals, not prostituting us out. I am seeking help for myself, and you should do the same. Now get out of my face! You, Mother, are worse than a bitch. You will join Father in the ranks of hell. I hope you have a good time down there together. I pray there are no children down there for you to abuse. One thing is for certain — you will never have the chance to abuse my children again."

She finished by saying, "You will quit treating Delores and Frances so badly. They do not deserve it. Our brothers are not gods; quit treating them like they are. Get Frances in school so she will have a chance to be something besides a prostitute. Remember, no matter what they do, it couldn't be as bad as you, Aunt Joe and Father have done. You have no right to judge them, no matter what they do. Wake up, Mother, before it is too late for all of you! Please do that for me!"

Vesta, was crying and walked away from my mother. There was nothing I could do to help her. My mother stood in the driveway screaming curse words at her and telling her what a bad person she had been all her life, even as a child.

Mother spit in my face and said, "You and Delores are no better than she is. You have no respect for anyone. Both of you are dirty liars and whores. You just remember that you will both pay for what you have done to this family some day. I will see to that if it kills me!" Then she stomped off into the house.

What had happened to the timid woman I used to know as my

mother? How would it be possible for any of us to continue to love and put up with her? I wondered what had caused her to change. It was now clear to me and to the whole world that Mother did not love any of us.

Chapter TEN

WHEN WHAT VESTA had said soaked into my mother's head, she ran to find the boys. Delores just happened by, or she would have been left behind. We quickly packed and left, leaving Vesta behind again. Mother took us back to Chicago. We stayed with Aunt Joe until Mother found a job and rented an apartment. It was a dump with mice and rats everywhere.

Delores became very wild. She took none of our brothers' bad treatment. The boys were brats as far as we were concerned, but Mother thought they could do no wrong. Mother and Delores constantly fought over the way the boys behaved. Delores joined a gang and hitchhiked all over the county. I seldom saw her, but when I did, she was very unkind.

Mother put us in school, and I was placed in the eighth grade. I had very little schooling up until then. My teacher did the best she could with me. Then Mother had a baby girl. She named her Rose Maria. I had to take care of her after school and at night.

Most of the kids in school stayed away from me. I met one girl, named Naomi, who was somehow different, and I liked her. I escaped from my brothers by taking Rose Maria to Naomi's house. Naomi's mother wouldn't let my brothers in her house. She didn't like the way they behaved. They helped themselves to her refrigerator and made a big mess, then didn't clean up.

One night that winter, I went to Naomi's house. Her mother was not home. Naomi was having a party and there were lots of boys there. Everyone made fun of me because I wouldn't take part in their sexual activities. To me, sex was a punishment, not something you did when your parents weren't present. I tried to take

Rose Maria and leave. One of the boys grabbed her out of my arms and wouldn't give her back to me. I tried to fight him over her, but he wouldn't let go and we were hurting her.

The boys decided that a boy named Lawrence would have sex with me. Lawrence was a virgin and they thought that I was, too. Several boys held me down while Lawrence learned how to have sex. Naomi tried to stop the boys, but several girls held her so that she was unable to help me. We never told any one. Naomi was not supposed to have anyone over when her parents were gone, and here she was having a sex party. She had me promise I wouldn't tell her parents before she let me in.

A few days later Mother said, "You won't be going to school today. We are going to see your father." She had gotten a lady friend to look after the other children. All I could think of was that I was going to die.

I told her, "Father is in prison. I do not want to see him."

Mother replied, "It's okay. Otis has made friends there. Some of them are his relatives. This visit has been arranged especially so that he can see you. It is off the books, so no one will ever know. There will be no record of this visit."

I said, "I do not want to go."

Mother answered, "You will go, like it or not."

I don't remember much about the trip to Arkansas. I kept thinking that Father was going to kill me, that there was no way out this time. How could Mother do this to me? All I could do was cry. Mother kept telling me to shut up and act my age. When we got there, we ate at a small restaurant, and Mother rented a room. She told me, "Take a bath and lie down and rest."

That night after dark, Mother said, "It's time."

I was too upset to even pay attention to what kind of a building we were going into. It seemed like Mother was dragging me down a street. All I could think of was that I was going to die. I remember Mother taking me into a room. The only furniture was a chair that Father was sitting on. There were some men outside the door. They told us to go in quickly. I don't know if Mother left the room or not. I was standing before Father, trembling like a leaf. He didn't seem to notice that I was scared to death.

Father said, "Take off your clothes and lie down on the floor."

He took off his pants and got on top of me to do his thing. I remember how hard the floor was and how heavy Father was. Then I pretended in my mind that Delores and I were tying Father up. I stuck a big fishhook through his penis. Delores climbed the tree, and I handed her the fish line. We managed to hoist him up off the ground enough to where he was dangling from a tree branch by his penis. He looked like he was flying to me. We tied the fish line to the tree very securely, and were throwing things at him, hoping his penis would fall off. It was just about to fall off when Father was through with me.

I came back to reality when Father said, "Can't you hear, you little two-timing bitch? I said to get up and get dressed."

For a while, I was confused and did not know where I was or how I had gotten there. When I heard Mother speak, I then remembered. Mother and Father talked. The men said, "It is time for you to go."

Then Mother asked them a question. One of the men said, "There will be no record of this. Nobody can prove anything."

Mother and I went back to our room where she told me to bathe and change my clothes. The next morning we boarded a train to Chicago. Something changed in me that day. I no longer cared what happened to me one way or the other. Maybe I was born to be a bitch. That's all anyone wanted me for.

We were home a week when Mother realized the whole family had crabs. The lady Mother had left the kids with had crabs and gave them to us. Mother bought medicine for the whole family, and she told us how to use it. I thought if I didn't treat them, maybe they would eat me up.

Paul Wilburn joined Mother after we visited Father. Paul and Mother said Rose Maria was Paul's baby. At this time, Mother was working at night. While Mother was at work, Paul would try to touch me or have sex with me. I would run around the bed and furniture until I was able to get out the door. Sometimes it was late when he came home. I had nowhere to go, so I went to the third floor of the apartments in front of us and slept on the back porch until Mother got home. Sometimes I got awfully cold.

When it was early enough, I went to Naomi's house. If I complained to Mother, she told me it wouldn't hurt me to make Paul happy. Paul never did have his way with me.

A couple of months went by, and I did not have my monthly period. I did not realize the significance of this at the time. I was still too ignorant to recognize the signs of pregnancy. I was happy I wasn't having my monthly period.

It was getting close to graduation. I knew that I did not deserve to graduate. But I had a wonderful teacher, and she acted like I was going to graduate anyway. Maybe she would have graduated me, I don't know. She bought me a graduation dress.

Then one day, Paul brought a man home with him. I heard Paul tell this man that if he ever wanted some young free ass, to just let him know.

Then Mother put on my graduation dress. I objected to her wearing my dress. She said, "Oh, hush up! When we get back, you can put the dress on and go out with Rex, yourself."

It was late when they got back, and I was asleep. Mother woke me, handed me my dress and told me it was my turn. I did not want to go anywhere. I just wanted to sleep. Mother made me get up and go out with this Rex. He took me out to eat. Mother made me go out with Rex almost every night after that.

Paul left and went to his mother's in McAlester, Oklahoma. Around the first of May, Mother told me that we were going to McAlester, Oklahoma, too, but that I would not be staying. I asked her why.

She answered, "You are pregnant. There is no room for you to stay with me. Rex is giving me three hundred dollars, and he is taking me and the other children to McAlester to join up with Paul, in exchange for you. You will be married after Rex fulfills his end of our agreement and not before.

I asked, "What am I, some kind of a horse?"

She slapped me in the face as hard as she could and said, "Shut your sassy mouth!" She then said, "No, you're white trash and will never be anything else. You're lucky this man will buy you when you have nothing to offer him."

Mother packed their clothes, and a week later we were on our way to McAlester, Oklahoma. We all piled into Rex's car, with a U-Haul trailer behind it. During the trip, Mother bought Rex anything he wanted to eat, but the rest of us did without. The trip was miserable for all of us. We were very crowded with the nine of us in one car. Rex, Mother and baby Rosie rode in the front seat; Delores, Orlaff, Dennis, Glenn, Elijah and I rode in the back seat of a 1951 Buick sedan.

I did not want to marry Rex. He said he was 34 years old, but he looked like an old man to me, and he treated me as if I was invisible. On the way to Oklahoma, Rex stopped the car along the highway and took a walk with Delores. When they came back, Delores bragged to Mother that they had had sex. Rex also admitted to this, but I did not care. Delores said she had done this so that maybe Mother would not make me marry him.

The day after we reached Paul's mother's house, Mother and Rex applied for a marriage license. Rex gave Mother three hundred dollars. A few days later, Mother took me down for the ceremony. I was wearing my graduation dress. My mother sold me into marriage when I was somewhere around the age of 13 to 15 – I did not know my birthday or true age. I was married May 9, 1955, on Mother's birthday.

Mother warned me not to say anything about how old I was. She told me, "I will answer all the questions." The judge questioned my age. Mother showed him a piece of paper and said, "This is all I have. We just moved here and I have not unpacked."

The judge was not satisfied. He did not believe that the paper belonged to me. He said, "She is too young to be that person."

Paul took the judge aside. They came back and the judge performed the ceremony. The judge made time to bawl Mother out from time to time. Shaking his head, he said, "She is too young! You should have more control over your children! You are not a good parent."

The judge walked away, shaking his head and mumbling under

his breath. Why couldn't this judge see that I was unhappy, and realize I did not want to get married to this old man? Why couldn't he see that I needed help? There was no help for the Patten children. No one cared if we lived or died. That's how I felt.

Mother explained what my duties as a wife were. She said, "You have no choice. You have to do whatever your husband tells you to do, no matter what it is. Sex is your first duty to your husband. If for any reason you don't please him, he has the right to punish you."

Rex and I slept on the floor with my brothers and my sister, Delores, that night. My brothers made fun of me the next morning. They said, "We heard you having sex last night. Thanks for the education."

My mother and Paul Wilburn thought it was a big joke and laughed for ten minutes. I was so ashamed that I refused to have breakfast with the rest of the family.

One lesson I learned from our marriage that day was that you couldn't depend on what was written in a document; it may or may not be true. It's only a piece of paper a person has written on. People lie to get their way or to accomplish whatever they are trying to do.

I washed Rex's clothes and tried to dry them on the stove. He was in a hurry to get out of there and head back to Chicago. I burned both his shirt and his pants while trying to dry them. He put them on anyway and said nothing about me burning them. For that, I was thankful. It was only my mother who fussed about me burning up his clothes. Rex stopped at the first store he found and bought another set of clothes. He had just brought one set of clothes for himself.

Both Rex and I were very quiet as we drove back to his parents' place on Clybourn Street in Chicago. I felt humiliated, stupid and dirty. I knew I had been sold to a man I did not even know anything about. I could feel that he was having second thoughts about what he had done. I took Rex's silence to mean that he didn't like me much.

What about his family? He had said we were going to live with his mother. I probably didn't have to worry about that. He was an old man to me. His parents had to be very old people; they would like me. I even enjoyed taking care of people.

I was ashamed of the way Mother had gotten rid of me. I knew my mother was thinking "good riddance," like I had heard her say about Vesta. I believed she had no shame or dignity at all. I no longer believed she was special, just that she was wicked. I thought Rex was feeling that he had been taken advantage of. I couldn't blame him. I was scared to death of what might happen next.

Mother had her three hundred dollars, her precious boys and Paul. That was all she cared about. All a girl was worth was the money a person could get out of her. And it didn't matter how little you got for her, or the pleasure anyone got out of having sex with her even when she didn't want to have sex. Now I had to be a slave to Rex and do whatever he wanted me to do. It turned out to be a better life than Mother had to offer. At least I had the opportunity to learn some things all people should know.

Chapter ELEVEN

REX AND I went back to Chicago and moved in with his parents. Mother hadn't told Rex that I was pregnant, and I wasn't showing yet. I didn't tell him either. When I realized the discontent this caused Rex, I felt Mother hadn't held up her end of the deal.

Rex's family was unhappy when he came home with me as his bride. His mother said, "She is just a child. She has no education. She came from a dysfunctional family. I have to teach her how to blow her nose. What is wrong with you? You are old enough to be her father."

My husband replied, "Teach her what she needs to know about being a wife and mother, and how to survive in life."

Even though I did not like Rex's mother, Wealthy, she taught me many things I needed to know. First, Wealthy took me in the bathroom and showed me how to take a bath. She showed me how to scrub my private parts. Using herself as a model, she asked me to demonstrate what she had taught me. I know she meant well, but she might as well have raped me. I hated her terribly after that. She wanted to make sure I was clean enough for her son.

When Rex and his family realized I was pregnant, there was hell to pay. Rex and his mother decided that I could not keep my baby. They said, "You have to give it up for adoption. You are too young to have a child. You are no more than a baby yourself."

I could not change their minds. Rex's mother said over and over, "You are too stupid and retarded to take care of a child. I am not going to raise this child for you. I wouldn't do it for one of my own daughters; I am too old. Why do you think your Mother pawned you off on Rex? She didn't want to raise your child either.

She should have taught you that sex is meant for married people."

Rex told her, "Shut up, Mother, that's enough. She is a person; treat her like one."

Wealthy considered me to be white trash. She was trying to reform me. I did as I was told. She taught me how to keep house, how to cook, how to care for my baby and how to shop. But it took a very long time for her to treat me like I was a good person and not a curse.

Rex's father, Bascom, was an alcoholic. He deliberately irritated Wealthy when he was drunk. Many times I saw Wealthy chase Bascom around and around the table with a butcher knife. Sometimes when Bascom was drinking, he crawled on all fours, barking like a dog, with Wealthy running behind him kicking his butt. They fought with frying pans, baseball bats and anything they could get their hands on. They never really hurt each other. They just acted like they were going to.

I thought to myself, "Talk about a dysfunctional family. What do they call this?" They would never admit it to themselves.

None of his family was ever very nice to me. When they visited, I tried to stay out of sight. Sometimes I went to see Naomi or just went for a walk outside. I could vent my feelings to Naomi. She understood and let me rant and rave all I needed to.

My husband, Rex, drank and couldn't hold down a job. He frequently beat up on his father while they were drinking. When he needed money, he robbed someone or stole what he wanted. He did a lot of gambling and fighting. He was also very prejudiced of other races. A lot of people were afraid of him. He was five-feet, eleven-inches tall and very skinny. He weighed 130 pounds. Rex knew how to fight. He fought with someone every time he walked out the door. He even fought with his brothers over who knows what.

Uncle Arthur was my mother-in-law's brother. He was a "wino," too. He was homeless and hitchhiked all over the United States. He came to visit his sister every year. Rex's parents never let him visit for very long.

I liked Arthur. He was different than the rest of them. We talked every chance we got. He told me about losing his four children.

I told him how much I wanted my child. He encouraged me to continue my education and not give up. He told me, "Everything is going to work out for you. Wait and you will see."

I went to see my schoolteacher who had bought me the graduation dress. I asked her if I could come back to school and she said no. The next day, I went to Walton High School and applied as a freshman. I lied about graduating in Bernie, Missouri. I started high school, listing Rex as my father and Aunt Joe as my mother. The principal let me start school before he had my records. He said he would send for my records. I was proud of myself.

In gym class the girls each had a shower stall assigned to them. The shower stalls had no doors. We were supposed to undress in our shower stalls, stand in line nude, walk up to the teacher and tell her what size of swimming suit we needed. Then we were to walk back to our shower stalls to put on our swimming suits. After swimming, we had to take our swimming suits off in our stalls, stand in line nude and walk back up to our teacher to give her our swimming suits. Then we walked back to our shower stalls and dressed.

I brought a blanket to put over my shower stall door, and a robe to put on while I stood in line. Then I walked back to my shower stall. The gym teacher did not like his. She took down my blanket and tried to pull my robe off of me. I fought her over my robe. When she did this, my friends in the classroom pulled her off of me. At this time, the school found out that I was married. Married people were not allowed to go to public school, so I was expelled from school. I was disappointed and felt like a failure. Wealthy explained that it wasn't my fault; it was the law.

One day, my mother-in-law gave me a set of pillowcases with a beautiful pattern on them. She told me to embroider them. I didn't know what she was talking about. I took the pillowcases and colored the pattern very darkly with crayons. Then I took wax paper and laid it on top of the pillowcases, so I wouldn't mess up the iron. I ironed the color into the pillowcases, and they were beautiful. My mother-in-law got very angry and told me how stupid I was.

Wealthy then taught me how to embroider, and later she taught me how to mend clothes when they needed mending. I learned how to vacuum, scrub floors and cook. She taught me how to get on the city buses and the "L" trains. She told me to always pin any money I had in my bra. She also taught me how to use a telephone. My mother-in-law taught me many things. She taught me how to use the machines that were new in my life.

I learned from her willingly. I even enjoyed learning. She had a lot of important knowledge that I needed and wanted to learn. Somehow I knew I needed knowledge in order to survive in this world.

Life was still hard for me, but it was better than it had been before I got married. Rex's mother liked to run me down and make fun of me to the other family members. This was upsetting and embarrassing to me. She didn't mind belittling me in front of anyone. She didn't seem to care if the things she said hurt my feelings.

At least now I had a washing machine to wash my clothes in. I had electricity. I had a real house to live in. Wealthy didn't have to like me for me to be happy. I had things I never knew existed. I felt like a person worthy of living.

I never talked back to her or gave her any unnecessary trouble like the wife of her younger son, Bobby, did. Her name was also Frances. Wealthy didn't like Bobby's wife either. She called her a red-headed bitch when she and Bobby weren't around. I already knew she talked behind my back, as well as to my face. I didn't understand that she was trying to help me grow up, but just didn't know how to go about it.

I craved ice cream during my pregnancy. Bascom went out one night to get some for me. My husband robbed him and took everything he had. My father-in-law came home carrying the top of the bag the ice cream had been in, even though he had taken a beating over it. His concern was that he had failed to bring me my ice cream.

My mother-in-law was angry with Bascom for going after the ice cream for me. I felt she should have been angry with her son for robbing his father. Didn't she realize that she would suffer too? Now they would be unable to pay their bills and buy groceries. Bascom didn't even have money for bus fare so he could go to work.

He would have to walk, and he seemed too old to walk very far.

Bascom was their whipping dog. I felt that if his family hadn't treated him so badly, then he probably wouldn't have drunk so much and acted like such a fool at times. He treated me like I was a person.

I learned my husband had been in prison for something. I was not told why; instead, I was told it was none of my business. I never learned why Rex had been in prison, or what had gone wrong in his first marriage. I wondered if he had any children by his first wife. Even Uncle Arthur wouldn't talk to me about these things.

The time for my baby's birth was getting close. Uncle Arthur tried to talk to Wealthy about my baby again. She was close-minded about this.

She told me, "I can see that you are trying hard to learn everything I am trying to teach you. You still have a lot to learn, but you are making progress. Give me the chance, and maybe I can make an intelligent person out of you. You are not there yet; you need more time. You aren't ready to start raising children yet. You need to know a lot more about life.

"Rex doesn't want you to keep this baby. You and your mother didn't do him right. He should have been told that you were with child. For the life of me, as dumb as you are, I can't imagine it being your own doing. You have to be the most ignorant girl I have ever met, without being retarded, and you definitely are not retarded. You could have made something of yourself, had you been given a chance. You are really too young to care for a baby. I don't have room for a baby anyway."

Uncle Arthur said, "I will gladly leave to make room for the baby. This girl is smart. You can teach her what she needs to know, if only you will."

I felt that, even though Uncle Arthur was a wino, he had more sense than all of us put together. At least he seemed to understand how I felt about giving up my baby.

He spoke as though he had a good education and, for some reason, just didn't use it. The one thing he did have was empathy for other people. Uncle Arthur believed in me when no one else did

– except for Mrs. Bermingham, and I would never see her again.

For the most part, Rex's family treated me like I had the plague. I tried hard to please them. Wealthy surprised me once when she said, "You have a good heart, and you do try to listen to what I have to say, but you are just too young."

Once, one of Rex's sisters, Jackie, gave me a doll to play with. Everyone thought it was a joke. I was embarrassed and ashamed; they didn't like me. I couldn't fit into their family, no matter how hard I tried to. It amazed me how much I missed my family, especially the children of my sister, Vesta.

I was also ashamed of the truth. I would have liked to play with that doll. I knew that if I did, his family would make fun of me. I still think about that doll today, and I still wonder if the baby Father killed was a boy or a girl. For some reason, in my mind I link them together. I did what I had to do. I tried to act like a grown-up, and set my desires to play with the doll aside.

No one seemed to see or care how lonely I felt. I didn't believe they could understand; they never had to feel this way. Now Rex expected sex from me, and I hated it with a passion. But my mother had said that was my first duty as a wife. I wondered how a man would like having someone stick something in them down there. I bet they wouldn't like it any more than I did.

I ran into Naomi while going to the corner store. We were glad to see each other. I invited her to visit me, but this made Wealthy angry. She told me, "Never invite anyone over to my house. You don't have that right, do you understand? This is not your home."

After my mother-in-law said that to me, I went to see Naomi once a week. Wealthy sometimes accused me of "catting around." I didn't know what she meant, but I knew she said those things when she was mad.

One day when she was in a good mood, I asked her what "catting around" meant. She answered, "It means fooling around with men in the wrong way."

This hurt my feelings and I said, "I am not a whore. You do not ever call me something like that again."

She responded, "No, you are not a whore, but you are the most ignorant and uneducated girl I have ever met. You are too innocent for your own good. Your parents taught you nothing. They must have kept you under lock and key to keep you so innocent."

I didn't have a big vocabulary. She explained a lot of things to me. I probably did seem stupid to her and her family. I had no people skills at all.

CHAPTER TWELVE

THE DAY CAME when I went into labor. It was early in the morning, and I told no one. My mother-in-law came upstairs to find out why I had not gotten out of bed. She always insisted I be up by 6:00 a.m. She found me in labor. My husband had been out all night drinking and had not come home yet. Nobody knew where to take me; I had not had any prenatal care. Wealthy called my brother-in law. He carried me downstairs to his car. My son was born in the car on the way to Cook County Hospital. I named my baby Thomas, and would call him Tommy.

Rex came to the hospital and signed adoption papers on my son. Rex didn't even stop in my room to see me when he signed those papers. I was asked to sign my baby's birth certificate, but I refused. I thought they were trying to trick me into signing adoption papers on my baby, so I refused to cooperate with them.

I was in the hospital for ten days. During this time, I was only allowed to see my son once. Then I was told, "Your husband has signed adoption papers on your baby; you can't see him." When I protested that I hadn't signed any papers, I was told, "You are under age. Your husband is your guardian. It isn't necessary for you to sign any papers. You are a baby having a baby. I don't understand how you got married in the first place. Someone had to do a lot of lying."

The night before I was to go home, I received a telegram from Rex. It must have been about 3:00 a.m. when the telegram was brought to me. It said, "Whatever you do, don't sign papers on my big boy. I have changed my mind. I want to keep my son. Signed, Rexford Monroe Carter."

I insisted on seeing my son. He was brought to me about 4:00 a.m. I took the blanket off my bed and wrapped my son in it. I attempted to walk out of the hospital. A nurse caught me. She gave me a shirt and some blankets to wrap my baby in. She got my clothes for me and made me sign some papers, which I was reluctant to do. I was afraid of being tricked and loosing my baby after all.

Something seemed wrong with this scene and I was taking no chances. I walked out of the hospital with my son. I didn't know how far it was to my mother-in-law's. It was late in the morning when I got there. I was very cold, but the baby seemed to be all right. I had buttoned him up in my coat.

Rex and his mother had a fit. I showed them the telegram. Rex had not sent that telegram. Wealthy said, "It is a mystery who sent this telegram."

Wealthy called the hospital, and wanted them to take the baby back. The hospital refused to readmit my son. The woman at the hospital said, "This is Friday. It is too late to do anything until Monday.

I was allowed to keep my baby for the weekend. I held him day and night. When he cried, someone complained. I thought about running away with him. What would I do for diapers? How would I keep him warm? I had nowhere to go. Where would we sleep? No, I wouldn't run away. I would do as my sister, Vesta, had done. I would let someone adopt him who would love and take care of him. To say goodbye to my son would hurt, but at least he would stay alive. I promised myself I would pray every night that my son would never learn where he had come from. And that he would never behave like my father had. I wanted him to grow up to be a good person, and have a good education so he could earn enough money for his family.

Arthur had left my mother-in-law's the morning I went to the hospital, after he had learned the sex of the child. On that Sunday morning, Wealthy received a phone call from the New York police. Arthur had been found in a New York City park, frozen to death on a park bench. In his belongings were a hand-written copy of the telegram that I had received at the hospital and Wealthy's address.

That was how the police knew to contact Wealthy. I would miss Uncle Arthur; he was like a guardian angel to me. The city of New York disposed of his body. I couldn't say goodbye to him.

Wealthy decided that since her brother had died to save my baby, then I could keep him. But I had to support him. They gave me some doll clothes that belonged to one of Rex's nieces. Rex stole six diapers for me.

Wealthy told me, "You will have to breast-feed your baby. We aren't going to buy milk for him. You will have to find a way to support him yourself. My brother died so you could keep this baby. Now prove to me you're worth the chance my brother gave you."

I promised her I was as worthy as Uncle Arthur believed I was, and I would prove it. I went out looking for work. I had to take Tommy and Wealthy with me. I went into a building and got an application for a job. Wealthy sat on the closest fire hydrant holding Tommy. I got the application and took it out to Wealthy. She helped me fill it out, and then I took it back into the company. The first job I got was with Montgomery Ward collating the catalog pages.

My mother-in-law got a breast pump for me and showed me how to use it. When I was at work and feeding time came, my whole dress would get wet and I would be standing in a pool of milk. I worked for several months.

One night Rex came home very drunk. Tommy was crying and I was trying to get ready for work. Rex hit Tommy with his fist so hard that he fell against the wall. I tried to protect my son. Rex shoved me out the door in my half-slip and bra, and he locked the door behind me. I waited until he passed out, and then I took down the clothesline in the front yard. I broke the window and crawled through it. I tied Rex up with the clothesline, took his belt and was beating him with it.

Because I did not pull down the blind in the window, the woman in the front apartment called the police. When the police got there, I let them in. They told me to get my baby and go somewhere for a couple of weeks. The police said, "The next time, remember to close the blinds and hit him once for us."

The police department was very familiar with my husband. The police drove me to the bus station so that I could board a bus. I had no place to go but my Grandmother Cahala's.

While I was there, Aunt Dorothy and I got up in the loft of the barn and bleached our hair. In the process of this, a bear came in the barn and we were stuck in the loft for a while. Grandmother Cahala was very angry when she saw what we had done to our hair. Aunt Dorothy also taught me how to knit and crochet in the loft of that old barn.

Grandmother told me during this visit that Father had made Aunt Lois pregnant years earlier. She made Aunt Lois get an abortion. Mother's brothers and sisters had children. I don't know how many, or what their names were. Aunt Fern and Uncle Guy were the only ones who would have anything to do with Father and Mother.

My husband figured out where I was and came after me. Since he didn't know about my Grandmother Cahala, I can't even guess how he found me, unless Aunt Joe had told him where Grandmother lived. One day he knocked on Grandmother's door.

Grandmother did not like him. She said, "Rex looks like Otis. No wonder Kitty sold you to him; he has to be some relation to Otis. How anyone could do this to her child, I don't understand. This is supposed to be the United States of America."

When I got back to Chicago, I no longer had a job. The next few jobs I asked for wanted proof of my age. I was asked to show my birth certificate, but I did not have one. Mother had told me that I was thirteen when I married Rex. My birth had never been registered. Even if it had been, I would be too young to get a job. I could prove nothing. I started babysitting for other people, but I could not make enough money to support my son. Tommy was five months old, and he needed baby food.

My mother-in-law again sat on fire hydrants while I looked for a job. I found a job at Dr. Shaw's Footwear Co. I did well there until my husband, while drunk, beat me so badly that I could not keep up with my work. Tommy had learned to crawl really well. I would have been fired anyway when I didn't produce a birth certificate and Social Security card by the deadline the company had given me. I didn't have these documents and didn't know how to get them. The only identification I had was my marriage license.

One day my husband drove us out to the suburbs of Chicago. He turned down a gravel road. Rex wanted me to get out of the car. When I did, he took Tommy from my arms and sat him down on the gravel road. He grabbed me and dragged me to the car. He held me so I couldn't get loose and he drove away. Tommy started crawling after the car. I finally broke loose from Rex and jumped of the moving car, skinning my legs and sides pretty badly. I ran back and picked up my son. His little legs were bleeding from the knees down.

My husband sat in the car and waited until I walked back to the car with my son. He was angry because I had gone back for the baby. He said, "I just wanted to see what Tommy would do and you ruined that."

So he beat me up. Between the fall from the car and the beating, I was in pretty bad shape and I was unable to work. He didn't seem to know or care that a job was hard for me to get without any identification.

Even so, I had several jobs after that. Each time, my mother-in-law sat on fire hydrants and helped me fill out the applications, and then waited for me to have the interviews. The company would give me three months to produce identification. When I didn't produce any, they fired me.

I weighed about 80 pounds and wore a size four shoe. People had to know I was lying about my age. If an employer refused to pay me under the table, I was out of luck. I couldn't work as a waitress because I had no balance. I was too clumsy. Aunt Joe once told me that having polio when I was younger was probably the cause of my balancing problem. Every three months, my mother-in-law sat on a fire hydrant while holding my son, and helped me fill out applications so I could find a job. People must have laughed at us.

One day in 1956, my Aunt Joe told me, "I registered your birth today. I made you two years older than you really are. Here is your birth certificate. I will take you down to the Social Security office to get your Social Security card tomorrow. I hope this will help you to find work easier." I was about 15 years old at the time, and Aunt Joe had registered me as being 17 years old. She didn't tell me my actual birthday, but she gave me the birthday of August 24, 1939.

I finally got to see what a birth certificate looked like, even though it wasn't the actual document. When I applied for a job and people asked me for my Social Security number, I didn't know what they were talking about. Now I would find out. I had always said, "I don't have one," and I was told to get one.

I asked Aunt Joe what a Social Security card was and why I needed it. She explained to me what I needed to know. It helped me to get into a nurse's aid class.

At the places I worked, the nurses gave me an oral report so that I could get by without knowing how to read much. I managed to get through the class by learning from observing, listening and looking at the pictures in the books. It was not as hard as the work I was used to doing. I enjoyed working. It made me feel like I was worth something for the first time in my life. I felt proud of myself. I was helping people who really needed help. To me it was an honorable job.

The people I worked with were nice and willing to help me learn what it took to do the job. I was eager to learn as much as I could as quickly as possible. I even did other people's work if it was something I was capable of doing. I felt more comfortable working than sitting around trying to be friendly. Most of my coworkers didn't mind my helping them at all. Mostly, I made beds, cleaned elderly people's bottoms and emptied and cleaned bedpans. I enjoyed staying busy. I felt like an adult. After I turned sixteen, it was easier for me to find work.

It didn't take long for Rex to demolish the confidence I had built up. He always reminded me how much I didn't know and where I came from. He enjoyed making me feel stupid. He and his mother constantly reminded me that I was from a dysfunctional family, and that I was nothing and would never become anything. They thought I was getting "too big for my pants."

This just made me rebel. But the way I rebelled was to learn more and to do better, so they wouldn't have so much to make fun of. As time passed, this worked for me. I learned a lot of necessary things to survive. I was becoming less timid than I had been before, and they didn't like it. I sometimes even stood up for my baby and myself.

The more I learned, the more independent I became and the more respect Rex's mother and his sisters gave me behind my back. Also, I began to learn some self-respect. I was winning. I was not as stupid as these idiots said I was. I didn't get drunk and fall on my ass, or stand in the middle of the sidewalk and fight like a fool. I refused to lower myself to their level. I did not get arrested for stealing, drunkenness or fighting. I felt good about myself. Father had not won; he had not changed what I felt in my heart. I had beaten him at his own game.

I have a lot to thank Wealthy and Bascom, my in-laws, for. Without them, I may never have grown up. I probably would be like the rest of my siblings. They never learned self-respect. They never learned to take responsibility for what they did. They raised their children the same way they were raised. Life is no good that way. I was learning a better way to live.

My mother-in-law taught me that there were many ways to find work. I did not have to stoop to prostitution to feed and support my children. Nor did I have to follow in my mother's footsteps and depend on welfare to take care of my children. I began to understand that Wealthy was just trying to help me grow up quickly, so my children and I could survive.

I felt much differently about her than I had before I understood this. She pushed me hard, but I still had a long way to go. I knew she didn't like me, yet she was helping me. She was rough and hard. But underneath that thick skin, she really had a kind heart. She just refused to show it. I think she knew what kind of a son she had, and she knew what I had to put up with from him and his friends.

I was not to complain. Rex said, "They are just playing. They are not really insulting you."

I complained anyway. They thought it was funny for me to hit one of them. Tommy once stepped on a live cigarette butt and, of course, he cried. Rex whipped him with his belt.

Rex took Tommy in the stores and held him against his shirt while he took packages of lunchmeat or anything else that would fit down his shirt. At night, Rex broke into people's houses and stole their money and jewelry. He took Tommy and held him in front of him.

"People will not shoot at me if I am holding a baby in my arms. You can understand that, can't you?" he asked me.

Chapter THIRTEEN

MY HUSBAND AND I moved out of my mother-in-law's house. His drinking got worse, and he brought home other men. They drank and played cards. Rex and his friends would throw lit cigarette butts on the floor during their drinking and card parties.

Rex would hold Tommy in front of him and steal, mainly jewelry and money. Rex did this from the time Tommy was born. It took all of our money to keep Rex out of jail. He couldn't hold down a steady job. We depended mostly on what Rex could steal and what he earned at his gambling parties to eat. I was lucky to earn rent money. Rex even loaned Tommy out to his friends to help them with their robberies. I was in constant fear for my son's life. My husband thought it was funny to use him as a shield.

I really couldn't complain, though. Life was better than it had been before I married. Life was pleasant when Rex was not home and when I was at work. I was enjoying watching Tommy grow and felt very protective over him.

When Tommy was only about 13 months old, I had potty-trained him, as I only had six diapers for him. One day when I had him outdoors, he ran into the woman's flower garden next door and urinated. This woman had such a fit that she threatened to call the police. This made me angry because I had thought it was cute. I stepped into her flower garden, picked up Tommy and sat down in her garden. I told her to call the police. I sat there and waited for them, but the police never came. I finally got tired and went home. I felt she was being unkind, but I have to admit I was being a brat.

I felt very grown up working and supporting my child. What

I really didn't understand was how much help Wealthy was giving me. My mother-in-law never threw this in my face. She kept me innocent about how much help she provided. My most important job was protecting my son.

Tommy was 19 months old when my second child was born. Again, I had no prenatal care. I was alone with Tommy when my daughter, Carol, was born before I could get any help. I had trouble making her cry. She was blue, so I did CPR on her. Finally, she cried. I cut the cord and tied my son in his crib. I then wrapped my baby up and walked four blocks to call the midwives' association. They brought a doctor to my house.

Carol had something in her throat that was enlarged. The doctor told me, "You must pump your breasts and thicken her milk with rice cereal." I don't know where I had learned to do CPR. I just did what I had to do to save my baby's life.

After Carol was born, I was hired at the Presbyterian Hospital as a nurse's aid. I was able to give more to my children. My husband continued to drink more often than not. He hit me frequently. I was used to abuse, so I was able to tolerate it. I believe I understood Grandmother's words to my father in the story he once told us. I felt free while I was at work. Life was looking better for me. I had once more gained a little self-confidence, and this felt good.

My mother-in-law spent the night with us one night. I slept in the crib with Tommy. She slept in the bed with my husband. I know nothing happened between them. She was just hiding from Bobby, her youngest son, for some reason. I don't remember why. I think he wanted her to give him some money for his rent. Bobby, like myself, needed help from time to time.

One year and one week later I went into labor with my third child. Again, I had no prenatal care. Because I was breastfeeding Carol and not having a monthly period, I had no idea when to expect this child.

When I went into labor, I was alone with Tommy and Carol. I did not have money for bus fare. I walked 18 blocks carrying Carol and holding Tommy's hand. Sometimes the labor pains were so hard that I had to stop and lean against a building before I could go on. I finally walked all the way to my mother-in-law's house.

By this time, I was definitely ready to give birth. My mother-in-law refused to let me into a bed in her house. She called someone to take me to the University Hospital. I couldn't stand it any more. The baby was coming; I couldn't stop it. While my mother-in-law ran around the house frantically telling me not to push, I crawled in her bed and gave birth to Phillip. She complained that I was ruining her mattress.

We were taken to the University Hospital, but I don't know who took us because there was so much confusion. I was so very tired that I didn't care about all the bickering that was going on. I simply needed to sleep. I was aware that my mother-in-law was fussing at me. Since I knew she didn't like me anyway, I really didn't care. I tuned everything out and went to sleep. I slept soundly.

I woke up in the hospital. All the time I was in the hospital, my husband brought Tommy and Carol to see me only one time.

Later, Wealthy told me, "You passed out from the lack of blood and from exhaustion. You didn't just go to sleep. You scared me to death. Only a fool would walk 18 blocks while in labor. You should have called a cab. I would have paid for it. Didn't you know I would pay for your cab in this kind of a situation? Don't ever do a fool thing like that again. You almost had that baby on the street."

When it came time for us to be released, Rex came to get the baby and me about 9:00 a.m. on the tenth day. Instead of taking us home, he went to a bar. I sat in the car for hours with the baby, while he barhopped. I didn't know where we were or how to get home. About 7:30 p.m. the next evening, a police car drove past me a few times. I watched for him to drive by again, and when he did I got out of the car and flagged him down. I told him how long the baby and I had been in the car. He asked me if I had anyone to go to. I told him I could go to my mother-in-law's.

The policeman called another police car to take me to my mother-in-law's home. I was running a high temperature, so my mother-in-law said. The first policeman sat outside the bar and waited for my husband to come out. They arrested him for drunken driving and endangerment of a child.

I was the black sheep of the family from that time on. It was not right for a wife to cause her husband to be arrested. I had committed the ultimate sin. Rex's mother explained, "You could be the cause of him spending the rest of his life in jail. You will never do something like this again."

Tommy was only three-and-a-half years of age at this time. Rex and his family seemed to take the fact that I had done something wrong out on Tommy because he wasn't Rex's child. I learned to stick a bottle in Tommy's mouth when these incidents occurred. I had to quiet him down quickly to keep him from getting punished. Rex knew the way to get me angry was to mistreat one of the children. When he was drinking, that was the tool he used to get my goat.

Phillip had colic as a baby, and he cried both day and night. Rex spanked him for the first time when Phillip was ten days old. I could no longer work because Rex would not stay with Phillip while I worked. Phillip's crying disturbed Rex's drinking and gambling buddies. They had to find somewhere else to hang out.

Rex was often gone for long periods of time. When he did come home and I complained about the children being hungry, Rex would take Tommy and use him as a shield and steal something for us to eat. I feared for Tommy's life. I tried not to complain that the children often had little or no food. I was forced to go to his mother for help. She never made it easy for me. It was always my fault in her opinion.

One day, Rex stole a bicycle and a kid's wagon. He fixed it so that I could attach the wagon to the bicycle. I put the children in the wagon and went anywhere I needed to go in this way.

On another occasion, Rex was home after having been out drinking for several days. I had no milk for Phillip, and I could no longer produce breast milk to feed him. He was screaming his head off.

Rex started screaming for me to shut him up, any way I could. I grabbed Phillip and said, "What do you expect? I haven't had anything but sugar and water to feed him all day. You never leave me with any money."

This was one of Rex's better days. He was drunk, but he decided that because Phillip was his real son, he would go out and get him a gallon of milk. Hours went by, and Rex didn't come back. I waited and waited. I felt strange; I was afraid someone would kill Rex that night. At the same time, I prayed to God that someone would kill him. This feeling frightened me. I had never before wished harm to come to someone. I felt very guilty about my feelings. But I just couldn't stop feeling this way. I think I both loved and hated Rex.

Early the next morning, a police officer knocked on the door and gave me a gallon of milk. He explained that my husband had been arrested for grabbing a woman's purse while she was waiting for a bus to go to work. When Rex ran from the police, they hit him with one of their sticks and hurt his knee. He was now in Grant Hospital. He had told the police that he needed a gallon of milk for his baby. The policeman said to me, "I brought you the milk as soon as I could."

Rex's father, Bascom, and his brother supplied Rex with wine while he was in the hospital. This made it difficult for the nurses to care for him because he was rude and cruel while drinking.

After Rex's knee healed, the police put him in jail. The landlord told me I had to move, and she gave me only five days. I had never rented an apartment before. Aunt Joe had moved, but I did not know where. I had a large baby buggy that I had gotten at a second-hand store. I could put all three of the children in it. I started walking the streets, looking for a place to rent. Most people thought I was crazy when I tried to explain my situation to them.

I then found one place with a photography office underneath it. This man was willing to let me live in his apartment if I would work for him as a model. I had never had such an offer; I was flattered. I felt that I would make plenty of money for the children and myself. I moved all of our belongings into the apartment, using my big baby buggy.

I was sure Wealthy would have to be proud of me now. I had no furniture, so I laid blankets on the floor and put my babies to bed. They were very tired, and so was I. We went right to sleep. I felt very proud of myself; I had found a job that should pay good money.

About eleven o'clock, someone knocked on the door. He said, "Pete, the landlord, wants to see you downstairs." I left my babies and went downstairs.

First, the landlord wanted me to take off my clothes. I wasn't about to do that. He told me I would have to undress at least to my slip in order to model for him. I undressed down to my slip. Then he told me to come over to him, and I did. He took both my arms in his hands. He told me that he would have me examined by a doctor. He said that a doctor would not be far from me at any time.

I did not understand what he was telling me. I asked him why I would need a doctor. He squeezed my arms hard and said, "I will send men up to your apartment. You will do whatever they want you to do. The doctor will keep you free from disease. I will collect the money and give you your share. I am the only one you will service for free."

He ordered me to take off the rest of my clothes. When he turned loose of my arms to take off his pants, I ran. This, I understood too well. I went upstairs and got my children; then I went down the fire escape and to my mother-in-law's. I told her what had just happened and what the landlord had said.

She informed me, "He is a pimp. It is a thousand wonders you were able to get away from him."

She screamed and yelled at me for being so dumb. She finally said, "Well, at least you had the good sense to get out of there and come to me. I didn't realize you were so naïve or I would have taught you about this kind of thing. That is probably more than that little red-headed bitch would have done." (She was speaking of her youngest son's wife.)

The next day she and Bascom went with me to get my belongings. I stayed with them until Rex got out of jail. I went back to work as a nurse's aid, and Wealthy babysat for me. Rex always took my money away from me.

Rex got a job at Max Factor. He sometimes stole lipstick, eye shadow and eyeliner from the company and gave it to me. He taught me how to use it. Rex's job did not last long. Between his drinking, stealing and fighting, he was in and out of jail. Wealthy watched the children while I worked. We got our own apartment, and Rex started having his drinking and card parties again. He became more abusive to the children and me while he was drinking. He was like a wild man.

One evening Rex got an ice cream cone for Carol. When she spilled some on her dress, Rex got so angry that he hit her and knocked her out of the car. When I objected to this, Rex showed me a gun. He said, "What the fuck are you going to do about it?" Carol was not yet four years old. She started having nightmares. (Years later, I learned her nightmares were really seizures.)

I ran into my Aunt Joe on the street one evening. I learned she did not live far from me. I had a black eye from Rex beating me. She advised, "Leave that son-of-a-bitch. He is a male chauvinist pig. La Verne's upstairs apartment is empty. I will help you get on welfare; this will help both of you." I thought seriously about leaving Rex. I was pregnant with my daughter, Vallerie, at the time.

I was tired of worrying about Tommy's life when Rex and his friends used him as a shield during their robberies. My babies would no longer be put in the trunk of a car when they got fussy during his barhopping sprees. I wouldn't come home from work anymore and find my children alone. I would be a fool not to take advantage of this. Maybe I could teach my children not to steal and not to be prejudiced like Rex was.

I had high hopes of bettering our lives. If I sat around and did nothing, my children would grow up to act like Rex. If they had the chance to grow up at all, I would be lucky. I had to do something. This might be my only chance to get my children out of the cesspool I had been born into.

I waited until Rex was in jail the next time. That took several weeks. Then I packed everything we had and moved into La Verne's upstairs apartment. I had to be careful to keep everything I packed hidden until I could get it over to La Verne's, just in case my mother-in-law came by, realized what was happening and tried to stop me. When I got all of our stuff out of the apartment, Aunt Joe hired some men she knew to get the heavy stuff out of the house for me.

It felt good to have my own apartment, without the worry about what Rex might do next. I felt I would be safe there, for a while at least, until Rex got out of jail. I didn't have to worry about one of my children taking a bullet for Rex while he was robbing somebody's house, or about Rex renting one of our children out to his friends for that purpose.

I felt safer being among family members. Life would be better for us now. My children would not be afraid all the time. I didn't have to walk very far to buy groceries and milk for the children. I thought to myself, "This is a good deal."

Chapter FOURTEEN

I MOVED UPSTAIRS, above La Verne, on Magnolia Street. Aunt Joe took me to the welfare office. She told the caseworker that she would like for me to see a legal aid lawyer. She said that I needed to get a divorce before my husband, Rex, hurt one of us. The caseworker said, "If she gets a divorce, the state will have to take her children. Her husband is obviously not fit to care for them. She is too young; her husband is still her guardian."

My Aunt Joe talked to the woman alone. I don't know what was said. Then the state sent me a check every month. Tommy started kindergarten. He loved going to school with his cousin.

Rex got out of jail and kidnapped Carol out of the yard one day. He took her to his sister Dorothy's house. When I tried to get help to get her back, the police said, "We can't help you. Legally, he has as much right to that child as you do."

While Dorothy was at work, I kidnapped Carol back. My children never played in the yard again after that. I was not as safe as I had hoped to be. He must have traced me through the school system.

My daughter, Vallerie, was born February 9, 1961. She was born at home, but I went to Grant Hospital after La Verne got home from work.

Rex started meeting me when I picked Tommy up from school. He gave the children candy, telling them how much he missed them and loved them, even crying sometimes. He talked me into taking the children to see him one Saturday at his apartment.

When I got there, I laid Vallerie down on the couch; she was too young to roll off. He then said, "You are not leaving this apartment," as he locked the bolt on the door. I tried to unlock it, but he overpowered me. He was now sitting on top of me, and I could not move.

While this was going on, Phillip had found Rex's razor in the bathroom and was trying to shave his baby sister. I was unable to get away from Rex to take the razor away from him. Once more, I had to rely on Tommy. I was scared to death that Phillip would hurt Vallerie. Rex just laughed.

Vallerie was just ten days old. I was screaming for Tommy to take the razor from Phillip. Rex told him, "If you go near Phillip, I will beat your goddamn ass. Let him kill the little bitch. Then I won't have to support her."

Tommy was so confused; he did not know what to do. Finally, I somehow managed to get free from Rex. Phillip had shaved the skin off his little sister's face. She was screaming, but not hurt very badly. With my five-and-a-half-year-old son's help, I managed to get the children out of Rex's apartment. Rex grabbed me before I could get out. He must have held me in his apartment for a half hour. He told me I was a "bought and paid for" wife, and that he could really make life hard for me if he wanted to. He was already doing a good job of that. He was making my life hell; I didn't want it to get worse.

Tommy had taken the children into the a hallway of an apartment next door. Tommy was five years old, holding a baby ten days old, standing in a hallway with his four-year-old sister and three-year-old brother for half an hour. No one seemed to notice.

When I managed to get out of Rex's apartment, I couldn't find the children. I screamed and screamed for them. Tommy finally answered and came out of the apartment where they were hiding. I can't begin to tell you how relieved I was to hear his little voice when he finally answered me. I breathed a sigh of relief. My children were all right. We had gotten away together this time. But could we get away the next time?

After that stunt, Rex tried to convince me to go back to him by buying a car for me. I accepted the car because I needed it desperately. I refused to listen to Rex or to go back to him, however, when he met me at Tommy's school.

Later that month, I was watching my children and La Verne's two daughters. Rex broke down my door and took Phillip. He was so drunk that he fell all the way down the stairs as he left. I ran to Aunt Joe's. She got the police and stayed with the children, while I rode around a the police car to find my son. I saw Rex's hat in the street and asked the policeman to stop. I got out of the car to pick up his hat, and heard my son crying. We found him under a porch a few houses from where I found Rex's hat.

Someone gave me a blanket to wrap my son in. The wind chill was 17 below zero. My son was wearing only a pair of pajamas, and he was freezing to death. Phillip was hospitalized with pneumonia a few days later. He was only 20 months old.

Phillip was already a very insecure child, and this didn't help him any. Instead, he became even more insecure. He was a heavy child and hard for me to carry around, but now he insisted that I carry him all the time.

I didn't see Rex for a while after that. One evening, I was watching La Verne's children again. This time I was downstairs in her apartment. I had the children sitting on the couch watching television. The front door was half glass. I saw a shadow pass by the door. I knew by the shape of the profile that it was Rex. I could see the shadow of the gun in his hand.

I told the children, "Lay on the floor, now!"

I had barely gotten the words out of my mouth when the glass shattered and the back of the couch was filled with bullets.

After this, La Verne was afraid for her children and asked me to move. I found a basement apartment on Griffith Street. The children and I were happy for a while, until Rex got into trouble with the law again. I had thought I was hidden from Rex. That proved to be a foolish notion.

It didn't take Rex long to bring me to my knees. One night in February, I woke up with a man standing over my bed. He said, "Don't be afraid of me, Frankie. Rex sent me to get his bail money from you. If you do not give it to me, I am to take Carol and keep her until you come up with the money."

I did not have any money and I told him so. He started toward the children's bedroom saying, "I will keep in touch every couple of days. When you have the money, I will return your daughter."

I said, "Like hell you will; get out of my house!"

I tried to fight this man to keep him away from Carol. I wasn't much of a match for him, but I did buy some time. When we got to the bedroom, the children were not there. The man became angry. He said, "I'm going to get something out of this besides a busted head." He raped me and left.

I immediately started looking for my children. I woke the lady in the apartment above me. She couldn't speak English. I saw a taxicab and hailed it. I asked the driver to please call the police for me. I looked all night for my children. I was approaching insanity and freezing to death.

When morning came, I was tired. I went to my Aunt Joe's house. Going up the back way was a little shorter. As I walked up the stairs, I could hear Phillip crying and Tommy telling him to be quiet, or they would be found. My Aunt Joe hated to do laundry. They wore their clothes until they were dirty, and then they threw them on the back porch. When they ran out of clothes, they went to a second-hand store and bought more. I found Tommy, Carol and Phillip hiding under the pile of dirty clothes. Vallerie was not there.

Tommy said, "She was too heavy for me to get her out of the crib. I emptied the clothes hamper on top of her. I covered her with Carol's blankets and mine. I hid her in the crib."

I hurried home. Sure enough, I found Vallerie buried under a mound of clothes, with blankets on top of her. She was safe and sound. She was still sleeping, as if nothing had happened. I thanked God that Tommy had used his little head. Vallerie was about 13 months old at this time, and Tommy was not yet eight years old.

Aunt Joe suggested that maybe Rex was able to find me so easily because I was on welfare. I filed for divorce, using Aunt Joe's address. I was afraid to stay in an apartment. Rex was able to find me too easily. I found a job in a nursing home and left the apartment, taking only our clothes.

I took my children to work with me. They slept in my car behind the nursing home. I did this for several months from about mid-March until the fall of 1963, checking on my children during my lunches and break times. I was about 22 years old at the time.

During the daytime, I took Tommy and Carol to school. I got a harness with leashes for Phillip and Vallerie that I fastened around my waist. I slept in Lincoln Park until school was out. When it was too cold to sleep in the park, we stayed in the car. I tried to always park in an alley, hoping Rex wouldn't find us.

I would pick Tommy and Carol up from school, do a load of laundry at a laundromat, feed my children and play with them a while, and then put them to bed in the car. I bathed my children at a barbershop. While we lived for several months like this, it really wasn't as bad as it sounds. We were safer this way, or so I believed. The only time I was not with my children was when they were in school, and then I wasn't far away.

I always gave Aunt Joe's address as my home address, and checked in with her once in a while. At times, Aunt Joe would let me bathe the children at her place, but she really didn't want us there. We were always careful not to stay too long in case Rex came looking for us. If he found us there, Aunt Joe would not help me protect my children or myself.

Rex was making it tough for me, but he would not win. I had no intention of letting him. I always had to look over my shoulder because I did not want to run into someone who might know him, or run into a member of his family. It was tough, but we were happy. To me, that was important.

Somehow I kept the children from realizing there were any problems. Rex's mother, of all people had taught me enough to be able to survive without his help.

Chapter FIFTEEN

IT WASN'T LONG until I realized I was pregnant again. I had not been with a man, except for the time Rex had sent a rapist to kidnap Carol. I continued to live in my car until I thought it was about time for the baby to be born. I think I felt safer living in the car.

I still took my children to work and they slept in the car. I had a small kerosene stove I had found at a second-hand store. I put it in the back of the station wagon to keep my children warm. I rolled the back windows down a couple of inches to make sure the children didn't suffocate. I knew this wasn't a wise thing to do, but anything was better than Rex finding us. Even the children feared that he might find us.

My brother, Dennis, came to see Aunt Joe, and he agreed to babysit my children. I rented an apartment and we moved in. I managed to find two beds, a stove that would keep us warm and a hot plate to cook with.

Dennis got out of line with me while he was drinking and tried to force sex on me, but he didn't succeed. I threw him out. He reminded me that it was a woman's job to make a man happy, that we really didn't have any say in the matter. He said, "You should have learned that by now. If you don't do what I want you to do, I will cause trouble for you. I will turn you in for leaving your children in your car at night. And tell the police you don't have a driver's license. They will arrest you and send you to jail."

Shortly thereafter, my daughter, La Donna, was born November 15, 1963. I delivered her at home, alone with my other children. When I went into labor, I kept Tommy home to watch Phillip and Vallerie. I sent Carol to go and get Aunt Joe. She lived two blocks from me. Carol did not come back. Aunt Joe had not been home, so Carol stood by her door for about three hours waiting for her. My half-sister, La Donna, who was about 14 years old at the time, came home from school for lunch and found her standing there. She came to my home and got the other children and took them home with her. I had already delivered the baby by this time.

Aunt Joe came over later that afternoon and told me that she had taken my children to my sister, La Verne's, house to stay for a week until I was able to watch after them again. Aunt Joe looked at the baby and said that she was doing fine; then she went home, leaving the baby and me alone. I named my baby La Donna because my half-sister, La Donna, was the first one to come to my aid after my baby had been born.

One day soon after, I walked out of the bathroom after taking a bath and found my brother, Dennis, walking out the door with my new baby. I asked him where he thought he was taking my baby daughter.

"I met a man who promised me three thousand dollars if I would bring her to him. Of course, I intend to split it with you," he responded.

I had to fight my brother for my baby. I wouldn't have won if the man in the apartment next to me had not opened his door to see what all the noise was about.

Rex found us about six weeks after La Donna's birth. Dennis had given Rex the key to my apartment while I was at work. I wondered if Dennis had hunted Rex down to get even with me for kicking him out. I was so tired of running from Rex. When he refused to leave, I did not fight him terribly hard. It seemed there was no way I could win this battle.

Rex asked me how I thought he was always able to find me. Then he told me, "I have lots of help. I belong to an underground gang. You can never get away from me." He again showed me a gun as proof of this. He said, "All the men I play cards with are members of the gang I belong to."

I felt that maybe he was trying to scare me. I thought people like that were rich and we were certainly not rich. I did not really believe him. However, I never forgot what he said, just in case it was true.

Many times Rex tore apart the apartment looking for money I had hidden. When he couldn't find it, he would beat me up. When he learned he could cash my checks without my signature, he met me at work and took my checks away from me before I could get home with them. When he did this, I couldn't pay for rent or buy food for us.

He didn't seem to care if the children went hungry. I was afraid he would retaliate if I called the police. I didn't believe everything Rex said about belonging to a gang, but I feared him a great deal. It was hard to know what he might do the next time he got drunk.

Aunt Joe wouldn't let La Donna babysit with Rex there. This left the children at Rex's mercy. It seemed as though he drank even more than he had before. Again, he began leaving the children alone when I was at work. We had to move because of his drinking, fighting and parties. The men he hung out with had no manners or dignity at all. They were dirty-talking men.

We moved to the third floor of an apartment building on Whitney Street. Rex seemed to hate Tommy, and he started teaching Phillip to do the same. He would sit Phillip on his lap and tell Phillip that when he grew up, he was going to fight and kill Tommy; that he would rob a bank and blame it on Tommy. If Tommy did not give his toy up to Phillip, Rex would whip Tommy. Rex told Phillip that Tommy was a bastard, a son-of-a-bitch. Rex did everything he could think of to turn Phillip against Tommy. I tried to protect Tommy, but I wasn't very good at it. My strength could not match Rex's. He was too strong, even when he was drunk.

Rex continued to teach the children to steal from stores, and to use the children as protection when he robbed someone's house. When we were in the car, if the boys had a problem or got too loud, Rex continued to lock them in the trunk. Once he spanked Carol for refusing to steal a sucker. I was very proud of her, especially when she told the store clerk that her daddy had some meat underneath his shirt. Rex was very upset when he got arrested because his little daughter had told on him. He treated her differently after she had done this.

One time, while we were at a Kentucky Fried Chicken restaurant, some African-American children were playing ball under the L train. Rex wanted to beat the children up just because they were black. I fought him over this, as I screamed for the black children to go get their father. Of course, I got beaten up, but the children did run away. Another time, Rex deliberately ran over a little black boy's foot while he was waiting for the light to change. He didn't even stop to see how badly the boy was hurt.

Rex hated black people. He taught the children to hate them, too. It is surprising how a young child can comprehend this kind of teaching. Several of my children carried this hatred with them throughout their lives. I couldn't shake off some of the things Rex had taught them.

Rex did many stupid things like this. I had been learning to read and write since Tommy started school. With the help of a Jehovah's Witness woman, I was teaching the children that what Rex wanted them to do was wrong. Tommy and Carol were old enough to understand some. But the difference in our teachings confused Carol a lot more than it did Tommy. Carol's nightmares got worse. Tommy seemed to grow closer to me. Tommy taught me what he had learned in school; I guess this helped us grow closer also. Phillip seemed to draw closer to his father; he tried very hard to please him.

When Rex forbade me to take the children to the Kingdom Hall, we sneaked down the stairs, climbed a fence in the backyard and went any way. I always paid a very dear price when we got back. But I felt like, finally, life had some kind of meaning. And at least once a week I had friends.

I took a typing and filing course in the evenings at a local high school. Some of the words I typed I could not even pronounce; I could read very little. But I was proud of myself. Rex beat me up quite frequently, which really did not help our situation. The two things that kept me going were school and the Kingdom Hall visits. The children and I looked forward to Sundays; this was our day.

One day, I came home from work and was met by the woman downstairs. She informed me, "I found your children on the fire escape."

Tommy said, "Daddy was being bad. We had to hide from him."

Carol said, "Daddy scared me. He set the stove on fire."

Rex was lying downstairs by the basement door, passed out and beaten up. He smelled of whiskey. I did not even try to get him upstairs; I let him lie there. I fed the children breakfast and took them to Lincoln Park.

When I came home one day and found Vallerie zipped up in a jacket, hanging from a nail outside the window of our third floor apartment, I had had enough. What I learned from Tommy and Carol was that after I had left for work, Rex took Vallerie's teddy bear and hid it. Vallerie had to have her teddy bear all the time, ever since the Kingdom Hall woman had given it to her. Because Vallerie wouldn't stop crying after repeated spankings, Rex drove a nail in the window seal, zipped her in her jacket and hung her out the window.

I quietly got my children out of bed and left, taking nothing else with me. I moved in with Aunt Joe. Her daughter, Bonnie, was a teenager by then, and was very mean to my children. Aunt Joe was not much better. She treated me as I had seen Father and her treat Mother. I was too afraid to fight her back. Aunt Joe and Bonnie beat on me, and I lost sight of my self-confidence. I knew I didn't stand a chance against them anyway.

I went to work in a punch press factory. I gave all of my money to Aunt Joe. She insisted on taking my car also. Each day, Aunt Joe gave me bus fare to go to work. I saw no way out of this. I gave all of my money to Aunt Joe, and she drove my car. I was trapped. I walked to work and saved my bus fare.

Then Rex found us again. Aunt Joe gave me the keys to my car and kicked me out. She told me, "I want no part of this; this is between you and him." Again we were living out of the car. This seemed to become a habit for me.

Before I could save the money to rent an apartment, Rex found out where I worked. It took him only about two weeks to find me. To this day, I wish I knew how. He started meeting me at work on payday and taking my check away from me before I could cash it. After he did this a few times, I could not feed my children. I had spent all the money I had for food to feed them. At this point I had nothing. I was becoming overwhelmed; I didn't know what to do.

We slept in a garage for two nights and the mechanics fed my children. Then they said that they couldn't do that anymore. They would get into trouble if we were caught there.

I found an empty house to hide in. It was so full of mice that I stayed awake at night to keep the mice off my children. I was afraid to stay in my car because I knew that Rex would be looking for it. We slept in that house for three or fours nights. I had nothing to feed my children all the time we were there. We could get water from the faucets in the house. But we were cold at night, and I had no blankets to keep the children warm. I had parked my car on the next block, hoping we wouldn't be found.

To pass the time, I mostly held the children and we sang songs. I would rock them while sitting on the floor. Sometimes we counted the mice in the house. We made a game of it. Tommy was about nine years old and he was a big help in chasing the mice away from us. La Donna, Vallerie, Phillip and Carol ranged in age from about 20 months through seven years old, and I was about 24 years old.

My children were crying because they were so hungry. I had no money. I couldn't work and leave my children with someone who would hurt them. I could no longer work and leave them in the car because Rex might find them. I was exhausted from staying up at night watching the children so the mice wouldn't get on them. I couldn't stand to hear them cry for food anymore. I didn't feel I could take my children back to Aunt Joe's. I was confused about Aunt Joe's attitude; she had promised to help me with the children. She had talked me into moving into La Verne's apartment house before.

I walked to my car with my children. I put them in the car and drove toward Navy Pier. I just didn't know what else to do to keep us all together. I went a little crazy for the moment, not knowing what to do. My intention was to drive my car off the pier into Lake Michigan, with all of us in it. I just could not stand to hear my babies cry anymore. They were slowly starving to death. I was going to do this because I loved my children so much, and they were suffering terribly. If I gave them to the state, then Rex might get them back and they would live a life of hell. I certainly did not want that to happen. I just did not know what else to do. However, I ran out of gas before I got there.

There was a policeman on the corner. I went to him to try and tell him I needed help, that my children were hungry and my car was in the middle of Wells Street, out of gas. He said, "All I can do is help you get your car out of the street." And that is all he did for us.

I knew what I was about to do was wrong, but I had to do it. I was desperate at this point. My children had to eat, and there was just no other way for me to feed them.

I looked up and down the block, and I saw a restaurant. I removed my children from the car. We walked into the restaurant, and I ordered breakfast for my children and myself. I fed my children and ate something myself.

When it came time to pay for the meal, I asked to see the manager. I told him, "I have no money to pay for this food. My children were hungry. They have not eaten for four days. I will wash dishes, or do anything else you want me to do to pay for the food we ate."

He asked me, "What are you going to do after you have worked enough to pay for the food you and your children ate? You must have somewhere you can go."

I replied, "I am going to finish what I started to do."

"What is that?" he asked.

I refused to answer him, but my little daughter, Carol, did. She told him, "My mommy is going to drive the car off the Navy Pier into the water." I had not told her what my intention was, but somehow she knew what I was going to do. I have often wondered how she had figured that out.

I told the manager, "I don't have any gas."

He questioned me, "Why? Why would you want to do a thing like that?"

I began to cry and told him what my husband was doing to me.

"Don't you have someone in the city you can go to?" he asked.

I told him I had my sister's phone number. La Verne was the only person I knew who could help me, but her husband wouldn't allow her to.

"Please give me her name and number," the manager said.

I gave him La Verne's phone number, and he called her. He asked her if I could stay with her. Then he said, "She is just a child herself. Is there anyone else she can stay with?" He wrote down a name and phone number. La Verne had given him my sister, Delores', number in Oklahoma.

He then called and talked to Delores. When he hung up from talking to Delores, he called La Verne again. He told her, "Tell your husband I will pay you to let her stay for two days. She needs to rest before she attempts a trip like this with these children. Just send me a bill." He gave her his address and hung up the phone.

Then he instructed me, "You are to stay with your sister for two days. I want you to stay the whole two days and rest. I am paying her to let you stay there. Don't let them make you feel any guilt. Will you trust me enough to take me to your car?"

I took him to my car. He told me, "Put the children in the car, and get in also." He went somewhere and got a little can of gas. He put the gas in my car. He then said, "Give me your keys." I gave him my keys. He drove my car to the gas station and filled it up. He then drove us back to his restaurant and gave me back my car keys. He asked me to take the children back in the restaurant and wait for him there. He left, saying, "I will be right back."

The manager left us and went out, telling me to stay there. When he came back, he took some maps from his pockets and traced a route from Chicago to Oklahoma City.

He informed me, "Your sister, Delores, and her husband are willing to take you and your children in and help you. You can get work there. They will help you get a job and watch after the children while you are working."

He gave me three hundred dollars for gas, food and hotels. He provided a way out of this mess. I was thankful for his help and for his concern for my children.

He made me promise I would never try to take my life or my

children's lives ever again. He made sure that I had his phone number in case I needed more help. He explained how he had traced the route that I should take to Oklahoma City. He told me to stay at La Verne's house for two days and rest. He had promised to compensate her for it. Then he made sure that I knew how to get to La Verne's, and then I left. I did stay for two days at La Verne's. She treated the children and me well. We enjoyed staying with her, and I was well rested.

While I was at La Verne's, she told me that Grandmother Cahala had stopped in Chicago on her way to Iowa. She was going to Uncle Bob's because she could no longer care for Grandpa Cahala and Aunt Lois by herself. She had said that she needed to see me very badly. Aunt Joe knew where I lived, but she had refused to tell Grandmother where I could be found. Grandmother died on the bus on her way to Iowa. I will never know what Grandmother had wanted with me.

I still feel badly about this at times. I loved my grandmother. When I was young, her home was the only place that I felt safe. I would have loved for her to have seen my children for the last time. But this didn't happen for me.

The night before we were to leave, I packed the few clothes that La Verne had given me into the car. Early the next morning, Rex woke us up by yelling for me. He had the hood of the car up, and he wanted me to come out and look at it.

Rex said, "The car will do you no good. It is in my name; you could never get tags for it. You are right to leave, but you have to run further than this."

La Verne called the police. When Rex heard the sirens, he ran down the street and got in another car. The car he got into was full of men. Then the police came. Rex had pulled all the wiring loose from under the hood of my car. There was no way I was taking that car anywhere. La Verne's husband asked if the police could arrange to have the car removed from his property, and so they did.

After the police left, I called the manager at the restaurant who had tried to help me. I didn't know his name. I told him how my husband had destroyed my car. I asked him to come and get his money because I could not use it in the way he had intended me to. I apologized for not being able to bring it to him. He told me to stay put for now. Then he asked to talk to my sister.

Robert, La Verne's husband, grabbed the phone and argued with the man on the other end. When he hung up, Robert looked at me and said, "You will stay here for now. All of you stay in the house."

Robert did not go to work that day. A couple of hours went by and the phone rang. Robert answered it and talked a while. Then Robert called me to the phone. It was the man from the restaurant.

He informed me, "I have called your sister, Delores. She and her husband have arranged to pick the children and you up. You are to wait for them there. You can pay the expenses of the trip going to Oklahoma City. Keep any money that is left. I have wired Delores the money to get here. She is on her way."

I thanked him and I promised to pay him back. I asked him for his address so I could do that. He replied, "Just remember the help I have given you, and help at least one person in your lifetime. That is the way you can pay me back."

I promised I would do that. La Verne's husband wasn't happy, but he let us stay until Delores got there. This was the last time I saw La Verne or any family from Chicago for many years. Some of them passed on without my knowledge.

Curly, Delores' husband, demanded that I give him the money I had. They were driving a Volkswagen Beetle. The children and I got in the back seat of the Volkswagen. The six of us rode from Chicago to Oklahoma City in the back of that small car.

We put the few things we owned behind the back seat. If anyone accidentally touched the back of Curly's seat, he got angry. He yelled, and if it was a child instead of me, he sometimes stopped and spanked the guilty child. We were miserable the whole trip. Curly stopped only to fill the gas tank. We were so jammed in the car that we could not help touching the back of his seat.

I know this story sounds like we never had a good time in Chicago or had any fun. This is not true.

There were days that I would take my children to Lincoln Park Zoo. This was free entertainment in those days. I have pictures of the two younger girls sitting on a sculptured bear in Lincoln Park. The children rode huge turtles. Phillip, especially, liked the turtles. Tommy caught his first fish with a string tied to a stick in a lagoon in Lincoln Park.

We went for walks in the rain. We made homemade pizza, stayed up late and ate our pizza on the back porch when Rex wasn't around. One night we even slept on the back porch, watching a weather balloon.

I took the children swimming at Lake Michigan Beach when I had the chance. I taught the children how to catch a ball. However, they never really got to run and play unsupervised.

My friend, Naomi, would come over, and we would jump rope on the back porch. This made the woman downstairs very angry. We baked pies one day and set them on the banister to cool. One of the pies accidentally fell on the sheets that the woman below was drying. She kicked up such a fuss and refused to accept our apologies that we threw the rest of the pies on her sheets. I thought she was a nasty old woman.

Naomi and I took our baby buggies and walked through the alleys acting like we were drunk when we hadn't had a drop to drink, just to hear the old ladies fuss at us. We went to the playground and the Kingdom Hall. In the winter, we made snowmen and threw snowballs at each other when it wasn't too cold.

These were the things I held close to my heart. I still cherish those days and memories.

It was June of 1965, and Tommy was nine years old when we left Chicago for Oklahoma City. Carol was seven, and was very quiet and timid, but sneaky. Phillip, who was six, was a very frightened child. If someone rang the doorbell or passed us on the sidewalk, Phillip would try to climb me like a tree, crying the whole time. This made it very hard when I had to ride the city bus with the children. Phillip wasn't as happy as the other children. He was quick to disagree on things, and he tried desperately to get his way.

Rex had been successful in making Phillip resentful of Tommy. Phillip also resented Vallerie. But he still stood up for them if an outsider ever tried to harm one of them.

Vallerie was three years old at the time, and was a tomboy. She always had to have her teddy bear. La Donna was just about 20 months old, and very spoiled. This was what my children were like when I went to Oklahoma City. I was approximately 24 years old when I left Chicago. This trip reminded me of my childhood trip when we had left Chicago.

Life wasn't easy for us, but we always managed to find something interesting to do. The life we were forced to live made us closer to each other than most families. The children looked out for each other.

This was the way life should be, but my sister had forgotten this. I believed that, together, Delores and I could succeed in figuring a way out of my situation. However, Delores had turned bitter. She no longer believed, as we did when we were kids. Her motto was, "Take advantage of as much as you can; take what you want, at any cost." She had also learned the value of money.

CHAPTER SIXTEEN

IN OKLAHOMA CITY, my sister, Delores, lived in a suburb called Del City. They had a two-bedroom house; it was filthy. Clothes were everywhere. It looked like dishes had never been washed. The walls were black with roaches. Chickens and rabbits were running loose in the house. On some days, Delores would bring a little pig in the house.

The first thing that I did was to try to clean up the house. Delores got mad. She said she liked the house just like it was. The children and I shared a bedroom. Curly laid down some household rules. The kids and I were to stay outside as much as possible. I was not to clean house. If anything was to be done to the house, the children would do it under Delores' supervision. They were allowed to correct the children as they saw fit. I was to work as much as I could to support my children, and give what I earned to Curly. I would receive an allowance. This sounded to me like Father's rules.

The first thing that Curly did was that he went to the state and got commodities. Then he took me out to find work. He had me get a job in two nursing homes at different hours. When I got paid, I signed my checks and gave them to him. He drove me to work for the day job. Then I took a cab to the second job, and Delores would pick me up from work.

This became a nuisance to them, so Curly bought an old car for me to drive. Curly helped me get a driver's license. It seemed as though I did nothing but work at my two jobs all the time. I saw my children very little.

When I was at home, Delores complained that I had stolen her birth certificate so that she could not adopt children. She wanted me to sign my children over to her and Curly, but I refused to do this. I stayed with them all summer. Delores finally figured out that she could not have my children. She complained that she and Curly had seen a judge about taking my children from me, and had been told that they could not.

I tried to explain to her that I loved my children. She cried and wanted me to sign my children over to her anyway. I refused. She said that the reason she couldn't have children was because Father had injured her during an abortion he had performed on her years earlier. I still wouldn't give my children to her.

I believed my sister, had forgotten what those days were like for us when we were young. How we stood up for one another against the world we lived in. The fact that my children were close to me seemed to irritate her and her husband. It may not have been possible for Curly to understand, but Delores should have understood our feelings. I wondered if Delores was jealous of my children, or maybe she had waited on that bridge so long ago and was still angry that I had never showed up to join her.

Delores bought me a beautiful black dress and insisted I start dating. I was not interested in dating. She reminded me of Mother when we were in Bernie, Missouri. I guess I hurt her feelings when I told her that. I was just not ready to date. I refused to date men to please her. Like Mother, she got angry when I refused to do what she wanted. When she told Curly, he threatened to kick me out.

To say the least, Delores and I no longer saw things eye-to-eye. I felt trapped, and didn't know which way to go, especially when it involved my children. Delores had become like the rest of the world – mean and impossible to please. She was almost as bad as my father had been.

My children complained to me about the way they were being treated. There was nothing I could do to help them. I worked as hard as I could to save the money to get out of there. Apparently, Curly had checked on my wages and insisted I give them all my money. I wondered if that was how Mother and Aunt Joe had found themselves trapped. But they could have gotten out of it when they went to Chicago, if they had wanted to. And they should have taken us children with them when they left.

I wouldn't let things go that far, if I had to sleep on the streets with my children. But Delores just said, "You owe them to me." No one would own my soul or my children's souls.

One day, Curly and Delores were not home, and my children were locked out of the house. Our clothes had been put in garbage bags and set outside. Curly had given Tommy a note telling me to leave the key in the car. Delores had given Tommy a piece of paper with Mother's address on it.

I was lucky that it was payday that day in both nursing homes. I walked up to the bank and cashed my checks. I went to a second-hand store, found some old suitcases, and then went back to Delores's house and parked the car. I put our clothes in the suitcases, and the children and I walked to the bus station. I bought tickets to Gridley, California, where the note said Mother lived. We had to wait hours for our bus to leave.

On the bus, the children told me that Curly had promised to buy them a horse if they would tell me they wanted to live with Delores and him. The children refused to do this. I believe that was what made them throw us out. Delores wanted my children, but they did not want her. Nor was I about to give them up, not even to my sister, Delores.

When I got to Gridley, I called a cab and asked to be taken to the address Delores had given to Tommy. The driver tried to tell me that I had the wrong address. He argued that this was his mother's address. We learned that this cab driver was my brother, Orlaff. He drove me to Mother's house. Mother didn't seem to recognize me. After I told her who I was, she allowed my family to enter the house. She was not happy to see me at all, and I found this disappointing.

I told her that Orlaff had been my cab driver. She became very angry and said, "Otis and his family are not allowed in this house."

I was confused and said, "Mother, I said Orlaff was my driver."

She said very hatefully, "His name is Otis Orlaff Patten. We call him Otis."

I explained that I had come to her because I had no place to go. I asked if I could stay with her. At first she said, no.

Then Paul came out of another room and said, "Let them stay for a while; we can get aid on them."

Mother said, "I have not told our children that she even exists. I don't want them to know."

Paul replied, "They are going to have to know. You can't just throw them out in the street. Tell the kids who she is."

Mother told the children that I was their sister whom she hadn't seen for a long time. I started a communication line for Delores, and Delores started one for Vesta.

Mother loved the three children she had by Paul. She took good care of them in a way she had never taken care of us. She said, "To me, the Wilburn children are better than the Patten children. If the Patten children and their offspring are going to live around the Wilburn children, they have to understand this, and they can help me take care of them financially."

I didn't quite know what to say to my mother without causing a problem. Mother had never legally married Paul. I resented the fact that she could say this to me.

A few weeks later, Orlaff came to the door and asked me to come outdoors and talk to him. He wanted me to go with him to get his children. He said, "My wife has already agreed to give them to me. We can make a lot of money working in the potatoes, if you will just come with me and help me."

I was uncomfortable at Mother's because Paul made passes at me every chance he got. Mother told me he meant nothing by this, but it still made me uncomfortable. I remembered what she had said in Chicago. I tried hard to stay away from him, but he often called me to him. Mother complained that I was a "bump on a log." She told me, "You should be dating different men."

I went with Orlaff to get his children. His wife, Ethel, gave them to him. She told him, "I am living with a Mexican man who is abusive to me and my children. I think they will be better off with their father."

Orlaff rented an apartment in Orville for two weeks. Orlaff's wife, Ethel, stayed with us until we left to go and pick potatoes. I didn't understand why she didn't go with us.

We set out for the potato fields. Orlaff seemed to know where he was going. Finally, he told me we were home. It was a five-room house with an outhouse and a hand pump. There were at least thirty people already living in that house. All but the cooks were men. The only furniture was a cook stove. Everyone slept on the floor. It was wall-to-wall bodies. I have never seen anything like it. There were several women who did all the cooking. The people's bodies were dirty. They had dirty mouths, and they cursed all the time. And most of them were drinking or on drugs. No one tried to hurt us, and no one made any passes at me. They just looked like bad people to me. I was afraid to trust any of them.

Those who went to work were up at 4:00 a.m., and in the fields by 5:00. Orlaff wanted me to take Carol, Phillip and his eight-year-old daughter to work with us in the fields the next morning. This would be leaving the other seven children with people I didn't know or trust. I refused; I wouldn't even let a child go to the outhouse alone. When one went, we all went. I took the children to the water pump and washed them, daily, as best I could without exposing them.

I complained constantly because I felt that this was a bad situation. Orlaff worked in the potatoes about two weeks. He got tired of my mouth and took us to Roseburg, Oregon. He didn't mince any words telling me that I had a big mouth, and that I had ruined his plans. In Roseburg, it didn't take Orlaff long to find a two-room shack, with a big closet, on the top of a mountain.

The house was full of mice, and the toilet did not work. We were completely isolated from any other people. A couple named Church checked in on us twice a week. They gave us three full-size mattresses, a couch, a wood cooking stove, bedding and some clothing. Orlaff slept on the couch, and the rest of us slept on the floor.

About halfway down the mountain, I noticed some two-by-fours lying in a pile. The next time they came, I asked the couple if they could get me a hammer, nails and some plywood. They brought me the things I had asked for the next time they came to visit. I made a full-size, three-tier bunk bed in the closet for the children and me to sleep on. It was better than sleeping on the floor.

The Churches helped Orlaff get a job in a graveyard, digging graves. Orlaff came home one day and asked me to look at his private parts. "There is something wrong. I hurt terribly down there," he said.

He dropped his pants, and his scrotum was one big boil. He had smaller boils on his penis; I put hot packs on him. The next time they checked on us, I let the Churches know about Orlaff's problem. They took him to a doctor, and he got two penicillin shots a day for ten days.

Next, Orlaff brought home a woman named Bonnie. She moved in with us. One day, Orlaff said, "I am going to bring some men home. They will be our customers. I will get the customers, and you and Bonnie will take care of them. We will split the profit equally, three ways."

Even though I understood very well what he meant, I made him explain exactly what he was talking about. Then I refused, saying, "I have never been a prostitute, and I never will be."

My brother told me, "You will be what I want you to be."

He left and came back with a man. I refused to satisfy this customer, as Orlaff called him. My brother told me, "Hit the road, Jack, and don't come back no more." He also told me that I was not taking any children, his or mine. Then he dragged me down the mountain by my hair. Whenever I freed myself, he just got another hold on me. When he got me to the bottom of the mountain, he told me to go and not come back. I walked the way I hoped was the closest to town.

After I got to town, I asked for directions to the Churches' ranch. It was down the highway several miles. It took me several hours to walk there. I told them I needed help getting my children and why. They called the police. The police met us at the couple's house. We went and got my children, who were crying and confused.

The police took Orlaff's children. My children and I went to the couple's house. Orlaff was arrested, and Bonnie was left there in the old shack alone. It was a good thing she had a car. The man who had come with Orlaff was gone. Orlaff gave the police the phone number of my brother, Glenn. The children and I stayed with the Churches until Glenn arrived to pick us up.

We were on our way to Salem. It was the summer of 1966. The city of Roseburg sent Orlaff's children back to their mother. We had stayed in Roseburg for quite some time, exactly how long I don't remember, but I was glad to leave. My brother was a bad person, as far as I was concerned.

Glenn lived in a trailer court. His wife, Betty, was disabled. She had no legs; they had been amputated just above the knees. Glenn was not working at the time, and they were on welfare. They had a storage shed that came with the trailer they rented. Betty's parents gave us two old bed frames and mattresses. We made a wall-to-wall bed that way. There was not enough room to stand in that shed, so we opened the door and crawled into bed. I lined our clothes against the wall, sitting them on the mattress in boxes close to the wall.

The first thing, Glenn applied for more commodities. I learned not to believe anything Glenn had to say because it was probably a lie.

I put my three older children in school. They had missed a lot and were behind. I found a job at a mushroom factory five miles from Glenn's trailer. I walked to and from work. When I got home at night, I was really tried.

It seemed that Glenn had been using my Social Security number and my birth certificate that Aunt Joe had gotten for me. (By changing the "e" in Frances to an "i," it became a male's name.) The name Louise could also be a male or female name. I was fired until I could get my Social Security straightened out.

When I came home that Friday and told Glenn what they had told me at the mushroom factory, Glenn insisted we move that evening. When I objected, he said, "We can't stay here now; I might go to jail." Glenn then said, "I rented a big house halfway between Mill City and Stayton, Oregon. We can move in tonight."

Glenn and Betty took their pregnant dog with them. The big

house already had old mattresses in it, an old wood cook stove and some dirty bedding. It looked like something Mother would rent.

Phillip stepped on a nail that Friday evening while exploring his new surroundings. I took our clothes out of the car. I had to leave them in the suitcases and boxes. I offered to help Glenn get their stuff out of the car. He told me their stuff could wait. I should have become suspicious at that point, but I didn't.

The dog had its puppies that same night. Glenn and Betty left the following Monday morning. They never came back. But I had noticed a school bus go by the Friday we had moved in. I hadn't felt things were quite right, so I took note of a few things that I hoped would be useful later on.

By Monday morning, the old dog's puppies began dying. Phillip's foot had a little red mark running from it. I knew he was getting blood poisoning.

Betty's father came over with his arms full of groceries. He laughed and said, "Glenn told me you were stupid and would trust him enough to go anywhere with him. I'll bet you believed him when he told you he rented this house didn't you? This house has been empty for years. Everyone in this county believes it to be haunted. He did not rent anything; he just moved you in here to get rid of you. If you will take me upstairs and make me happy, you can have these groceries to feed your children. There is more where these came from."

I grabbed a piece of wood by the stove and started swinging. He dropped the groceries and ran for his truck. I never saw that man again. This man had children older than I was. Why is it that some men only think of what's in their pants? They do not think of a female as being a person.

On Tuesday morning I got up early and got the children ready for school. I had nothing to feed them. I wanted to be early enough to catch that school bus. I had no clock, so I guessed at the time. We were at the crossroads waiting for that bus a while. When I saw it coming, I stepped out in front of it to make sure it stopped. The bus driver did not want to let us on the bus. As we were arguing, I had the children get on. He finally let me on, too.

We went to Mill City Grammar School. I walked into the office to register my children. Then I talked to the school counselor. I told her the situation I was in. The principal took Phillip to a doctor. My children were all fed lunch. I was given food for their supper and breakfast. We rode the school bus home with the older children. I had started the ball rolling by telling someone I needed help.

Glenn and Betty had left me in a pickle. I really wasn't sure how I was going to get out of this mess. I found it hard to believe my brother could have done this to me. Glenn and Betty never came back to the old house, not even to see if we were all right or had food.

Three days later, Phillip's teacher brought the children home. They had found a furnished apartment for us in town, and had come to help us move in. The apartment was seventeen dollars a month. There was a job washing dishes in a restaurant for twenty dollars a month. I gladly accepted the town's offer. The children were happy, and they worked hard to catch up with their schoolwork. I finally felt like it was safe to let them play like children should.

I felt independent again. It looked like we were going to be fine. I worked hard, but I had never worked as a waitress before. I have never had any balance, and I fell very easily. I was not a good waitress and I knew it. Why the lady who owned the restaurant kept me on, I had no idea. She kept saying, "You will get the hang of it sooner or later." I may have gotten a little better, but I was never a good waitress. I was thankful to this woman for her patience with me.

I was good at taking care of people, but there were no hospitals or nursing homes nearby. There was a hospital in Stayton, 17 miles away. The closest nursing home was in Salem, 42 miles away, but I had no transportation. There wasn't even a doctor's office in Mill City. I was stuck with trying to learn how to be a waitress. I tried hard, but I just wasn't cut for it.

The little city was beautiful, and I loved it. But there were no jobs available that I was qualified to do. This shamed and embarrassed me to no end. It made me feel stupid and not fit to be a good mother. I needed more education to care for my children the right way, and I knew it.

CHAPTER SEVENTEEN

A JEHOVAH'S WITNESS came to town and knocked on my door. I started going to the Kingdom Hall again. This little town did not like Witnesses. The people in town started letting me know that. The minister of the church threatened to withdraw my job. He told me that the church had been paying most of my rent. He said I could either drop this Witness lady, or all the help the town had been giving me would be withdrawn.

I didn't like that. No one had told me before that the town was helping me. No one was going to tell me whom I could talk to. I didn't listen to the minister. The minister complained to me again saying, "This town does not like Witness people."

I ignored the town's warning. The principal in Mill City accused Tommy of breaking and entering, destroying property and stealing some money. We had been at the Kingdom Hall at the time the school robbery had taken place. I proved that my son was innocent.

I lost my job, which I was no good at, and now the rent was sixty dollars a month. We worked in the strawberry fields that summer. We enjoyed life. The country was beautiful. There were plenty of trees and flowers. There were a lot of places to swim. We worked hard, but we also played hard.

The Witness lady suggested that I move back to Salem. "There are more opportunities in the bigger city," she said.

She took me to the welfare office in Salem. I explained to these people that I wanted to work. I was ashamed to except charity when I was able to work. They gave me a house in a low-income housing project. They suggested that I go to school, instead of trying to work with no education. When school started for my children, I also started school to get my GED. That part was easy. The hard part came after I got my GED and I started college.

Vallerie started Head Start that year. The state helped me to get my GED. I applied at different colleges throughout the state for LPN grants. I received one in Pendleton, Oregon, for the coming school year. While the children and I were in Salem, we worked in the fields and bought a car. We saved as much money as we could for hard times.

Mother's live-in boyfriend, Paul, passed away that summer. He was having gallbladder stones removed. The doctor had said, "He died from fright. He was so afraid of the surgery that he had a heart attack on the operating table."

Mother called the police station to notify me. She wanted me to come home for the funeral. Paul's children were coming from Missouri and other cities, and she didn't want to meet them alone. I had one of my friends from the Kingdom Hall check my car over to make sure it would make the trip safely. I quickly gathered a few clothes we might need while he was working on my car. Gas at the time was nineteen cents a gallon; I filled up my car tank.

The children and I drove to Gridley, California, for Paul's funeral. Phillip was quite the little navigator. Tommy couldn't read the maps, but Phillip could. He was so proud when I asked him to sit in the front seat and help me stay on the right highway.

When we got there, Paul's family was coming from all parts of the country. The family from Missouri would be arriving at Travis Airport in two hours. Dennis and Glenn had gone to meet them. We told the children to go outside and play. I helped Mother finish cleaning the house. Mother was on pins and needles. She didn't look good in the face; I was afraid it was more than just being tired.

The Red Cross called to say that Elijah would be arriving later that night; he was in the Army. While I was helping Mother, my brother, Orlaff, took my daughter, La Donna, to the mortuary to see Paul without my knowledge. He told her that the bugs and worms would eat Paul's flesh, and that his bones would turn to dirt. He said that Paul's hair would continue to grow and would come out of the ground as brown and yellow grass. I knew that La Donna had become afraid of dead grass, but I didn't know why.

Some of Paul's family arrived. Later that night, Elijah arrived. They all started drinking. My brothers fought over who was going to wear Paul's suit to the funeral. Some of Paul's daughters rented motel rooms about four blocks away. Children were fed and put to bed; my children were quite tired. I stayed up to help Mother wait on these people.

Paul's brother, Walter, was one of the first of Paul's family to arrive. The men stayed up most of the night drinking and fighting over who was going to take different articles of Paul's clothing. The biggest issue was who was going to wear Paul's new suit. Paul's brother, Walter, constantly made passes at me, and talked dirty from the first hour he had arrived.

The next day was pure hell. I helped Mother wait on people and clean up after them. More of Paul's family arrived, and everyone was drinking. Arrangements were made for a neighbor to look after my children during the funeral. Mother did not want my children to attend the funeral for some reason unknown to me. I didn't argue with her about this.

That evening while I was washing dishes, Walter walked up behind me and grabbed my butt with one hand, and my breast with the other. I flew into a rage and started hitting him with a frying pan. Mother stopped me.

Walter said, "She is a beautiful woman. All I wanted is a little peace of ass to console me. I miss my brother."

Mother tried to make me go into the bedroom and have sex with him. She said, "It won't hurt you any; he just lost his brother. It isn't as if you are a virgin. I'm sure you have had plenty of men by now. Stop acting like a baby."

Paul's son, Johnny, jumped up and dragged Walter out in the yard by the nape of his neck and beat the pants off him. When he was through with Walter, he came back into the house and bawled Mother out. I was going to leave, but one of Paul's daughters said, "You are too upset to be driving with five children." She gave her motel room to the children and me. She shared her sister's motel room with her.

The next morning, even Paul's daughters were drunk. I was the only one sober enough to drive Mother through the funeral procession. I helped Mother clean up after the funeral, and got ready to leave. Mother came to me and wanted money to send my brothers home. I gave her what money I had.

The children and I went back to Salem and worked in the fields to earn the money to buy gas for our trip to Pendleton, Oregon. My children worked hard, with very little compensation, maybe a bottle of pop at the end of the day.

The children were teaching me how to play baseball while we were killing time before our trip to Pendleton. I swung at the ball and hit Phillip with the bat, and knocked his eye out of its socket. Phillip had been standing too close to me. We spent the rest of the day in the hospital emergency room. The doctor was able to fix Phillip's eye; there would be no complications.

Not long after the funeral, Rex found us in Salem. Salem had a summer program for the Head Start children. Vallerie wanted to go, so I let her. That evening, I had to go to Vallerie's Head Start party; it was the last day of school. They were having a party for the kids and parents. The older children had worked in the field after school that day, and they were tired. Rex came while I was gone. How he had found us again, I do not know.

The children let him in. He whipped Carol because the dishes were not done. I came home to some very upset children. I called the police, and Rex ran. Rex didn't leave Salem. Instead, he would sleep in our garage after I had gone to bed. He tried to sneak in the house at night and then get in bed with me. Our fighting would awaken and frighten the children. By the time the police would get there, he was gone and we would look like fools. Our garage caught on fire one night. I believed that Rex was responsible for that. I have always believed that my brother, Dennis, contacted him and told him where we were.

The summer of 1967 was about over, and we went to Pendleton to find a place to live. I rented a house on the airport grounds. I located the schools and visited the Kingdom Hall. I found a lady to watch La Donna, who was almost four years old now, during the days until Tommy, almost 12, got out of school. Carol was ten, Phillip was nine and Vallerie was six years old at the time. We were ready to move to Pendleton. We went back home and packed our belongings. I was excited about being able to go to college. I was 26 years old at this time, although my identification papers still listed me as being two years older.

Carol stepped on a nail and developed blood poisoning in her foot. This delayed our departure for three days. I kept Carol lying down in the back of the car, as the doctor had ordered.

Finally we were on our way. Then, I had car trouble in Roseburg, and this delayed us even more. The police in Roseburg did their best to help me. They rented a motel room for us, and had a mechanic fix our car the best that he could. They also saw to it that we had food to eat, all at no cost to me.

I explained to the policemen that I had traded a 1957 Chevy in for this Ford station wagon because the doctor had said Carol could make the trip if she could get plenty of rest. There wouldn't have been room for her to lie down in the Chevy sedan. I had discussed the trip I was planning to make with the car salesman, who had ensured me the car would make it.

As I talked to the Roseburg police, I could see they seemed to be angry. One of them asked me for the name of the car lot I had bought the car from. He said, "You have bought a lemon. The person who sold you this car knew it was no good. They took advantage of you."

I had canned eight hundred quarts of various foods to be sure that we had something to eat that winter. The mechanic told me, "You will never make it to Pendleton pulling that much weight."

I donated my canned goods to the community center. We were on our way again, with a police car following behind us to make sure we made it. The police followed me to the county line, where another police car was waiting. I made it to Pendleton. The old car barely made it up the mountain to the airport. It died in front of the house I had rented, and refused to start, so it couldn't even be backed into the driveway.

Chapter EIGHTEEN

SCHOOL STARTED THE next day for all of us. We made arrangements for someone to pick me up to enroll in college the next morning. One of the men's wives who had come to help me was a schoolteacher. I was to put the children on the bus in the morning, and she would handle things after they got to school. The person who picked me up would take La Donna to the babysitter's. I didn't worry about unpacking anything; we just set up the beds. Everything was handled. We went to bed — the boys in one room and the girls in the other room.

The next morning we all went to school. Vallerie broke her collarbone the first day. The school took her home and left her there alone. When I got home she was asleep. I knew we had all had a hard time the last few days, so I let her sleep. When I woke her for supper, she cried and one shoulder was lower than the other. I had seen this before; I knew what was wrong. I found an unwilling neighbor to take me to the hospital. Later, we became acquaintances.

I had trouble keeping the boys out of the hangars at the airport. For their safety, I had to find another place to live. One of the brothers from the Kingdom Hall fixed my car. This was a great help. I was a young mother with five kids and started out needing too much help. Some of the people at the Kingdom Hall gave us the cold shoulder for a long time. They did not want to get involved with us. Without their help when I first arrived, I don't think I could have made it.

It was at this time that Tommy started taking charge of the other children when I was not home. Carol mothered Vallerie and

La Donna. Phillip became very resentful of Tommy and hurt Vallerie every chance he had.

The overseer of the congregation took my boys in hand. He could see I could not handle them, and this helped me a lot. He even bought the boys each a pair of boots one winter, which they desperately need. He tried to understand my sensitivity about wanting to be able to support my own children, and gave the boys chores that they were capable of doing. He sometimes paid them a little money.

I found a duplex in town, not far from an elderly Witness couple named Elda and Lon. They fell in love with La Donna. Elda babysat for me until she found a girl named Rita who needed a home. Rita had a baby out-of-wedlock and her parents had kicked her out. She moved in with me, and I let her use La Donna's crib for her baby. Several months went by; we were doing fine. I was doing well in school, and the children were, too. We were making friends at the Kingdom Hall. Elda and Lon picked us up three times a week to go to the Kingdom Hall meetings. I was beginning to feel comfortable with my surroundings.

Tommy would be twelve years old that October. He complained about Rita watching him urinate. He said he did not like it, and he couldn't see why it was necessary. I asked Tommy if she had ever touched him in the wrong place, and he said, "No."

I told Rita that my children and I needed more privacy, and I wanted her to move out. Tommy was old enough to watch after Carol, Phillip and Vallerie until I got home. Elda and Lon would watch over La Donna. I gave her two weeks notice and told her, in the meantime, I wanted her to stay out of the bathroom with my sons.

The next Sunday morning, Elda and Lon came to pick us up for the Kingdom Hall meeting. Rita said, "I will be gone when you get back."

My response was, "Okay, but leave my baby crib." I followed Lon down the driveway. We were going to have a potluck supper that day after the meeting, so I had food in my car. After the meeting and the potluck, the children and I went home.

I found the police waiting for me. Rita had told them that I had chased her and her baby down the road to her mother's house with a butcher knife. They took me down to the police station and left my children with Rita, even though Elda and Lon told the police that this was not possible, that I had been with them all morning. They had been with me from 8:45 a.m. until 3:00 p.m., along with 17 other people at the Kingdom Hall.

The police said, "You may need to prove that if charges are pressed."

Elda and Lon said, "You can bet your boots on that."

The police said, "We have to arrest her and hold her for now." The police put me in a cell, but they never shut the door. Then they took me down to the state mental hospital.

A caseworker came to see me and said that I was under investigation because La Donna had told her preschool teacher that when people die, their hair continues to grow after they are buried. She explained that the hair turns into yellow and brown grass. I tried to tell her that I did not tell my daughter that. My brother had told her that at my stepfather's funeral. She said all of this would be investigated.

She then said there was an "assault with a deadly weapon" charge against me. She told me, "You are in a lot of trouble, and there is a possibility of losing your children to the state. I know this isn't easy to do, but don't sleep all the time." I tried hard to keep busy by talking to people, and walking up and down the halls – anything just to keep myself busy.

The state paid Rita to care for my children. A caseworker checked on them once a week. I became quite upset. I tried to tell the caseworker what Tommy had said to me about Rita watching him urinate. This woman acted like she didn't believe me, or else she just didn't care. Then she said, "Tommy will be placed in a foster home for his protection."

The state kept me two weeks for evaluation. When they released me, Dr. Murphy said that he found nothing wrong with me. He said that I was not crazy, and that he didn't understand why – anyone else who had been forced to live my life would be. But he also told me the law said that I had to be on probation for a year. If anyone had a complaint on me, for any reason, then I would be put back in the mental hospital for at least a year, and I might never get out.

I didn't understand how this could have happened because I had done nothing wrong. Dr. Murphy said that people around there didn't take to Jehovah's Witnesses. The charge of an "assault with a deadly weapon" was never brought against me. The one thing I did know was that small towns shouldn't have been allowed to get away with this stuff. It was not right to kick someone when they were already down.

The state gave me back my children. Rita moved in on the other side of the duplex that I lived in. I couldn't go back to college that year; I was too far behind and could never catch up. Elda and Lon put in a phone for me, in case of emergency. I started looking for another place to live. I didn't want to live next to Rita, and I didn't want her around my children. I didn't quite accomplish putting any distance between us, as I had been trying to do.

About three weeks went by before I could find another house to live in. I was in the process of moving, and it was getting dark. I had stopped working for the evening. Elda called and told me a caseworker had called her, and had told her to get over to my place and get my children. She said the state was coming to get me. Elda told me to leave my children and get out of the house. I grabbed the children and headed for the car.

I saw car lights turn down the road. We were living along the railroad tracks. That road was the only way in or out of town; it was a dead end. I gave La Donna to Carol, and told the children to go inside and wait for Elda and Lon. I knew they were on their way and would be there within five minutes.

As I turned to run, I saw car lights turn down the gravel road. I thought it was the police. I ran down the railroad tracks. Then I saw the police lights flashing behind a car turned crossways on the road. I lay down between the tracks. I was told later that one of the elders of the congregation had turned his car crossways on the road and pretended to have a bad battery to give me a chance to get away. He made the policemen push his car off the road.

The police ran around the house with flashlights and walked up and down the railroad tracks looking for me. It was dark and hard for me to see what was happening. The police did not go as far as the curve in the tracks, which was where I was hiding. I couldn't stay there long; a train was coming. I had to get off the tracks.

I walked to Elda and Lon's. They were already there with my children. I gave Lon my car keys, which I had in my pocket. He went to my house, threw some blankets in the car and brought my car to me.

On my way out of town, Rex had apparently found me again, somehow. He stepped onto the road in front of me. There was no way I was going to stop. I just kept right on going. He jumped out of the road just before I hit him. I was thankful that I didn't hit him because, if he had not moved, I wouldn't have stopped. I was too afraid of losing my children and going to a mental hospital, for God only knew what. I did not know what I had done wrong. That was the last time I ever saw Rex.

I was frightened and confused, and I wasn't sure which way I should go. Unless I went to Mother's, we would be living in the car. So I headed toward California, knowing what kind of a welcome I would receive. There was no other way out for me. I was afraid the police would pick me up on the highway, so I took as many back roads as possible. Several times, I got lost doing this.

Someone "upstairs" must have been with me one more time in my life. I had managed to get my children to California safely. I didn't understand why the police should be after me again. I had done nothing wrong. I was not the only Jehovah's Witness in town. Why were they picking on me?

I was told by a caseworker in California that it was because I was a young mother, alone with five children, and was "easy picking." She commented, "Most young women wouldn't have been able to outsmart them the way you did. Instead of becoming frightened, you used your head." I was frightened. I was scared to death, even if she didn't know it, but I didn't say anything.

I had to lower myself to accept welfare once again. The caseworker was a nice woman. She said, "We have a college in Yuba City. You can go to school there. You may have to wait until next year. Can you do that?"

Well, I would have to wait. There was no other choice. I swallowed my pride and accepted their help. My children had to eat.

Chapter NINETEEN

THE CHILDREN AND I were back in Gridley, California, and had moved in with my mother. All we owned were the clothes we were wearing and a few blankets. I knew that we were not welcome, but I didn't know where else to go.

Ethel, my brother Orlaff's wife, came to visit Mother. Ethel and I moved into an apartment together in Orville. She convinced me that if I did not get aid on the children, then Mother would — that it was better for me to receive welfare checks on my children than it would be for Mother to; that Mother would spend all the money on her three children, and mine would do without. She said, "I tried it; your mother will take advantage of you and your children. She did the same thing to me."

I applied for welfare. Mother had been drawing welfare on my children. Then the checks were transferred to me.

I knew my mother did not want or like my children or me. Ethel's little sister had accused Orlaff and Paul of molesting her when she was nine years old, while they were drinking. Ethel had believed her sister and left my brother, taking their children with her. I now knew why Mother didn't want Ethel and her children in her house.

I asked, "Why are you giving your children back to Orlaff, if you believe this?"

She answered, "My boyfriend mistreats them."

I moved after living with Ethel for less than two months. Ethel liked to stay out late and she brought men in and slept with them. She also was using drugs. I did not want my children to be around that kind of behavior.

Mother had a Mexican neighbor named Rudy. He had many friends in Mexico who wanted to come to America. Mother informed me, "You can make a lot of money if you will listen to Rudy. He wants you to marry the Mexican men who manage to get across the border. They will pay you one thousand dollars for each man you marry. Two weeks later, they will take you to Reno and you will get a divorce. The next week, you will marry another man. If you keep this cycle up, you can make two thousand dollars every four weeks. You don't have to have sex with any of them."

I wondered if Mother had any morals at all. Did it make a difference to her that this was wrong and that I might even go to jail? What did she think would happen to my children if I went to jail? I really didn't want her taking care of them.

I told her, "Mother, this has to be against the law."

She responded, "It is not against the law unless you get caught. Who is going to know what you are doing? This is the only way these men can become citizens of the United States. Girls do this all the time."

I replied, "Mother, I am not going to put on a man and then take him off like he was a set of clothes. When I marry, I intend to stay married 'until death do us part.' I will not deliberately break the law."

She became very angry with me. She believed that money was more important than my children. She later accused my daughter, Carol, of stealing my half-sister, Rose Maria's, jewelry. Mother turned my place upside down, but she found no jewelry in my home when she ransacked it.

Rudy turned out to be a very good friend. He respected my values and respected me as a person. It took his help to get my mother off my back about his offer.

Around this time, a woman gave us her German shepherd dog named Silver. The dog was refusing to eat or drink because the woman's little girl had died. La Donna was about the same age as their daughter had been. The dog quickly took to our family. At first, she would only eat out of La Donna's hand. Silver would let no grown person come near my children. She was very protective toward them.

I needed to get away from my family. My brothers would just walk into my house and eat, or simply carry the food we had out of our house.

I rented a little house in Live Oak. I applied at the college in Yuba City and I was accepted. I taped all the lectures and studied until late at night. When I went to bed, I played the tapes. Every time I woke up at night, I would rewind the tapes and play them again.

I graduated from Yuba City College in 1969. I was 28 years old. My children's ages ranged from six years to almost 14 years at this time. My children were so proud to have a nurse for a mother. They shouted it every chance they got.

It was during this time that my mother had a heart attack. I kept Rose Maria, Paul Jr. and Loretta. Paul Jr. was truly a brat. He refused to go to school, and he fought me if I insisted. At night, I physically had to find him and threaten to call the police to get him off the streets and into bed. Then, half the time, he would sneak back out the window. He really gave me a hard time.

When I called Glenn, Delores and Curly and told them that Mother had had a heart attack and was in the hospital, they all came to California. They stayed at Mother's house and got so drunk that they vomited all over the beds, floor and bathroom. My little sister and my children helped me clean up the mess after they left, before Mother came home from the hospital. I was quite angry with them. I was having a hard enough time going to school and taking care of eight children – my five and Mother's three. This was very disrespectful and thoughtless on their parts.

While I was in school, Mother let the children swim in the canals. La Donna might have drowned in a canal if Silver, the dog, had not pulled her out of the water. When one of my children got in a fight with another child, Silver knocked the other child down and sat on him until I came to rescue the child. She frightened many children, but never bit one. Silver was the best present anyone could have given us.

We went to visit Elda and Lon in Pendleton, and decided to move back. I got a job in the same hospital that I had been incarcerated in. Elda and Lon helped me buy a house trailer. I rented a lot 17 miles from Pendleton in a wide spot in the road called Powell Butte. We had only two close neighbors, the Weygands, who owned the property, and another family who seemed to be dirt poor. I went back to California to get our belongings, but I did not tell my family I was leaving.

I never found out why the police came after me the night I fled Oregon. But I was told that if I had not fled, I would have been let go the next day because Rita's mother took her to the police and made her tell them she had lied both times. The truth is, I wouldn't have bet on the fact that I would have been released.

Chapter TWENTY

I WENT TO an Army supply store and bought a 12- by 16-foot Army tent and an Army bunk bed. I took old railroad ties and 2"x 8's by eights and built a floor off the ground and walls slanted upward toward the top. Someone gave me an old rug to put on the floor for warmth. I took twelve poles, dug holes and poured cement in the holes. Then I took a tarp and attached it to the poles over the tent. I bought two second-hand chests of drawers, an electric heater and a very heavy electrical cord. I had made a bedroom for my boys, and the dog stayed in the tent with them. When it snowed that winter, we pushed up on the tarp to dump the snow off the tarp.

I worked at night when the children were sleeping. We were happy there until the fall of 1970. I thought life would be good here. The boys loved having the tent as their own private space.

Shortly after we moved back to Pendleton, Carol started acting oddly. It had been years since she had had a nightmare. She started acting the same way she had acted during the time she was having her nightmares. I thought that it was defiance because of the other things she was doing. The people next door had a young boy named Jimmy visiting them. Carol started sneaking out at night to see him. The boys and Carol began fighting when I was not home. Many times I worked double shifts to make ends meet. I was at my wit's end, not knowing how to control her.

Tommy and Phillip told me that Carol left the trailer every night. Carol would deny this. People I knew in the area told me Carol was out on the highway hitchhiking at night. She also denied this. Betty, a so-called friend of mine, complained that Carol would come to her house to use the phone. Jimmy had gone home, and she was calling him long-distance. When I tried to talk to her about these things, she gave me a blank stare and acted confused, just as she used to do during her nightmares, except that she was awake.

I was later told that Betty had performed an abortion on Carol. When I learned of this, I was very upset. I don't believe in abortions. They both denied this and I had no proof. I no longer took my children to Betty in bad weather.

One day we were on our way into town to do some shopping. We were going down the mountain into Pendleton. Carol suddenly stiffened and grabbed me around the neck. She had her foot on the gas pedal, on top of my foot. I could not get her foot off the gas pedal, and we were flying down the mountain. I was taking up all four lanes, trying to stay on the highway. I managed to slip the car into second gear. I was trying to get her arms from around my neck when she bit my finger; I had to have six stitches in it. She had her arms so tightly around my neck that she was choking me. I was having trouble even seeing the road.

The other children were in a car ahead of me with a woman from the Kingdom Hall named Jenny. She was taking them home with her to play with her grandchildren. I almost ran into the back of her car. I could not stop the car. I was in town now, so I blew my horn to let people know I had a problem. All of the other cars pulled over and stopped, getting out of my way.

I finally turned off the car, but I had no steering and we were still moving. Carol started convulsing, and I still could not get her foot off the gas pedal. I did manage to get my finger out of her mouth and her arms from around my neck. Going up the mountain had slowed the car down. As I approached the hospital, I put the car into first gear and pulled the emergency brake. This brought the car to a stop in the hospital parking lot.

Jenny had realized there was something wrong and had followed me. She went into the emergency room to get help. She took my children home with her for a few days. Carol was diagnosed with epilepsy. She stayed in the hospital a few days to have her meds adjusted. She was put on 90 milligrams of Phenobarbital and 100 milligrams of Dilantin. This helped, but didn't stop her seizures altogether. When she had a seizure, it frightened all of us.

I had torn up the transmission in my car that day. Betty's husband offered to fix it for a fee. I used to take the children to Betty's on stormy days because the house trailer was not much protection. They had a pond there that the children liked to play in.

They also had an epileptic son. One day their son had a seizure, and my children ran to them for help. Betty's husband told them that he would be all right, that it was just the demons in him trying to get out. I explained to my children that this boy had the same condition that Carol had. Betty needed to give him his medications.

Their cats would get on the roof of their house and scream the way cats do when mating. Betty told the children that the screams were the demons screaming. She told them, "Our house is full of demons."

I did not know that they had told the children about any such nonsense as demons. The children did not tell me because they knew I would not let them go over there and swim, which was the only recreation available to them at that time.

Tommy once jumped headfirst into their pond, hitting his head on a rock. Betty and the children did not tell me this until Tommy's head started swelling and he complained of a bad headache. I took him to a doctor. He had a fractured skull, and infection had set in. Tommy had a fifty-fifty chance of recovering and he survived. I had thought these people were my friends.

One day it rained, and Vallerie had grabbed hold of the trailer door. It shocked her so badly that she could not turn loose of the door handle. I knocked her hand loose with a broomstick. I then took her to the hospital to have her checked out and to make sure that I didn't break any bones when I knocked her loose. Also, I wanted to make sure that the electric shock had done no damage.

Vallerie was okay. It happened to be payday; I was paid every two weeks. I cashed my check and took the children to the ice cream parlor. I paid for the ice cream. When I got home, I did not have my wallet. I let Betty know about it. She let the whole congregation know about it also. People started bringing over groceries to help me.

At first I appreciated this. I felt my children wouldn't suffer after all, but when one of the men from the congregation embarrassed me, I no longer wanted their help. He brought over some groceries and said, "If you have told a lie to get extra help, Jehovah God will know it. That is what I believe you have done."

The overseer of the congregation said he thought Carol had stolen it. I took all the groceries they had brought to us and set them on the steps of the overseer's house with a note telling him thanks, but no thanks. I then went to see if I could get some commodities. We ate commodities for the next two weeks.

Someone put my wallet in the mail with my entire identification, minus my money, and mailed it to the overseer's house. Whoever took my wallet knew that I went to the Kingdom Hall. Trouble seemed to follow me and people said it was because I was a single mother. They believed that I should marry, even if I didn't care about the person.

One time, on my day off, the children were playing hide-and-seek. Carol could not be found. It was getting dark and we still could not find Carol. I was afraid she was in the wheat fields having a seizer, so I called the police. By the time they got out to Powell Butte, it was dark. We must have had 100 men looking for Carol. They took flashlights and, walking only a few feet away from each other, searched though the wheat fields. They ruined Mr. Weygand's wheat crop.

They finally found her hiding in an underground potato cellar. She looked to me like she was having seizures. Her eyes were blank and glazed over. She did not respond when spoken to. But the police said that she was high on a drug called "purple haze." I did not believe them; I wanted to take her to the emergency room. The police said, "You have three days to get her out of town, or we will put her in juvenile hall."

One of the men from the Kingdom Hall said that I needed a man who would turn me over his knee three times a week, and that I was spoiling Carol rotten. I wasted no time trying to get out of there. Betty's husband put trailer brakes on my car and hooked the trailer onto it.

I have no excuse for my daughter's behavior when we lived in Powell Butte. What I do believe is that when a child acts out and does the things that Carol was doing, there is usually an adult behind the child encouraging them to be naughty.

We left Powell Butte and headed back to Oklahoma City. I wrecked my trailer on Horse Mountain in Portland, Oregon. Betty's husband hadn't put the brakes on right, which caused them to burn out, so the police told me. I had not traveled 100 miles yet. We were thankful to escape with our lives. I believe someone "upstairs" had to be looking after us that day.

I had the choice of going off the cliff or taking a cow path through a wire fence. I took the cow path. My trailer was weaving so badly that it was pushing the car down the mountain. When I turned the car into the fence, the back wheels of the trailer got caught in the ditch. The trailer came unhitched from the car, and flew over the top of the car. The car turned over, and the trailer came down where the car had been. The house trailer split in two pieces. The dog and cat inside the trailer survived.

An ambulance came and took us to the hospital. Silver, our dog, wouldn't let the ambulance workers near us. I finally got the dog under control, and we got in the ambulance. Silver freed himself from the man who was holding him and jumped in the ambulance with us. We could not get him out of the ambulance. I am sure he was the first dog to ride in an ambulance. Our only injury involved Vallerie, who had a huge hole in the palm of her hand.

While we were waiting for the insurance to settle up, we stayed with some Witnesses in Portland. The insurance company totaled out my car. On the advice of the Witness brother, I bought my car back from the insurance company for one hundred dollars. The Witness brother fixed up my van.

We continued on to Del City. We slept on the ground at national parks for a few nights. I stopped when the sun shone in my eyes because I couldn't see to drive. I tried to sleep during these stops, while the children played. This worked for us.

Chapter TWENTY-ONE

I DIDN'T NOTIFY Delores when I got to town. The year was 1971, and I was about 30 years old. Tommy was 16 by then, Carol was 14 and Phillip was 13. Vallerie was ten years old at this time and La Donna was about eight.

The children slept in the van for two nights before I found an apartment on Cherry Street in Del City. I got two second-hand bunk beds, three chests of drawers and a television to keep the children occupied. I put the boys in one bedroom and the girls in the other. I bought no other furniture at that time. The stove and refrigerator came with the apartment. The apartment had central air and heat. I found a full-time job and a part-time job. This gave me a good start. In a short while, we would be fine and I would be back on my feet again. The apartment was small, but we would survive this problem.

Usually, when I got home from work, it was the girls who were up. This time the boys were up watching TV, and the girls were still asleep. I went to bed in the boys' room. I was asleep in a few minutes. Tommy came in and woke me up, telling me to "get the hell out of his room."

I was tired and frustrated. The kids were beginning to act out, fighting with each other when I was not there. The younger children complained that Tommy abused them while I was at work. Carol was sneaking out at night. I couldn't stop her. I had to work, or they would have starved to death.

I went to the closest furniture store and bought myself the first new bedroom set I had ever had. Then I went to a hardware store and bought a door handle. I went back home and had Carol help me move the boys' bunk beds into the living room. I went in and lay down on Carol's bed until the doorbell rang. The bedroom set was delivered, and I put it in what had been the boys' room.

I then said, "Now, you boys stay the hell out of my room!"

I went in my bedroom, locked the door and went to sleep. I was beat. I seldom got that upset with the children. This time I had, and I hoped what I had done had taught them a lesson. I was a person; my blood was red. I laughed and cried like everyone else. I could even get tired like other people. I was not a machine.

I thought that maybe the children were feeling their oats because we were so crowded. So I started looking for a house that I could afford to buy. I received a government low-income loan and bought a four-bedroom house on Terry Way.

Tommy got a job assisting the janitor in the high school. He gave me half of what he earned for his expenses. One day Curly, Delores' husband, saw Tommy as he was walking home from work. They stopped and talked, and Tommy told them where we lived.

I learned that my sister, Vesta, had moved from New Jersey to Midwest City, another suburb of Oklahoma City. She had six children, was single and was an alcoholic. This was the first time I had seen Vesta since we watched her three babies being taken from her in Bernie, Missouri. She told me that Betty and Pearl had died from polio. All she knew about William was that he was mentally disabled. She didn't know where he was, or even if he was still living.

Vesta still felt the pain of losing her children. I could see it in her eyes, even though she tried to hide it. I could still feel the pain, too. I believe that Vesta never got over having to put her children up for adoption.

I got to know Vesta as a person. She told me how much she had suffered at the hands of our father. She also told me how many times she had wanted to help me and my other sisters. But she explained that she was afraid to do so. She told me, "I realized how much you younger kids resented me. If only I could have made you understand how lonesome I got in those days."

She apologized for not being able to help us. I finally realized that my oldest sister was as much a victim as the rest of us. Her life as a child had made her an alcoholic. She still felt helpless and hopeless, and she was still very confused. She was afraid to let her children out of her sight.

Tommy was old enough to want to drive. He gave me three-fourths of what he earned, with the understanding that I would save half toward his insurance, and use the rest as I saw fit. I realized that Tommy was a good boy; this made me proud of him.

Tommy and Billy, Vesta's oldest son, became very close. For some reason, this made Tommy feel his oats a little more. He bullied the other children even more. Vallerie and La Donna were getting old enough that they did not want Carol constantly trying to mother them. I believe that mothering them made her feel like she was helping. When they refused her help, it hurt Carol's feelings.

Carol started running away. She got on drugs, using her body to obtain the drugs. She told one of her counselors that she ran away because she could not do these bad things in her mother's house. She said that she refused to defile her mother's house in that manner. She said that her mother was perfect, so when she felt the need to do these things, she felt she had to run away. Phillip began to act out also. He was jealous over Tommy having a job because he was not yet old enough to work.

A police officer named Stanley took Carol into his home, with my permission, to try and help me straighten her out. He and his wife did try very hard. Carol was a handful, even for two people.

Stanley was shopping at Gibson's store, and he had asked me to pick Carol up there because he and his wife wanted a little time alone. They were not waiting at the front door for us, like he had said they would be. They had shopped a little longer than they had meant to. Across the street from Gibson's store was a Goodwill store. It was raining so I took the other four children across the street to the Goodwill store to wait. You had to be a member to go into Gibson's, and I wasn't one. All I could do was wait for them in the car or in the Goodwill store.

Tommy had almost saved enough money for his car insurance, and he had given it to me for safekeeping. As we waited for Carol to come out of Gibson's, Tommy was looking around the

Goodwill store. He found a couch and a chair that he wanted, and he wanted me to buy them. When I told him I could not afford to buy anything, Tommy yelled as loudly as he could that I was just cheap. I still refused to buy the couch and chair. Then he started running though the store, yelling, "My mother is a cheapskate!"

I realized that he was just trying to get his way by embarrassing me. I got mad and didn't let it happen. I felt guilty later, but I never told Tommy that. Instead I asked, "Tommy, do you really want that couch and chair bad enough to act like this?"

He answered, "Yes, I do. We need a couch and chair."

I bought the couch and chair. I did need living room furniture, but Tommy was being quite embarrassing and acting like a fool. We joined up with Carol and I took everyone home. I didn't say a word to Tommy about his insurance money.

A few weeks later, Tommy wanted me to give him his insurance money. He was ready to buy insurance for himself.

I asked him, "What insurance money?" I told him that he had wanted that couch and chair so badly that I had thought he wouldn't mind paying for it. I asked him how he had expected me to pay for the couch and chair, since I had told him I had no money. He was angry, but he never verbally abused me in a public place again. That was a hard lesson to learn.

Tommy started over and finally saved enough money for his insurance. I then allowed him to get a driver's license and to drive my car when I was off work.

Carol did not stay long with Stanley and his wife. Carol and her friends broke into his liquor cabinet. The couple came home and found their house full of drunken teenagers. Carol went to a juvenile hall called Taft, about 120 miles from Oklahoma City.

Vesta was married to a military man named Bural Jolly, who was also an alcoholic. He had two little girls of his own of whom he had custody. I didn't agree with their lifestyle, or the way they treated their children. Bural's daughters went back to their mother after a couple of years because Vesta and Bural had mistreated them that badly.

It was a match made in heaven. They were both alcoholics; no one else would have put up with that. Because of their drinking, they did a lot of fighting and many foolish things. But Bural stayed with Vesta through thick and thin. Years later, he was by her side when she died. Even though he was a drunk, he was there for her.

Chapter TWENTY-TWO

I RECEIVED A call from Yuba General Hospital, telling me that Mother had had a vein stripping, and that she refused to get out of bed until I got there. They said she could develop blood clots if she did not start moving around. I talked to Mother on the phone, but she refused to cooperate. Mother gave me her address.

I left Phillip, Vallerie and La Donna with Vesta. Tommy and I went to Yuba City, California. My car gave out along the way. I hired some people to take us on to Yuba City, and they took us right to Mother's door. I left my car sitting along the highway. That was all I could do. I didn't believe it could be fixed quickly enough.

When I got to Mother's house, I understood why Mother had wanted me to come. My brother, Glenn, and his family were living with her. When they left, they took Mother's furniture and all the food in the house with them. Mother's three children were alone and hungry. Mother's next Social Security check wouldn't come in for three more weeks; she had just received one before she went to the hospital. She had cashed it and Glenn took it away from her, along with the furniture he needed.

The first thing I did was to get some groceries to feed my brother, sisters and son. I went to the hospital and insisted that Mother get up at least twice a day. This caused considerable discomfort, which was to be expected after this kind of surgery. I stayed until Mother was home again.

I bought a second-hand bed for Mother to sleep on, a bunk for the girls and a mattress for Paul Jr. I made sure there were groceries in the house. They would have to eat beans, macaroni and commodities until the first of the month. That was the best I could do.

I had to have enough money to get home. Tommy and I rode a bus home. Financially, this put a strain on me for the rest of the month. I was able to overcome this, though, with some difficulty.

Ever since I had graduated nursing school, I had saved for a rainy day. I put away ten percent of what I earned for emergencies. No matter what, I did not touch that money for anything else. God knows I had enough emergencies for 20 families. I needed a car now, and I let Tommy pick it out. He wanted a Barracuda, so that was what I got. I had to start my emergency fund all over again.

When I saw Carol, I tried to give her everything she wanted so that she would know I loved her. Then Phillip decided that the way to get what you wanted was to misbehave. When he told me this, I began to realize what I was doing. At that time, I tried to even things out as much as I could. But it was too late; Phillip had become a brat. He refused to take baths. If we wanted to go for an outing as a family, Phillip refused to come. He tried to make things as difficult as he possibly could. Talk about being an ornery teenager – he certainly was!

Rose Maria married and moved to Reno, Nevada. Mother moved from California to Delores' house. Delores and Mother had a falling out. I came home one morning to find Mother and Loretta in Carol's room. Paul Jr. was sleeping on the couch. A couple of days later, I came home and Mother had moved my boys' bedroom furniture into the garage, and had bought a bed for Paul Jr. Mother had moved him into my sons' room, and moved my sons into the garage. My boys assured me that they didn't mind sharing with Grandma. They said they liked it in the garage.

Mother received a Social Security check each month, but she didn't help with expenses. I now had three more people to care for. I went to work double-shifts again. There were times I was so tired that I did not know which end of me was up. Then Mother moved Elijah, his two kids and his girlfriend into the garage. She had my boys sleep in my bed at night.

During the weekdays, my children were in school when I got home. When I was home, Elijah would take his family to Vesta's or Delores', so I would not know they were there. This went on for several months.

Mother complained because I couldn't buy steaks and bacon and eggs for them to eat. I couldn't understand where all the food was going. All I did was work and I couldn't make ends meet. I continued to put ten percent of one of my monthly checks back for emergencies each month. This habit saved Carol many times. I could always send her money to get home on, or to go get her myself.

I had taken one of my dresser drawers out and taped a brown envelope to the back of the inside of the dresser and put the drawer back in. I did not know anyone knew I had hid money there. I came home, paid my bills and slept. I did not know I had more than Mother and her two children in the house. Mother got angry when I took off work for Carol's sake.

Carol had run away from Taft several times. The authorities would find her and put her back in Taft. One morning, Taft called me at work and wanted to see me at 3:00 p.m. that day. I took off from work to change my clothes and rest a while. Taft was a long drive — down close to McAlester, about 120 miles away.

I came home and found Betty asleep on my couch. Glenn was lying on the floor with his three children. Mother had moved my brother Glenn and his family in. She was convinced that they would be allowed to stay, but I said, "He has one week."

This week turned into several months. Glenn refused to leave and Mother took his part. Glenn ran my phone bill up to nine hundred dollars, so I had the phone disconnected. When he complained, I told him to get a job, I couldn't pay it. He claimed he couldn't find work.

One Sunday I arranged for someone else to work my day job. I came home at about 8:00 a.m., and everyone was asleep. Glenn's family was asleep in the living room. My boys were asleep in my bed. I went out to the garage. I found Elijah and his family, along with my brother, Dennis. At this point, I blew my cool and threw everyone out but Mother. This made Mother quite angry; she accused me of being selfish. I tried to explain to her that I had all the people I could support.

On my next payday, I went to put my ten percent into the envelope. The envelope was gone. I asked Mother about it, and she said she had divided it up between my three brothers. She said, "What else did you expect me to do? They have to eat."

I told her that I could not support the whole family. She stayed with Delores for a couple of days, but she didn't stay long because they didn't get along. Then she moved back to my house while I was working.

I bought Curly's Volkswagen bus. I had to make payments because Mother had taken my emergency money. During this time, Vesta's son, Billy, got sick with leukemia. Vesta moved to San Antonio, Texas, so that Billy could get better care. Billy got sicker, and died two months later.

Vesta called and wanted me to come down immediately. Billy's death was painful for her. She said to me, "I am going crazy. I need someone here. Promise me you are leaving now, or I am going to kill myself."

I promised her that I was on my way. She said, "Please bring Tommy and come down. Don't bring Mother. I can't handle having her right now. Please don't tell her in the same words I used; think up an excuse. Don't bring Delores and Curly either. Don't tell them anything."

Vesta refused to let Mother or Delores attend the funeral. She and Mother still hated each other over the things that had happened when we were children. Vesta and Mother still argued every time they were together over which one had had the right to love Father. Vesta was taught as a child that she was Father's wife in another life. He would never let go. I think she also believed that Delores and Curly wouldn't control their drinking while they were there. Vesta had promised me that she and Bural, her husband, would not drink while I was visiting.

Tommy was still working, helping the janitor after school and on weekends, but now he had more hours. Tommy had a date and had just taken my car keys and was planning to go to a movie. He had already left the house and was pulling out of the driveway. I asked Vesta to hold on. I was wearing only my slip and bra, but I ran out of the door and down the street to get Tommy's attention. I really don't think anyone saw me; I didn't see anyone. Tommy saw me and stopped. I told him about Billy, and he came back. He called off his date without wasting any time. That was the only time, except in Chicago when Rex shoved me outside, that I was outside half-dressed. I just had to catch Tommy.

We both quickly made arrangements to take off work. It was easier for me to get off work than it was for Tommy. I had to talk to the head janitor of the school to get Tommy excused from work. The man had thought Tommy was lying. Tommy and I left to go to Billy's funeral, leaving the other three children with Mother.

It was very windy. I drove the Volkswagen bus and, because of its shape, I could hardly hold it on the road. On the way back, the Volkswagen bus caught on fire under the dash. The firemen got upset with me because I had tried to put out the fire. They told me to always carry a fire extinguisher in my car; they said that everyone should carry one.

Mother moved my brother, Dennis, back into my house while I was gone. When I protested, he wouldn't leave. I hate to admit it, but I was afraid to call the police on him. I was afraid of what he or Mother might do in retaliation.

Tommy got sick and started passing out at work. He refused to let me take him to a doctor. I was told I could not force him to go; he had to consent, which he would not do. He finally told me that he had lumps under his arms, in his groin and other places on his body. He believed he was dying from leukemia. He said, "I am not going to leave you with a huge hospital bill. You can't pay, so stop hounding me to go to a hospital."

I became quite desperate at this point. I begged him all the time to let me take him to a doctor. Finally Tommy said, "You need help taking care of these kids. If you will get married, I will go to a doctor."

The hunt was on; I had to have a husband. A new man named George was delivering medicine at the nursing home where I worked. The first night he delivered medicine, he said his car would not start. I loaned him my jumper cables, and then he said he had no lights. I told him I couldn't help him on that one. I watched him as he drove down the street. After he got down the street a way, he turned on his lights. I took that to mean he was interested. A few days later, he asked me to go out. We didn't have much of a courtship. Tommy approved of this man, and I knew by the way he treated my children that he was a good man.

Mother wasted no time letting me know that I did not need a husband. She said, "Your son is just spoiled and wants a father, and thinks he has found a way to get one. A man who would marry a woman with five children has to be crazy or have something wrong with him. He drives a truck, delivering drugs to nursing homes and hospitals. You don't know how many or what kind of drugs he may be taking."

I reminded her of the time she had wanted me to marry a different man every two weeks for money. Mother wouldn't let up on the subject. Finally I said, "This time, Mother, I will use my own judgment. I am no longer thirteen years old." She then shut up.

Mother called Delores, complaining about the terrible man I was about to marry. Curly came over and gave me a four-hour lecture on how careful I should be about marrying the first man who came along. When I didn't listen to him, Delores tried her hand at discouraging me. I told them to mind their own business. My son's life might depend on the decision I made. They were convinced that Tommy would overcome this.

My children heard all these discussions and were confused, especially Phillip. Tommy was planning on going to Oregon after graduation. In Phillip's mind, with Tommy gone, he would be the man of the house. Phillip was really looking forward to this. My family played on Phillip's feelings. Phillip didn't comprehend that his brother was sick and might not make it until graduation.

It seemed that Mother didn't care that my son was sick. She didn't even try to help me convince him to go to a doctor. Mother didn't care about Tommy; or maybe she felt as she did about Vesta – good riddance to bad rubbish.

Chapter TWENTY-THREE

GEORGE AND I went to Wichita Falls, Texas, and were married on November 28, 1972. I was 31 years old at the time. George was a few years younger, at 27. George had a seven-year-old daughter by his first wife, Linda.

I hadn't known George for very long, but I married him so quickly because Tommy would not see a doctor unless I married someone to help me take care of the younger children in case he died. Tommy thought he had leukemia. Vesta's son, Billy, had just passed away with leukemia, and Tommy had similar symptoms.

Tommy went to the hospital the day after I got married. It turned out that he had rabbit fever, which he had contracted after getting a scratch while trying to catch a rabbit. He would have died had I not taken him to a doctor. George spent a great deal of time with Tommy while he was in the hospital.

George is a good man. He is a quiet man and is like me in that he doesn't always stand up for his own rights. He is pleasant to be around and seldom gets upset. I like to tell people that God threw away the mold after He made George because George is the only decent man alive today. I also like to tell people that George has more morals than any virgin girl.

George and I had little privacy at this time. Sometimes after work, we drove to Thunder Bird Lake in my Volkswagen to be alone. One night George drove off the boat ramp. Don't let anyone tell you that a Volkswagen will float. Take my word for it; it does not.

Phillip resented the fact that I had married. He got arrested for stealing candy from a store. At this time, Phillip was working at a Sonic restaurant on Sunny Lane Road, and he kept all of his wages.

He did not make much, but he had money in his pocket and could have paid for the candy.

Mother did not like George and ran him down every chance she got. I finally got the phone bill paid, and the phone connected again. I found it hard to provide adequately for my children because the rest of my family kept me financially and emotionally dragged down. They were in the gutter and they tried to keep me there.

Tommy was in his senior year in high school. Phillip was in eighth grade. Phillip, at this point, could have gotten a job through the school, but he did not want to.

I got pregnant, and Mother was not pleased. She constantly wanted me to kick George out. She wanted us to raise the baby by ourselves. She said that if I made George leave, there would be no more babies. She would keep the house and take care of the children, and I could work. Mother even tried to make me believe that George was illegally selling drugs. She also tried to make me believe that he was unsafe to be around the children.

Carol continued to run away from Taft every chance that she got. I cut down on my working hours so I could visit her more often. I felt she needed me.

On one occasion, Carol was allowed to come home on the weekend to visit, but I could not get off work. I came home from work that Saturday morning and, as always, checked on my children. When I opened the door to the room Carol was sleeping in, I found my daughter lying on the bed nude. My brother, Dennis, was kneeling beside her, his hand on one breast and his mouth on the other. I flew at him in a rage. George ran out of our bedroom to see what the problem was, and Dennis ran outside to the driveway. He stood there yelling for Mother to give him some money so he could leave. I was trying to hold George back because he wanted to kill Dennis for what he had done.

Dennis had been in a truck accident earlier in his life, and he had a steel plate in his head. Mother had said, "If he falls or bumps his head, it will kill him." I was afraid for George to fight Dennis. I was afraid that George might accidentally kill him.

Mother was standing there, saying that she would deny that Dennis had touched the child if I called the police. Mother gave Loretta some money, and Loretta went through the garage and gave it to Dennis. Dennis stood in the driveway a while longer and goaded George by saying, "Come on, you coward. Come on out and I'll kick your ass!"

It took all of us to hold George down. I asked Mother to leave, but she refused. She said she had given all her money to Dennis to get away on. I did not force her out on the street with nowhere to go, but I was very tempted to. I reminded myself that she was my mother. I couldn't throw her out.

Time passed, and George and Mother still didn't get along, I was so angry with Mother; the anger didn't go away. I came home one evening to find George sitting on the steps of our house. His clothes were scattered all over the driveway. He said that Mother had thrown him out. His explanation was that Vallerie, my daughter, was sitting in the big chair. Loretta had wanted the chair. Vallerie refused to get up, so Loretta pulled her out of the chair by her hair. Vallerie cried and Mother spanked Vallerie for crying, telling her that if she had gotten out of the chair in the first place, Loretta would not have pulled her hair. George picked Loretta up out of the chair and sat Vallerie back into it.

Mother and George got into an argument. Loretta called George a fucking son-of-a-bitch. At this point, George picked Loretta up and turned her over his knee and spanked her bottom. Mother threw George's clothes out on the driveway. She told him that this was not his house, and that he did not have the right to correct any child in it. Then she told him to get out and stay out.

George and I picked up his clothes and went into the house. The moment we entered, she started screaming at George to get out. She was trying to tell me her version of what had happened. At the same time, Loretta tried to tell me her version, using foul language when referring to George. George kept quiet; he didn't even defend himself.

Finally, Mother put her arm around me and said, "This man is nothing but a bum. Put him out; we can raise the baby. You don't need him. All he wants is your house."

George stood and said nothing. So I asked him why he would let Mother throw him out of our home. He said, "Your mother is right; this is your house. It is not mine."

Mother had fixed a meatloaf for supper, and it was sitting on the kitchen counter. I picked up the meatloaf and threw it in George's face. I told him, "What is mine, is yours; what is yours, is mine. You are supposed to plant your feet firmly on the floor and protect what is ours. Go get cleaned up and come with me."

We went to the mortgage company. I had George's name put on the deed to the house. I went home and showed it to Mother. I told her that from now on, she would do as George said. He was now the man of the house. Mother got mad and went to Delores', but she complained that Delores' house was too dirty for her to live in. Shortly after that, she went back to California with Paul Jr. and Loretta.

Graduation time was getting close. Tommy would be graduating from high school. Phillip would be graduating from eighth grade. Tommy's graduation was to be one evening, and Phillip's was to be the next. I let George know of my intentions to give the Barracuda to Tommy for his graduation. He asked me what I intended to get for Phillip. I had intended to get him a nice bike, but between my mother and my brothers, I didn't have the money.

George said very calmly, "We'll see what we can do about that."

George got several paper routes, and he asked the boys to help him deliver them. They used my Volkswagen bus, which George had fixed, leaving the sliding door open so that they did not have to get out of the car. George would drive very slowly down the streets, and the boys would throw the papers from the car. Every day before George went to work and the boys went to school, they would throw papers. George got up at four in the morning to deliver papers while also holding down a full time job.

George rebuilt the engine in the Barracuda, put in a new transmission and put new brakes on it. He completely rebuilt that car for Tommy. The boys didn't know why this was being done. Tommy wanted to go back to Oregon after graduation. He thought he was getting the Volkswagen. George bought Phillip a dirt motorcycle because he was not old enough to drive on the streets. George had hoped this would make Phillip happy, and he would stop being such a brat.

When graduation night came for Tommy, Phillip refused to go. We did everything we could to make him understand that we would be going to his graduation the next evening. Nothing helped; we couldn't make him go.

While we were at Tommy's graduation, Phillip tore the doors off my kitchen cabinets, and punched holes in the walls with his fist. He ransacked the house looking for the car keys to the Volkswagen and George's car. He had intended to ram the cars into each other, wrecking both of them. We were very angry when we came home.

I gave Tommy the keys to the Barracuda, and he was truly elated. He had been made to believe George was fixing it for me. Phillip stormed out and didn't come back until late that night.

The next day we went to Phillip's graduation. He pretended very hard not to be proud, but he was. I took the family out to eat, while George went and got Phillip's motorcycle and parked it in the driveway. Then he joined us at the restaurant. Phillip was truly surprised when we got home. But this did not change his behavior. He was now jealous because I had given Tommy the Barracuda. Soon, Tommy left for Pendleton, Oregon.

Phillip was mad at me for marrying. He said that I had cheated him out of being the man of the house. That summer, he stayed out too late on his bike and I scolded him for it. Phillip hit me as hard as he could in the stomach. He had me on the floor before George knew what was happening. George pulled him off of me, telling him that he could hurt the baby I was carrying. Phillip remarked, "What do you think I'm trying to do?"

At that time, I became afraid of my son Phillip. Curly and Delores offered to take him, and I allowed it. Phillip was not with them long when he stole their car and ran away. I was not told that

Phillip had run away. Whenever I called to talk to Phillip, I was told he was out, busy or plain not home. Whenever I went over to Delores' to see him, I was told he was visiting someone, or that he wasn't home. I got the idea that they just did not want me to see Phillip. I felt like my family was falling apart, and I was helpless to do anything about it.

Carol was 16 years old now and had run away from Taft again. This time they did not find her. Carol called me from Kansas City, Missouri. She said she was in a mental hospital there and was sneaking the call because she was not allowed to use the phone. I got the name of the hospital out of her, but she did not know the address. Then someone came in and took the phone away from her. George and I went to Kansas City, Missouri, looking for Carol.

When we got to the mental hospital, they said that Carol was not there. I wanted to look through the hospital wards for her and they refused to let me. They claimed there were no minors there. I threw a fit and raised a big fuss.

George said, "Come on, honey, let's just find a phone and call the police. If that doesn't work, I'll contact a lawyer."

At that time, they decided to let us go through the wards. I found Carol half-dressed on a mixed ward, with men and women. They claimed she had been thrown from a moving car in front of the hospital. They did not know that she was a minor. The hospital tried to refuse to give her to me. George again threatened to get a lawyer. They gave her to me, telling me to seek psychological help for her.

When I got home, I took her to the University State Children's Hospital. She was admitted to the children's psychiatric ward. The hospital diagnosed her as a paranoid schizophrenic. The University Hospital could not hold her either. She propositioned the orderlies. When the orderlies took her out to do their thing, she ran from them, and she was able to get away. Several orderlies were fired for this.

Then Carol was picked up in Fort Smith, Arkansas, hitchhiking nude. The police called and asked me to bring her some clothes. Carol had refused any covering that the police had offered her. Instead of taking her to the hospital, we took her to George's mother, Ruth, in Wichita, Kansas.

I petitioned the court to get custody of Carol back. The state was not doing any better than I was. I refused to tell the state where she was. The state threatened to put me in jail until I told them where Carol was. I refused to tell them, and they did not put me in jail. The judge agreed with me. He said they were not doing as good a job as I had been doing. He gave us custody of my daughter.

I did everything I could to control Carol, without success. Carol even tried to get in bed with my husband. He spanked her butt and sent her out of the room.

Our daughter, Georgiannia, was born September 1, 1973. I went back to work when Georgie was three days old. One morning, I came home to find George sitting on the side of our bed, holding Georgiannia. George looked so very tired. Since it was a weekend, I asked him why he was not in bed. He said, "The baby quit breathing during the night. I had to give her resuscitation. I wanted to make sure she didn't stop breathing again."

I asked him why he did not take her to a hospital. He said, "I didn't know what to do, so I just watched her breathe until you got home."

George was pretty upset. The baby cried, so I breastfed her. George gave her formula at night while I was working. Because I needed to calm George down and decide what our next course of action should be, I started to fix a bottle for our baby. I noticed something in the can of powdered formula.

Carol was on 90 milligrams of Phenobarbital for her seizures. She had dumped the whole bottle of Phenobarbital in the baby's formula. I knew, at this point, not to let the baby sleep. I knew Carol ate the baby food as fast as I could buy it, but I never dreamed she would drug our baby. Carol said, "If you can afford to buy baby food for that baby, you can afford to buy it for me." This made it impossible to keep baby food for Georgie.

George put a chain around the refrigerator and through the door handle, and padlocked the refrigerator to keep the baby food safe. I became afraid of what Carol might do to the baby when I was not looking. I think George was afraid too. Georgie was about eight months old when I realized that Carol was pregnant.

I saw to it that she had the necessary medical treatments. I tried to buy her the foods that she craved. But she was so hateful and contrary that she refused to listen when I told her she needed to stay off the drugs. I could not understand how anyone could deliberately allow these things to be done to their body when they did not have to. I just found it hard to have a lot of compassion for her during this time. For this, I am sorry.

One day, a lady from the Board of Health came out to see me. I personally knew Peggy; I had worked with her for a time. Peggy told me that Carol would not be allowed to keep her baby. Carol had told her counselor that as soon as the baby was born, she was going to Kansas City and find the tallest building she could, and climb up on the roof and drop her baby between two tall buildings.

I was at a loss for words. I didn't know my daughter thought that way about her child. I said, "My husband and I will adopt her baby."

Peggy told me, "You can't have Carol and the baby together. Your baby is not safe with Carol in the house." I knew that Peggy was right, but there was nothing I could do at the time.

George's mother, Ruth, called and wanted us to come to Wichita. She told us, "I am sick and need someone to take care of me and Alice."

Alice is my sister-in-law, born June 2, 1951 with Down syndrome. Ruth kept her in a bedroom where she sat cross-legged, 24 hours a day, and rocked back and forth in her bed. Ruth was dying of cancer, so we put our house on the market.

Carol had her baby November 25, 1974. He looked black; the doctor said he was addicted to drugs. I rented an apartment for Carol and made sure she had plenty of food. I helped her get a job. We hired a lawyer, and Carol signed adoption papers on her son. Christopher became George's and my son.

I knew Carol had it rough during this time, but I saw her often, until she joined a religious cult and moved to Oregon. She was 18 years old. I notified my brothers who lived in Oregon and asked them to keep their eyes open for this religious group. Carol had some problems adjusting to the group. She found my brother, Glenn, and moved in with him and his wife.

I am not sure what happened there. At one time, Carol told me that Glenn had taken advantage of her sexually. During this time, she was taking illegal drugs pretty heavily. Today, she tells me this is not true. My children have a way of thoroughly confusing me at times.

When Christopher was two weeks old, we moved to Wichita. Leaving Carol behind was one of the hardest things I have had to do. It reminded me of leaving Vesta behind. I allowed Carol to visit her son, but every time she did she gave Georgie or Christopher something that made them sick.

One time, Carol had just left when I noticed Georgiannia had no life in her eyes; they were blank. I could not get her to respond to me, and she could not sit up. I took her to the hospital. The doctor said she had been given LSD. He said I was to call the police when Carol came to visit the next time. Georgiannia had seizures that the doctors called flashbacks until she was 13 years old. Carol joined some kind of a cult that she traveled with for several years. Instead of calling the police, I tried to help her any way I could.

I had become pregnant again, but had told no one about it. I miscarried and nearly bled to death while George was at work. Richard, George's brother, carried me into Riverside Hospital and laid me on an empty gurney in the hall. I don't know why, but he told no one I was there, and I was unconscious from the loss of blood.

The hospital administrator found me and did the necessary surgery, not even knowing who I was. I woke to find him sitting in my room. He explained how he had found me and what he had done. He told me I had the right to sue him, but I would have died if he had not done the surgery. He asked me to please sign the consent forms and date them for the previous day.

I signed the consent forms and dated them as he asked. I thanked him for saving my life. I told him that I had two babies at home, two teenagers and a dying mother-in-law; I couldn't afford to die myself.

George's mother, Ruth, died when Christopher was five months old. Those were the hardest five months of Vallerie's and La Donna's lives. Ruth weighed 350 pounds, and she was bedridden most of the time, but my children were not allowed to make themselves a sandwich when they were hungry.

George had two brothers and two sisters. His oldest brother, Bill, was awful; he even mistreated Georgie, who was only 17 months old. No one helped out with the expenses. Ruth received Social Security for herself and Alice. The money we had was equity we had received out of the house we had sold. George finally got a job at a gas station six weeks before his mother passed away.

George would not stand up to his family. When I complained about his family, he yelled at me at the top of his lungs. He could yell more loudly than anyone I had ever heard. I soon learned that George did not like to talk to me about much. This, again, made me feel stupid. When I tried to talk to him, he would yell. When we went grocery shopping and I tried to talk to him, he sometimes yelled. So I tried to stop talking to him. I was sure glad to see his family go home. Now things would be peaceful again, or so I thought.

Paul and Jane were George's friends. They came over at least once a week to play cards. All they could do was talk about Linda, George's first wife. They talked about which rooms she and George had slept in, how she liked this, how she did that, and the places they had gone together. Somehow, I believed they knew this upset me and thought it was funny. Well, it wasn't funny to me, and I wondered how George would feel if I continuously talked about Rex and ignored his request to stop.

The house wasn't mine; it was Linda's. I never did feel at home in that house, even though it was supposed to be George's and mine. I tried to talk to George about this, and he yelled. It was not easy to live in another woman's shadow. As our children got older, when I tried to talk to him about the children or tried to get him involved in their lives, George either yelled or became mute.

What I didn't know then and do know now, is that George was unable to handle stress, so he avoided any kind of confrontation, no matter who the person was. Don't get me wrong; George was an absolute angel in everything else, except in raising the children. That was my job. George wanted no part of it because he was unable to handle any stress.

George's oldest sister, Frances, died in March 1976, one year after his mother had died. She died from a D and C, which doesn't happen very often today. Her body was donated to science. Her death was very hard for George to accept.

We took the children to her funeral in Omaha, Nebraska. I was pregnant with our son, Timmy, at the time. We stayed with George's niece (Frances' daughter) for a few days so that George could collect himself. George took both his mother's and his sister's deaths very hard.

Before Frances' death, George's family had wanted me to come to Omaha because they wanted me to lay my hands on Frances, believing I had some kind of healing power. They also had tried to get me to try this on Ruth before she died. I told them on both occasions that I would not dishonor God by trying such a thing. I do not believe in these things. George's family still blames me for their deaths.

In Wichita, George had been working at making couches and chairs to sell. He also had been working at a cab company owned by a woman named Opal. George bought a car and put it on the cab line; he drove it himself. George was now a private owner, which meant that he owned only one car, but had started on his way to becoming a fleet owner. A fleet owner owns more than one cab, but does not own the company. George did all the mechanical work on the car. This gave us more money to provide for our family.

At this time, Delores lived about 15 miles from a small town called Seminole, Oklahoma. It had a small hospital and several stores and gas stations in it. I was not fond of her husband, Curly. I didn't feel he treated my children and me right at a time I needed help in the worst way, but I tolerated him. I still loved my sister; she could do nothing to stop me from loving her.

Delores called me and told me that Curly had died of a heart attack. She wanted me to come down. It would have taken me about five hours to drive to Delores' home. I was pregnant and two weeks from my due date. I didn't want to go. I was afraid I would go into labor in her dirty house. I could just picture the roaches crawling, and me screaming to get them off of me.

Delores was upset with me for not attending Curly's funeral. I knew the whole family would be drinking, and possibly fighting, and didn't want to put myself in that kind of a situation. On top of that, I couldn't stand the thought of cockroaches crawling all over me, even up inside me. I was worried that the baby might get some kind of infection.

I promised to see her as soon as possible after the baby was born. I went into labor the next morning. Alice, my sister-in-law with Down syndrome, refused to leave the room. She was the second one to hold Timmy after his birth.

Chapter TWENTY-FOUR

MY SON, TIMMY, was born March 13, 1976. He was a breech baby. George had to help me deliver him, and Timmy would have died without George's help. He had to be turned around and I couldn't do that by myself. George was a very proud papa. Timmy is his only biological son, and he worships him with all his heart and soul. In George's eyes, that boy could do no wrong.

After Curly died, Delores called us at least once a week and wanted me to go to her house. George had kept her in cars, and he fixed her cars when necessary. She called me when she was sick or just when she was lonesome. I borrowed Richard's house trailer so that we didn't have to eat or sleep in her house. Delores had adopted two girls, Debbie and Judy, who were about eight and nine years old at this time. I brought Delores and her daughters home with me; they stayed several months at a time.

Curly had left her quite a bit of money. Delores gave me three thousand dollars I had asked her for to start a business with. She made me promise I would come and see her once a week first. I paid her back within six months. Plus, for interest, George and Richard made her a beautiful flowered hide-away bed with a matching chair.

George continued to work making furniture, which enabled him to save enough money to gradually add more cars to the cab line. The drivers paid us for the use of the cars. If a driver didn't pay us, George called me and I had to take the car away from the driver. When the word "no" was uttered, I had to do it. I got so lonesome, sometimes I truly thought about running away. After I got away from Rex, I had to talk to people sometimes, and I began to enjoy it. I wasn't ready to handle rude drivers that tried to get in bed with me, though. Some of them even tried to pay me to have sex with them.

Delores kept me running between her house and mine. Delores and I made several trips to California to see Mother during this time. Mother couldn't remember her name or address when she went to the store alone. I was very worried about her. My brothers ate her food, but did not worry when she was gone for hours. I wrote her name, address and telephone number on a 4"x 6" card and put it in her purse so when this happened and the police picked her up, they would know who she was and where she lived. She told me the police had to bring her home a couple of times, and they had trouble finding out where she lived.

She always had her house full of my brothers and their families, Loretta and her children, and she also babysat for Rose Maria's son and friends of Loretta's. I always left her with at least a week's supply of groceries and as much money as I had when I went home.

One winter Mother called and said, "Loretta's husband has beat me up and thrown me outside. I have nowhere to go."

I told her to go to the senior citizens' center. I knew that was within walking distance of her home. I said, "I will pick you up there."

I left immediately and drove straight through. I brought her and Aunt Lois (Mother's sister) to Wichita. After she was here three weeks, she wanted to go back. She said Loretta's husband, Johnny, would have been cooled down by then. I couldn't talk her out of it. She was worried about Loretta's children because both Johnny and Loretta used and sold pot. I took her back to California the next weekend. Delores was very cruel to her while she was here. This made Mother sad; she did not stay any longer.

Carol came home, but she was not there long when she gave Christopher a whole bottle of codeine cough syrup. I really don't think she meant to hurt him. I called the doctor and he told me to make Christopher vomit. Georgiannia became very lethargic. I took her to the hospital, and they said she'd had an overdose of Dilantin. I realized that Carol could not live with us. I could not watch the children closely enough.

The next day, I took the papers I had received from the Children's University Hospital and went to the welfare office. The caseworker I talked to said she could help Carol if I would bring her into her office. The next day I took Carol to the welfare department. They gave her an emergency check. I found an apartment for her, gave her landlord my phone number and bought some food for her. The state sent her to school, gave her a monthly bus pass and a monthly check. Carol's landlord called me many times when she was having a seizure. I would hurry over to take care of her.

Carol began to grow up. She still needed a lot of help, but she was trying to learn to care for herself and to do what was right. Carol finally found work, and was very proud of herself. She started going to church.

George and Linda's daughter, Teresa, was 14. She was graduating from eighth grade. We attended her graduation ceremony. George and Linda talked and decided that Teresa would come live with us. However, we had said nothing about Linda moving in with us. Linda was George's first wife. I didn't mind having Teresa; she was George's daughter. He had helped raise enough of my children. I owed him this one.

Linda and Teresa came from Oklahoma City and moved in. It was kind of weird living with my husband's ex-wife. Linda lived with us for three months. While she was there, Delores called and said she was sitting in front of the emergency room doors with her two adopted daughters. She was afraid to go home. She was afraid she would have a heart attack.

I went to her and while I was gone, Linda tried to get in bed with George and he threw her out of the house. George's brother lived in the business that we owned. Linda moved in with him. I didn't feel as awkward in the house after that, but I still could not make it home. George's friends still came over to play cards with George. They still talked about old times, which always included Linda, and this still made me uncomfortable. I believe the thing that really bothered me was that no one seemed to care about my feelings. In fact, I believe all this talk was designed to make me uncomfortable.

Teresa was a handful. I guess you would call her the typical teenager. The difference was that I was not her mother, and she did not mind telling me that. She wanted to stay out until 2:00 a.m., and George wouldn't say anything to her about it. She finished high school. She stayed with us until she was married at seventeen. She had a baby boy, and then she divorced a year later. She moved in with us; then she remarried a year later. Teresa went on to divorce and marry several times, and had three children. However, she managed to stand on her own two feet and needed very little help.

Tommy came to Wichita with his wife to find work. They had two small children. Tommy and his wife got into a fight. He was abusing his wife; I saw him hit her. I called the police, but his wife refused to press charges. My son would tell you this was not true, but it was.

My house was becoming like my mother's – people moving in and out at will. I realized how my mother felt when my brothers did this to her after they were grown.

Vallerie and La Donna began feeling their oats. I became afraid of my daughters. Vallerie wanted to be emancipated. I wanted her to finish out her senior year of high school.

La Donna had a social worker call on her sixteenth birthday. The social worker said, "Today, La Donna is 16 years old; she wants to leave home. You have no legal right to stop her if you try."

I did not try to stop her; it was hopeless. I felt like I had failed to raise my children to be decent people. My daughter will never know how badly she hurt my heart that day, or how much I would miss her. She was too young to understand that she was ruining her life.

La Donna didn't finish school. At first, she moved in with her sister, Vallerie. Later, she moved in with a man fresh out of prison for sexually abusing a four-year-old child. I later took her to Oklahoma City to live with her brother, Phillip, because she refused to come home.

Phillip was living with a girl named Margie. They had two children, Phillip and Michelle. Phillip and Margie drank heavily, took pills and smoked what they called "weed." After a few months, Phillip called and asked for bus fare money to send La Donna to her brother, Tommy. There, she married a boy named L.G. Nelson.

Chapter TWENTY-FIVE

VALLERIE GOT MARRIED to Rodney, an alcoholic. They moved to Fairview, Nebraska. The next time I heard from Vallerie, she needed financial help to keep her house. We later received a call from a woman's shelter, asking us if we would come and get Vallerie and her son.

We brought Vallerie home; she was very wild. One weekend, she went back to Nebraska and stole the furniture Rodney and she shared. It was not paid for, and she took it across the state line, not realizing that was wrong. To keep Vallerie out of jail, we paid the $2,040 owed on the furniture..

After being in our home for almost nine months, Vallerie gave birth to Megan. We kept her two children most of the time. Vallerie stole my checkbook and took her friends to Silver Dollar City. Vallerie could sign my name exactly like I did.

Megan was about two months old when Rodney, Vallerie's husband, showed up. Vallerie told Rodney she would get back together with him only if they lived in our house. Rodney and Vallerie showed up with a caterpillar. I felt something heavy hit the house. I ran to the door to see what was happening, and saw that the porch was gone.

Rodney said, "George gave me permission to build an apartment under the house."

I was frantic. If George had given them permission, I had no right to say anything; it was his mother's house.

They told me to keep the children in the back of the house. Next, the windows in the front of the house went crashing down. Soon, I had a 13-foot hole under the house, with a plank over the hole where the porch had been, leading to the front door.

Rodney and Vallerie got into another fight. Then Vallerie filed for divorce. They both ran off, leaving behind a 13-foot hole, with dirt piled up to the roof on both sides of the house, for us to take care of. George was surprised when he got home. He had not given them permission to make an apartment under his house.

The hot water tank and the heater were already under the house in a little 4'x 4' dug-out place sitting on concrete. They had bull-dozed around that; if they had hit it we would have had no heat, air or hot water. We did not have the money to fix the house, so George and his brother put jacks under the house and plastic over the south side, and we continued to live there.

A few months later, I alone at home with Vallerie's two little ones and my three children. Timmy was getting dressed. Suddenly, he said, "Mommy, I can see outside."

I opened the bedroom door and saw that the whole east side of the house had fallen down. The only thing holding up the floor was the hot water tank and the stove below. I softly tried to coax five-year-old Timmy to come to me. I was afraid to step on the floor as I thought maybe my weight would make it fall in. Finally, I got Timmy out of the room and all the other children out of the house. I was lucky the whole house didn't cave in.

I went to neighbors who called my husband at work. George and his brother, Richard, jacked the house up. They, too, were sur-prised the the whole house hadn't caved in. That is the only time I ever heard my husband speak of religion. He said, "You do have someone 'upstairs' looking out for you, don't you?" I guess I had voiced that phrase to him several times.

We had to fix the house now. George and I, with the help of our two small boys, built the walls inside and outside of the basement. But when it came to the sewer, George didn't know how to fix it, and we had to hire someone. The contractors wouldn't work on the house with the children in it. In the meantime, I had received a call for help from one of my daughters, and I thought I could solve both of our problems.

My daughter, La Donna was pregnant and having problems.

I took my children and went to visit La Donna and her husband, L.G., in Salem, Oregon, to see if I could be of any help to them while the contractor was working on our house. I was welcomed until all the money I had was gone. The way they spent money, it didn't take long.

La Donna told me, "You and your children have to go somewhere else." She then said, "Your children are making me miserable. I am afraid I am going to lose the baby."

I was upset. I had been waiting on her hand and foot while her husband was at work. I also had taken care of her two small boys. I don't believe her husband knew anything about this since whenever he came home from work, he fixed supper, cleaned the kitchen and bathed his boys. Whenever La Donna asked me to drive her to the store, all she bought was candy for herself. She was already grossly overweight. I tried to get her to eat healthy foods, which she refused. I think that maybe this "meddling" was what had upset her, not my children.

I called Tommy and asked if we could stay with him for a while. Then I called George and asked him to send me enough money to go to Tommy's. We stayed with Tommy until the house was safe for us to return to.

We all enjoyed being at Tommy's. He had two boys the same age as our boys. Tommy was a little rough around the edges and was what I considered a male chauvinist pig. By this, I mean he didn't have the sensitivity toward his wife and children that I believed they deserved.

He was too quick to punish his boys, and when he played with them, he played very roughly. When one of them cried because Tommy threw the baseball too hard, he called them babies or girls. When I said something about the fact that he was being too rough on the boys, he was proud of it. He said, "I am making my boys tough. They are not going to be sissies."

I had heard this nonsense before; he sounded like my father. He felt like I was butting in where I had no business, and maybe I was. I went for a walk in the woods to regain control of myself.

I tried to talk to Tommy about the way I believed he was mistreating his boys. We didn't fight over this, like the rest of the family would have. It just made both of us uncomfortable. Tommy thought I was interfering, and I wasn't sure; he could have been right. I backed off the subject to avoid any problems that might develop if I continued to let him know how I felt.

My children loved it at Tommy's. He treated me okay, too. At this time, he tried to be the proper son, and insisted he was not hurting his boys, when I knew he was. He just enjoyed being the head of the house too much, or so I thought. It was safer to go home as soon as possible.

I loved the state of Oregon, and hated to leave all the beautiful trees, mountains and waterfalls. I knew I would never walk through the Oregon woods again. George hated the mountains; this would be my last trip.

I also missed my husband and needed to get back home. So George wired me the money and I drove back to Wichita, Kansas. It was a rough trip. Georgie had several seizures on the way home, so I drove as long as I could without stopping. I drove for 17 hours straight, trying to get my daughter back to her doctor.

The walls that we had fixed did not leak, but wouldn't you know it – the part we hired someone else to do did leak. We now had a 17-room house with a leaky basement. But at least we had our home back.

Chapter TWENTY-SIX

I HOME-SCHOOLED our children, mainly because of Georgie's flashbacks. Delores's daughter, Judy, got married. Delores and Debbie (her second adopted daughter) moved in with us. I couldn't continue to teach the children at home, because Delores was cruel to both my children and to Debbie. I can not begin to explain how awfully she treated this child. She was definitely Father's daughter.

Debbie, in turn, mistreated my children and me, also. I did what I could to help Debbie, but she stole everything she could from our house. Delores got angry when I complained, and shoved and screamed at me.

She said, "Debbie is my child and I will do what I want with her."

I called SRS several times. The lady on the phone told me all I could do was tell Delores to leave. I didn't want to do that. They had no place to go but that filthy house they came from. I allowed myself to be a rug under their feet because I loved my sister. To get along with my sister, I let Debbie slap me around. I see now how wrong that was. Delores said that I owed it to her to support her and Debbie because of the punishment she took for me as a child, and I tried to repay that debt to her satisfaction.

Georgie and Debbie got into all kinds of trouble. They started leaving the house at night. I nailed the windows shut. I sat outside of my daughter's room in a lawn chair all night. Debbie went to SRS and complained. They told me what I was doing was illegal, and that I had to stop it. So we put an alarm system on the doors and windows. We had a large German shepherd dog, so then they crawled out the doggie door.

Debbie and Georgie ran away together once. Debbie ran away many times and got pregnant. She gave birth to a baby boy that she named Carlos. Delores later adopted him. George and I supported him, though we were allowed no say in his upbringing. Delores refused to even let him sit in the same room with us unless she was present.

Delores had a heart attack, and she had to have a balloon treatment through her arteries and veins to clean them out. At night, when George was home and the children were asleep, I walked to the hospital and visited Delores. We lived about a mile-and-a-half away. I had just gotten home from visiting Delores one night, and was sitting at the kitchen table drinking a glass of milk, when Debbie came up from behind me and put a knife to my throat.

She said, "I could cut your fucking throat and get away with it because I am a minor."

She held me there for at least ten minutes, cursing and telling me not to make a sound. She told me how much she would enjoy killing me. I said nothing; I just sat there like a statue, afraid to move.

When she finally put the knife down, I shoved it off the other side of the table. I jumped up and slapped the tar out of her. This woke up my husband, and he came out of our bedroom. Debbie ran from the house. My husband told me to call the police, but I refused to do that. I didn't want to hurt or upset my sister for fear it might make her have another heart attack. All I wanted was a little peace in my life.

The next night, when I went to see Delores, she started screaming and yelling at me, telling me to get out of her room. She gave me no chance to explain. She said, "Debbie has already told me what you did to her. You waited until I was in the hospital to mistreat her, didn't you? If I die, it will be your fault."

When she got out of the hospital, Delores, Debbie and Carlos moved in with Vallerie for a while. Then Delores came back home, and Debbie married an African-American man named Jim. I believed this was to spite Delores, who was very prejudiced. Debbie was half Indian and Delores never let her forget it; she mistreated her because of her race.

Georgiannia started her senior year of school. Debbie called me one day and said, "Georgie, is no longer lily white and pure. Jim and I took care of that."

When Georgie came home, her right arm and both her legs were skinned up. I asked her what had happened, and she said, "I fell down the stairs. Just leave me alone."

She locked herself in her bedroom and refused to even let me care for her scrapes and bruises. I felt it was better to leave her alone until she was willing to talk to me. That never happened. She became very mean and uncontrollable instead.

At this time, we owned thirty cars on the Best Cab line. We had changed the furniture store into a garage so that George could keep the cabs running. We had hired a mechanic to help him named Jerry.

Jerry's girlfriend, Sally, was 59 years old. She asked if Timmy, who was 14, could help her cut wood. I saw nothing wrong with this, and at first, neither did Jerry, our mechanic. But after a while, Jerry and Timmy no longer got along when Timmy helped in the garage after school and on weekends. Timmy quit helping us on the paper route. Sally often brought him home late, saying they had worked late. Timmy helped her cut wood, so I thought, for three years. He was arrested a few times for being out after curfew. We had to go down to the police station and pick him up at all hours of the night.

This made it difficult for George; he was tired all the time. George wanted to be Timmy's friend, and wouldn't correct him for anything he did. If he wasn't called for Timmy being out after curfew, he was worrying about him. George underwent a great deal of stress. He was at his wit's end with his boys. He didn't seem to understand what this meant to their father's health.

Chapter TWENTY-SEVEN

ONE MORNING, GEORGIANNIA refused to help with the paper route. She said she was leaving home; then she started to cry. I sat down in the big chair and pulled her down in my lap. After a lot of coaxing, she told me she was pregnant; but she would not tell me who the father was. I told her that three heads were better than one. We would work this thing out together. She then told me that the baby would be black, and that she wanted an abortion.

I then remembered what Debbie had said a few months earlier, and I finally understood what she had meant that day. I remembered the sacks we had buried when I was a child and the effect they had on my life. As an adult, I sometimes wondered what that lost baby of mine might have been.

I told her that an abortion was not an option. My daughter hated me for this, but I thought she would get over it. I was wrong; she still hates me. I still believe I did the right thing. I will always believe abortions are wrong. A counselor tried to tell me it was my daughter's choice. I didn't think so; she was too young to understand the loss she would feel.

Delores wanted me to put Georgie's child up for adoption. She did not want to raise Carlos with a black child. I looked into the possibility of adoption and was told that because the baby would be of mixed race, it would be hard to place the child with adoptive parents. The child would probably be raised in foster homes, and most likely passed from one home to another. I couldn't live with that. Her baby deserved a better life than that.

One of Teresa's husband's family members wanted to adopt the baby. They had just had a baby and thought they could teach Georgie's baby to be a servant to their child if they trained it from birth. Well, I wasn't going to allow that. Georgiannia was not ashamed to display her hatred for this child.

She said, "I want my child to have a bad life because it has ruined my life."

I did everything I could to help Georgie bond with this child. I took her to buy a crib for the baby. She refused to even look at them, so I bought the most expensive one in the store. I bought a baby buggy that Georgie could use for many babies, but she just gave it away.

I painted the room the baby was to use, but Georgie refused to help. When it came time to put the crib up, she wouldn't help. I tried to get her to go shopping for baby clothes, but she refused. I went alone and bought the clothes. When I got back, I asked her to put the clothes away. I heard Georgie screaming. I ran into the room, and she had thrown the baby clothes all over the room. She was bumping her head against the wall. I quit asking her to help prepare for the baby. She graduated from high school. We gave her a car for her graduation gift.

That summer, she started college with 15 credit hours. She wouldn't listen when we told her that was too many hours. She dropped down to three credit hours and didn't tell us that she kept the refund. I began to wonder if I was wrong in not letting her have an abortion, but I just couldn't do it.

Audriannia was born September 27, 1990. Georgie would not even touch Audrie, so George and I took guardianship of the child. Georgie verbally voiced her hatred of Audrie. Delores took Carlos and went to live with her daughter, Judy. She did not want to raise Carlos with a black child. Georgie went back to college, taking only three hours. I took complete care of Audrie.

Georgie started acting like Carol had when she was young. She gave her body to anyone who would have her, not for drugs, but just to show me she could. I think she tried to have sex with all my male drivers. I tried to take her to a counselor, but she refused to go.

Opal, the woman who owned the cab company, wanted to retire after her husband had died. George and I were considering buying it because of the number of cars we had on the line. George was the largest fleet owner in the company, with 33 cabs.

My son, Phillip, wanted George to buy him an 18-wheeler. He told him, "If you can afford to buy the cab company, you can afford to buy me a semi-truck."

We tried to explain to him that we would have to borrow the money for the cab company. He responded, "You can borrow the money to buy my truck."

We told him that would be impossible, so he started destroying our taxicabs. He put sugar in our gas tanks, flattened the tires, keyed every taxi we had so that we had to repaint them and smeared eggs on our cabs. He threw glass bottles at our garage doors, filling the driveway with glass.

He hated my little granddaughter, Audriannia, for no other reason except her skin was black. He tried to force us to put her up for adoption by abusing her when he had the opportunity. I feared opening my door to him, so he sat on our steps and waited for us to come home from work. When we unlocked the door, he pushed his way in; we were unable to stop him.

Delores was gone about three months and then came back. She never allowed Carlos to be in the same room with Audrie. Delores came and went from our house frequently. Delores stayed with us most of the time because she and Judy fought when she tried to live with her. Judy refused to carry her food to her and run her to the store every time she wanted to go. Those were the kinds of things that Delores expected from me, and I was stupid enough to do them.

Also, she expected us to put up with anything Carlos did; it didn't matter what it was. Though she mistreated him herself, we didn't have the right to complain when he broke our windows, or messed up our computers. She kept coming back to our house because, as she said, "I am happier with you."

When Delores got angry, she locked herself and Carlos in her room and acted like she was starving herself to death. But we knew she got up at night when she thought we were asleep and ate what she wanted.

Chapter TWENTY-EIGHT

I ONCE LEFT Audrie with Georgie while I went down to scrub the garage floor. I had barely gotten started when Georgie called and said she had been throwing the baby up in the air and failed to catch her. The baby was lying on the floor, not moving. She asked me what to do and wanted me to come home.

I told her to call 911, and that I was on my way. I called Phillip's wife, who lived next door, and told her to get over to my house quickly and call 911 if necessary. I left, leaving the garage open, and drove with the gas pedal to the floorboard. I blew my horn and did not stop for anything; I ran every red light.

When I got home, Georgiannia said, "Well, that's one way to get you home."

She walked out the door. Margaret, my daughter-in-law, said, "I found nothing wrong when I got here." Audrie was playing on the floor. The police hadn't been called; I was thankful for that.

Georgiannia moved in with a woman named Joan. I did not like her. I saw Joan and Georgie kissing on the mouth while standing on my front porch. When they visited, Georgie had nothing to do with Audrie. Joan was all over the baby. She was the one that held Audrie and played with her.

Joan seemed to have an uncanny domination over Georgie. Georgie did what Joan told her to do. Something just didn't seem right with their relationship. I wondered what had happened to my little girl; she seemed to have no conscience. I said nothing. I didn't want to start an argument; it would have served no purpose.

George and I bought the cab company in October 1990, but

we didn't take it over and run it ourselves until January 1991. I was about 50 years old at the time, and George was about 46.

Phillip told us, "If you will stop wasting your money on that little black bitch [he was referring to Audrie], you could afford to buy my 18-wheeler truck for me." I couldn't convince him it was impossible. He believed we were loaded with money.

Audrie was two years old when Phillip was sitting on our door-step one day, drunk and waiting for us to come home from work. Phillip followed us in the house, trying to pick an argument. He threw my end table at Audrie, who was sitting in the big chair, as he called her a "nigger bitch." George threw his body over Audrie, and the table hit George in the back. Phillip then grabbed George around the neck and was choking him. George managed to whis-per that he could not breathe.

Phillip laughed and said, "I am going to kill you."

I called the police, and then I ran back in the front room to get Audrie. Christopher (the grandson we adopted) came home and stopped Phillip by knocking him on his rear. Christopher told him, "If you get up, I will knock you down again; so please don't get up."

Phillip crawled out the front door before the police got there. When the police arrived, George was shaking all over and crying. The police called an ambulance.

George is a severe diabetic, and getting upset affects his blood sugar level. When the police arrested Phillip, he saw the ambulance and laughed, saying, "I killed the old man. Now Mother will get my truck."

I couldn't make these children understand that we had no money. We just had good credit. We took out a loan to buy the cab company. Phillip continued to try to keep us from succeeding in the cab business by destroying our cars in any way he could. Phillip was an adult; he should have known right from wrong, but he was an alcoholic and did stupid things.

Timmy was also acting up very badly and cursing at me, his teacher and even his school principal. I could not do anything with him, and George refused to get involved. George would not even go down and talk to his principal. He didn't feel it would help any. George believed that Timmy was defying any and all authority. The more we tried to tell him what to do, the more he would rebel. George wanted Timmy to love him, not hate him. Timmy was becoming unmanageable. It became necessary for me to watch what I said in front of him, or I would get cursed out and belittled by him.

I took Audrie to work with me from the time she was born. Timmy always found at least an hour a day to spend with her; he loved Audrie as if she was his own child. I was beginning to get suspicious of Timmy and Sally's relationship. I could not make myself believe that an older woman would molest a little boy. I brushed my suspicions aside; I wish I had not done that.

We had kept Georgiannia in vehicles ever since she had graduated high school. I gave her $125 a week to take Audriannia out once a week. I am sensitive to the sun, but Audrie needed to get outdoors sometimes, but I also hoped that by spending time with Audrie, Georgie and she would form a bond with each other. Georgie would not take her out for less than $125.

When Audrie was about 14 months old, I was taking an accounting class at the vocational rehab school. George was not feeling well. He was asleep, so I did not wake him. Georgiannia was there, and I asked her to watch the baby while I was in school.

When I got home, Georgie grabbed her stuff and headed out the door. As she went out the door, she said, "By the way, she ate a whole box of rat poison." I grabbed her and asked how she knew it was a whole box. Georgie said, "I watched her eat it."

I then asked her why she had not awakened her father, or called me at school. She replied, "I wanted her dead; she should be dead."

I frantically called the poison control center, and they told me to make Audrie vomit, which I was unable do. I made Georgie go with me to the emergency clinic, and Audrie vomited on the way. I worried about leaving Audrie with Georgie after that.

I started teaching Audrie how to count when she was about three. When she was four, she could read first grade books. George and I were proud of her; she was a very bright child. This seemed to irritate Georgie.

Georgie had taken Audrie home with her for the weekend. When Audrie got home, she told both Delores and me that a man had undressed in front of her by the couch. She wanted to know what that thing hanging between his legs was. After that, we had trouble with Audrie wanting to kiss passionately on the mouth. This surprised us; we wouldn't let her kiss us this way. That was the last time I let Audrie spend the night with Georgie. Georgie only wanted Audrie because her friend, Joan, wanted to see her.

Audrie was about four when Georgie ran a stop sign and hit a tow truck. She totaled her car. George bought her another one. A couple of weeks later, my van was stolen out of our driveway. We suspected our mechanic or one of my son's friends had stolen it. George had to get me another car.

Georgiannia decided that the car George had gotten for me was better than the car he had gotten for her. She wanted to know why I had to have the best of everything. She demanded that we buy her a brand new car. I told her we couldn't afford new cars for ourselves. She put her hands on her hips and told me we would do it or she would take Audrie away from us. I told her when she was ready to take Audrie, to just let me know and I would help her pack Audrie's clothes. She assured me she meant what she said. I told her I did also. Georgie stomped off, saying that Audrie was full of demons and she would have to find a way to get them out of her. Georgie said no more to me about wanting Audrie, and we went on with our lives.

One day we received a subpoena. Georgiannia was seeking custody of Audriannia. George and I fought our daughter in court over our granddaughter because we knew that she only wanted her to spite us. Georgie had refused her at birth. I had to pay Georgie to take Audrie out to play. Because of the things Georgie had said and done, we were afraid for Audriannia's life if Georgie took her.

We loved both our daughter and granddaughter, and wanted to do what was best for both of them. The question now was, what is the best thing to do? We followed our hearts; we didn't know what else to do.

Going to court against your own children is not a very easy thing to do. They hate you for the rest of their lives. Someday, maybe she will understand why we had to do what we had to do. You can't take a child away from people who love her, just for spite. It is also wrong to use a child to try to get everything you want from your parents or anyone else.

It made me sick to my stomach to hear the stories they told the judge. I wondered how anyone could make up those horrible things they said about me. There were times when I was speechless because of the questions Georgie's lawyer asked. I was under the impression that the court and the religious system were separated. That a person couldn't be prosecuted because of their religious beliefs, unless it was doing someone harm.

My daughter's lawyer handed me a Bible and asked me to look up several scriptures to explain; the judge said nothing. My daughter admitted believing she had sex with the devil and the court still considered her sane. I was horrified when she said that Audrie was full of demons and she had to find a way to remove them from her. This was wrong in my book. I thought religion and the state had to be kept separated. I have learned that schoolbooks don't tell children the true facts of life. They are told what the government wants them to believe.

When they teach government to our children, they teach that our system is fair and equal. This is not true all of the time. It may be that judges are supposed to have rules to follow. If so, most of them do not follow them. A judge can do as he pleases, whether it is right or wrong. Legal documents are just what some man or woman writes down. Yes, they have to be followed, but that does not mean they are truthful or right. I received a fair judge when we went to court on Audrie, but that is not always the case.

Chapter TWENTY-NINE

VALLERIE CAME TO visit me. Her son, Kenny, and some friends had vandalized someone's property. The judge had ordered them to pay three thousand dollars each in restitution. Her husband had refused to pay it for Kenny, who was 15. Vallerie wanted me to take guardianship of him and pay the three thousand dollars.

I talked to Kenny, and he said, "Believing in God is a weakness. There is no way I am going to anyone's church. I will ride my bike anywhere and anytime I want to, and there's no way you can stop me. I will come and go as I please."

So I told Vallerie I could not take him, and this made her very angry. Her remark as she walked out the door was, "But you can afford to fight Georgie in court over *this*," pointing at Audrie. Vallerie and I didn't speak for years after that.

A few days later, Carol came to visit me. She was a lot more plainspoken than Vallerie. She wanted me to home-school her son, James. But James was to be allowed to watch his television shows. He could not write, so I had to do all the writing for him. He had trouble in math, and I was to give him the answers in math. He could not read as well as Audrie, so it would be helpful if I would read his lessons to him. He was not to be punished in any way. If I would do this, she would say anything I wanted her to say in court.

I told Carol, "I will not home-school your son. When I teach a child at home, I expect him to be ahead of the public school system, not behind the public school system. And as for the court, all you can do is tell the truth."

I explained that I would not fight Georgiannia over Audrie if I believed that she loved her and wanted her for the right reasons. I felt I had good reason to fear for Audrie's safety if Georgie took her at this time. Not once had she said, "I love my daughter." Instead, she held her over our heads, and threatened to take her away from us if we didn't give her what she wanted.

Around this time, Mother came to visit. I arranged for a family gathering so that all the children and grandchildren could see their grandmother. She was older, and I felt it might be the last chance they had to see her.

One day, Georgiannia told Amy (one of my employees), "I am pregnant. The baby belongs to Kevin [one of my drivers]. I have to break up with him; he is married and living with his wife. This will not look good to the court. If I expect to win in court, I will have to look respectful."

Well, I was in for a big surprise. Mother left and the court day came. I felt that I had done nothing wrong and that no one could possibly say anything bad about me. I hoped my family would show their love for me. There were many times I felt that this did not happen.

True to Carol's word, Vallerie and Carol testified against me in court, twisting and turning any and everything I had said to them as children or adults to suit their purpose. They tried to make me sound like a crazy person, using the very things they knew would hurt me the most. They used my Jehovah's Witness association against me, and said that I had taught them to believe in demons. They said I had told them Betty's son, Eddie, had demons in him and that was why he had seizures. They said I ran up and down the streets half-naked. Vallerie said I told them that cats had demons in them. Vallerie accused me of holding a wake for Audrie while she was still alive, when Mother visited.

I guess I was pretty stupid. I did not know what she meant. I read a religious magazine called *The Awake*. Another magazine I read was *The Watchtower*. I asked Vallerie what she had meant when she said I had held a wake for Audrie. She laughed and said that a wake was a party held for a person after they are dead. Georgiannia said I had taught her to have sex with the devil. That she had had sex with the devil many times. They twisted my faith in every way that they could.

The trial went on for several days. I became so confused while sitting in the witness stand that I was unable to think or answer questions asked of me.

George went to the bathroom. A police officer came in and asked for me. When I got outside of the courtroom, I was told George was having trouble in the bathroom. When we got to the bathroom, George was crawling out of the door. George crawled to the elevator, with me trying to help him up. Everyone came out of the courtroom. I asked if someone could please call an ambulance.

Vallerie and Carol came and shoved me against the wall, away from George, saying, "We are nurses; we can help."

Vallerie was trying to make him eat some candy. George tried to crawl away from them. George finally managed to whisper, "Leave me and my wife alone."

I heard Georgiannia and Joan laughing. Georgiannia said, "We will win now, for sure."

By this time, Vallerie had stepped away from George, and she also agreed that they would win. The ambulance came and took George to the hospital. George's blood sugar was in the 800s; candy might have killed him. The ambulance driver immediately started an IV and gave him some insulin.

The trial continued after George got out of the hospital. Georgiannia failed to take custody away from us. My daughter had nothing to do with me after that. Whenever I saw her, she was very hateful to me.

Audrie had a tonsillectomy and adenoidectomy done through outpatient care at St Francis Hospital. I put Audrie in daycare. She seemed to love it; the daycare continued to help her learn to read better.

Georgie got married to Frank Welton. They had a baby girl they named Coleen.

My brother, Elijah, passed away. No one had enough money to bury him. The funeral home would not even embalm him. I was not notified until a week after his death. Mother told them if they did not notify me, she would hitchhike to me. She said, "Get hold of Frances; she will take care of things."

Rose Maria then let Mother call me. I caught the next flight out, taking Audrie with me. When I got there, Elijah was black and he stank when they put him out for us to view. The funeral home director said that all we could do was cremate him. I paid the bills.

Mother was upset that Elijah had to be cremated. But she was also happy that he had been taken care of. She insisted that his ashes be buried, and this was done. She also wanted me to have my hair done for the funeral.

Tommy took me to a beauty salon. On the way to the salon, he insisted on knowing who he was. He accused me of lying to him all his life. Tommy insisted that I tell my life story to his congregation, some of whom I knew from when I lived in Oregon. I refused to do this.

Tommy and Rose Maria had been talking to my brothers. They told them some of the things that had happened when we were kids, and they had told them that Rose Maria and Tommy were sister and brother, which was not true. My brothers told my son half-truths. Instead of being ashamed, my son was proud of what he thought – that he was a Patten.

I could not tell my son that he did not belong to my father because I did not know. I could tell him that Rose Maria was not a Patten. I had always believed that Tommy belonged to my father, but I could not prove it. Anyway, I did not want Tommy to know this. I refused my son's request. He got so angry that I told him to take me back to Mother's, without getting my hair done. I was so angry; I just wanted to leave.

When I got there, I started packing. I called Portland to see when the next plane was leaving. The plane wouldn't leave until the next morning. I called a cab to take me to Portland. Mother wanted to know what was going on. I couldn't tell her, so I just said nothing. Tommy came in and Mother asked him why I was leaving. She told Tommy that I had called a cab.

Tommy called the cab company back and canceled my cab saying, "I will drive you. What time does your plane leave?"

At supper that night, Tommy sat at the table calling himself a Patten and claiming to be proud of it. I was so ashamed; I just wished I could die. If my son only knew what I couldn't tell him, he wouldn't be acting like such a fool. My half-sister, Rose, was also claiming to be a Patten.

They said, "We are brother and sister. Why don't you just tell us the truth?" But we were not brother and sister.

I got up from the table and I went outside. I couldn't listen to their stupidity any longer. What had put this nonsense in their heads in the first place?

I left the next morning before the funeral, not telling Mother why. My son and Rose Maria sat in the front seat of the car, and I sat in the back. My son did not speak to me the whole two hours it took to drive to the airport. My feelings were hurt.

I heard nothing from Rose Maria or Tommy until Rose Maria called and said, "I am taking care of Mother and Aunt Lois. Mother has had several strokes. She is all right now. My transmission has gone out in my car. I need three thousand dollars to fix it. I have to have transportation to get Mother to and from the doctors. Also, I need transportation to keep food in the house. Can I borrow the money?"

I sent her the money. After all, she was taking care of my mother and I needed to help make her as comfortable as I could for as long as she lived.

The only time I heard from a family member was when they needed something. It got to the point where my husband began to resent them. When I received a call from any of them and my husband answered the phone, he would say, "Who is it and what do you want? How much money this time?" Then he handed the phone to me. To hear my family talk about George, he was a very bad man. I couldn't blame him for the way he felt. My family had been using us for years.

Chapter THIRTY

WHEN TIMMY WAS seventeen he moved in with Sally. Timmy admitted to us that they were a couple. He admitted that they had been having sex since he was 14. He said that if we tried to do anything about it, they would deny that she had ever touched him. I couldn't comprehend how a woman in her fifties could have sex with a fourteen-year-old boy. I called her "Antic Bitch." Timmy lived with her for three years.

Then Timmy met Misty, who had three children by another man. They got married and Misty became pregnant with their first child. Timmy, our son, said, "I need eight thousand dollars for her prenatal care. We have no insurance, and a doctor won't touch her without the money in advance."

George and I gave him eight thousand dollars, which took almost all we had. We learned later that they had used the money to redecorate their house. Timmy filed for bankruptcy, and then bragged to me that he didn't have to pay us back. He said, "The law says you lost your money because I have filed bankruptcy." That was the last time we accepted behavior like this again.

It was about this time that I found three bags of what I thought was marijuana in Christopher's closet. I told him he had to leave our home. I took the weed and dumped it in an industrial garbage container. When I threatened to call the police, Christopher admitted that Vallerie and he had planted weed on the property where George owned an old building that he was using as a garage. I hired our mechanic to get rid of it. He said that he took it out in the country and burned it so no one could smoke it.

Christopher moved in with my son, Timmy, and his wife. Timmy brought Christopher back to my house and dumped his clothes in the middle of my living room floor. He called me all kinds of filthy names.

Timmy's wife said, "I have been in four different mental institutions, and you are the craziest person I have ever met. Christopher is your responsibility. You can't throw him out without a court order and that will take months. You have to keep him." I just threatened to call his parole officer. I will not have drugs in my life.

One day after work, the Dallas police called. They asked if a Frances Armbrust lived there, and I said I was speaking. There was a pause. They asked if I had named a daughter after myself. I said no. The police then ask me if I knew of anyone that would be carrying my identification. I immediately thought about Debbie, but I told them that she was a young woman.

The caller said that they had found a body that was so mangled they could not tell the age of the victim. The police said the body had been shot in the back of the head at least 30 times. It had no face left. It had been shot in the torso at least 60 times. I asked them if it was possible to run a fingerprint check. I was told the policeman didn't know; that the body was in bad shape; she had been shot with a machine gun. They believed that it was gang-related because the car had been physically tipped over into a ditch in an attempt to hide it. The police said it took more then one person to do that.

I told the police that I knew Debbie's fingerprints were on file because she had been arrested before. I asked them to call me back if it proved to be Debbie. I also asked them to give me the chance to tell my sister first. Because she had heart trouble, I wanted to soften the blow as much as was possible.

Delores was in North Carolina with Judy at the time. The police called back; it was Debbie. I called Delores and talked first to Delores and then to her son-in-law. Their biggest worry seemed to be that they did not have clothes for the funeral.

Delores called the next day and said she needed fifteen hundred dollars to cremate Debbie and have her remains sent to Seminole. She also gave me her son-in-law's measurements for a suit and his shoe size. She gave me her dress and shoe size, and Judy's dress and shoe size. Judy had three boys and a girl. She gave me their sizes, as well as Carlos' sizes. She asked if I would buy their clothes and take them to Seminole, Oklahoma, the following Tuesday. I agreed to do this.

They were planning to drive and it would take a few days. She asked me to get the money to her as quickly as I could. Delores figured it would take about five days for me to get the money to her and for Dallas to send Debbie's remains to Oklahoma. They felt they had plenty of time to drive. I waited for her to call and tell me she was there before I started down. I had no choice but to take Alice and Audrie with me; Delores knew this.

I sent the money and went shopping for their clothes. I had the clothes in Seminole on time. I was asked to stay for the funeral. We had to wait three days for Debbie's remains. There was no funeral. They dressed up and took Debbie's ashes and scattered them over Curly's grave. Carlos did not want to touch his mother's ashes. Delores slapped him in the face a couple of times, called him a baby and made him take his mother's ashes in his hands and sprinkle them on his grandfather's gravesite. I felt very much out of place and used.

Delores and Judy tried to keep their children away from Audrie. Audrie got angry and slammed the door, accidentally hurting a puppy. Judy wanted to whip her, but I wouldn't allow it. Everyone got upset with me and told me what a brat she was. I didn't see it that way. I believed the adults were being unfair.

It was a hard few days for Audrie. Every time she tried to play with a child, an adult called the child away from her. They didn't mind asking for my help, but they were so prejudiced they could not tolerate my little granddaughter. She needed to be allowed to play with the other children that were present. I felt very hurt, and so did Audrie. I took Audrie and went home.

A few weeks later, Delores and Carlos showed up at our door saying they had no place else to go. Delores and Judy had a fight and Judy threw her out. Delores refused to allow Carlos to be in the same room as Audrie.

Delores home-schooled Carlos. I got so tried of hearing her yell at him and beat him that I suggested putting him in the private school I had Audriannia in. I told Delores she could help me at the cab stand, and she liked this idea. While we were enrolling Carlos in school she said, "You will have to pay for the private school," in front of the administrator. Even though I knew she had thirty thousand dollars in a bank bag at home, I really wasn't surprised. This was the kind of thing that Delores did to George and me all the time.

One morning I went to work. About 10:00 a.m., Timmy and Misty came in. They wanted me to pay Timmy fifteen dollars an hour to stay home and take care of Misty and her children. I refused to do this. They cursed, calling me a "crazy, mother-fucking witch" and everything else they could think of, while both pounded their fists on my desk.

Everyone in the office came running to see what was happening. My dispatcher asked if I wanted her to call the police. I said, "No, they will calm down in a bit."

When all of my employees went back to their offices, Timmy picked me up in his arms, carried me outside, and threw me in the sand. He said, "Go home and tell Dad not to come to work. I am taking over the business now, and I don't want you or Dad here getting in my way. I intend to make a lot of changes."

I carried a set of keys around my neck. I unlocked the door and went back into the business. Timmy was sitting at my desk. I said, "Son why don't you just bide your time. Your father and I are not going to live forever."

Timmy said, "Yeah, but you are not dying fast enough to suit me. I want the cab company now."

We fired our son. That was a very hard thing for us to do.

Two months later, he came to us, crying. He was about to lose his house, and his children were hungry. He could not find a job because his parents had fired him – that is what he told us. We took pity on him and hired him back. He continued to refuse to do as we wanted in our business, and we found he was taking money under the table from some drivers. He gave them the best orders for a certain percentage of their income, which was unfair to the other drivers.

I asked that his wife stay out of the business because it was bad enough for Timmy to act like that. She would come into the business and Timmy would show off for her, and she would also curse, scream and pound on my desk with her fist. Timmy shoved me against the wall several times. They never physically hurt me, but they set a bad example for our employees. We could never get it through Timmy's head that we owned the business and he worked for us.

I was tired of this kind of behavior. It caused our drivers, as well as my office help, to disrespect me. I couldn't run a business with everyone disrespecting me. Our sons were rude to the customers and drivers. Neither George nor I could make them understand they were ruining our business. When we tried, Timmy cursed us like he was a sailor. Christopher also said, "Fuck you," and continued to do as he pleased.

Georgiannia and Frank wouldn't get off their butts to do anything. In fact, we had a couch in my office that made down into a bed. Frank came to work to sleep. That was all he would do all day, unless he was working on his car or his mother's car. He took parts for their cars from our garage and never paid for them. I couldn't keep office help because Georgiannia was hateful to them, and so they quit. I had a hard time keeping up with everything. George had his hands full taking care of his sister, Alice.

While I was running back and forth to California, trying to help care for my mother, George put a young man in the office who literally stole us blind. When I left, we had $300,000 in the bank. When I got back, we had $20,000 in the bank. No one could account for where the money had gone. All my books were messed up. I couldn't make heads or tails out of them. I was forced to hire an accountant to straighten out our business. Even the accountant couldn't find where the money had gone.

This young man George hired had seemed very nice and willing to please us. Beware of people who are trying to "kiss your ass" — they may have something else in mind every time.

I believe it is a mistake for parents who own a business to hire their children. It doesn't seem to work out very well. I am looking forward to being able to retire and hand that business over to our sons. At that time, they will learn how much work a business really takes.

Chapter THIRTY-ONE

ONE DAY GEORGIE came to us and said, "I want Audrie. She is old enough to help me do housework, and I need her to watch Coleen."

Georgie was expecting another child. She said she would be going to court to break our guardianship. We talked to our lawyer. Our lawyer said that because she had married and had another child, the judge would rule in Georgie's favor. Also, the judge would not care what Georgie's reasons for wanting Audrie were. We would not be able to prove what her reasons were. Our lawyer told us it would be better to let Audrie go and live with Georgie rather than to break the guardianship. She told us to talk to Georgie and see if she would agree to this.

Georgie agreed to do this, but only on her terms, which were unreasonable. She would agree if I would give both Frank and her a job, paying them each ten dollars an hour. Also, I would have to buy Audrie's clothes and allow Frank to fix their cars and his parents' car at our garage. If we did all of this, then we could see Audrie every weekend.

We gave Georgie what she asked for. This worked for a few weeks. After a few weeks, Georgie would say, "Audriannia is being punished," or "We have planned a family outing." So we didn't see her very often the whole four years they had her. We missed her terribly. We had no idea that she was being mistreated.

Georgie called the cab stand one day and asked if we had picked up Audrie and Coleen. We hadn't picked up the kids; they were missing. I asked her if she had called the police, and she said they had not. They had just noticed them gone. It was two in the afternoon when she called. I alerted all the cab drivers in Wichita to watch for them. Most of the drivers knew Audrie. Georgie called the police, and I called the police.

A truck driver had picked the girls up on I-35 at 8:00 that morning. Georgiannia claimed Audrie had run away. What had really happened was that Coleen was throwing a fit to eat. Audrie said they could not find anything in the house to eat. She went in and woke her mother for help and Frank spanked her. A little while later, Coleen started throwing everything she could find on the floor. Audrie again woke her mother and Frank spanked her again. So Audrie made each of them a bottle of ice water and tried to walk to the cab company, down I-35, the only way she knew how to get there because that was the way that I drove to work every morning. She was coming to me so that I could feed her little sister. The girls spent three days in the children's home because Audrie was only trying to get food for her little sister.

Later, when Audrie was at my house and had told me what happened, I told Audrie I would show her how to fix something for Coleen to eat when her parents were sleeping. I proceeded to fix grilled cheese sandwiches in the microwave.

Audrie put her hands on her hips and said, "Grandma, I can't do that. Our bread is all green and crumbly where the mice have been in it. I can't feed that stuff to Coleen."

After that, I noticed bruises on Audrie's breasts; she was just beginning to develop. Audrie said she did not know how they got there. One time, Audrie complained that her chest hurt. I looked and there were several bruises on her breasts. They looked like fingerprints. Audrie denied that anyone was touching her there. I called Georgie and talked to her. Georgie told me it was from carrying her heavy book bag back and forth to school, so I bought her a book bag with wheels. There would be no excuse for marks on her breasts now. Those bruises stayed on her for a long time.

One evening after I picked Carlos up from school, I took him to the cab company. He went out in the garage and found a can of black spray paint. He sprayed the mechanic's truck and the white part of some of our cabs. He drew a picture of a stick person and wrote his name under it on a small trailer we had in the yard. This child painted everything within his sight. He was just being a kid, but he needed to learn that this was called vandalism, and was against the law. People went to jail for doing this kind of thing. Delores didn't see it that way.

When George saw this, he was not very happy. We could not use the cabs he had messed up. They had to be repainted again before they were allowed to be on the streets. This was a city law. This put our drivers out of work. It cost us money in not being able to rent the cabs, plus it cost a thousand dollars per car to repaint.

George came in my office, where Delores was sitting. He had Carlos by the nape of the neck. He told Delores if he ever saw Carlos in the lot with his cars again, he would "spank his ass." This made Delores angry, and she denied that Carlos had done such a thing. But when we got home, she took a belt to Carlos, telling him that this was what we had wanted her to do. She whipped him that morning and night, telling him she had to whip him because that was what we wanted. When I tried to stop her, she just whipped him harder.

One night, as she was beating on Carlos, Delores told him that his mother was a thief, a prostitute and a druggie, and that she had deserved to die the way she did. She said that she was thinking of taking him out in the field and just shooting him, and then shooting herself.

I guess I finally got up the nerve to say something to her. I said, "I have had enough. You are not to touch that child again. One of my part-time drivers is a police officer. I am going to ask him if he can fingerprint Carlos and see if he can get fingerprints off the can of paint used to mess up our cars. If Carlos's fingerprints are not on the can, George and I will apologize to Carlos. If his prints are on the can, you are to shut your mouth and quite mistreating the child. I am through tolerating this kind of abuse. He made a mistake. Forgive him for it; we have. I want this abuse stopped now, or I am going to call the police on you."

The next morning when I went to work, I met Tom, the police officer, in the parking lot. He had brought his wife to work, who at the time was my office girl. I asked him if he could lift fingerprints from the paint can. I explained to him why I wanted this done, and asked him if he could do this without getting Carlos into any kind of trouble. I told him that I just needed to make some peace in my family.

Tom said, "Yes, I can do this. I will bring the van to your parking lot and do the dusting on your premises."

At that time, Delores came running over to us, kicking Tom, the police officer, in the knees, and cursing at me. Tom said, "For your sister's sake, I will not arrest you."

Delores then got one of my cab drivers to take her to the school and pick up Carlos. When I got home, Delores and Carlos were gone. A box of rat poison was on the floor and my two little Pomeranian puppies were foaming green stuff from their mouths. I called my husband, and he came home and took them to a vet. We did save their lives, but it cost $900 per puppy. Her dog was locked upstairs, so it couldn't get to the rat poison. We were quite angry with her. George swore he would never again let her in our home to live.

A few days later, Delores called from Vesta's house and said, "Have the authorities been looking for me yet?" She then said, "My son-in-law's father will be over to pick up all my things. Pack them and have them sitting on the front porch for him."

I packed all of her stuff and carried it downstairs; she had used the upstairs bedroom. I stacked everything neatly on the porch, including a heavy oak desk. When he got there, all he took was the two-pound dog. She must have had a semi-truck full of stuff. We called the veteran's store and had them pick it all up.

Delores's daughter didn't want her mother to move back with her. Delores was upset because she said the flag that had covered her husband's casket was among her things I had gotten rid of. I tried to apologize, but she refused my apologies. There was nothing else I could do. To expect someone to pack your personal items and pay for shipping them to you is asking too much in the first place.

Delores went to California to stay with Rose Maria and Mother. Shortly after Delores moved to California, Rose Maria called and said, "I need $2,500."

I said, "I do not have it."

Rose Maria said, "Dig deep down in your bra; you will find it."

I did not send her any money. She hadn't told me that Delores was there, but Vesta had told me she went to California. Rose Maria wanted to rent a bigger apartment. Rose did not tell me this. I knew that Delores and Carlos were there, and I figured she needed it because of them. I learned why she wanted the money after I went to California — she had wanted it to support Delores and Carlos, and to buy some knickknacks to sell at a garage sale.

I knew Delores had money. I had taken her to the bank where she drew out $9,000 a day, until she had $33,000. I saw no reason why they should need financial help at this time.

Rose Maria said, "I am going to call you every month for her half of the rent; she refuses to help out with any expenses."

I said, "I can't support them any longer. I have been doing that for twenty years. It's your turn now."

I no longer felt that I owed it to Delores to support her and her grandson after they had poisoned my dogs and treated me so badly. George had said he wouldn't have them back in our home again. I refused to ask him to support them somewhere else. That didn't seem fair to me. Rose Maria, on the other hand, thought it was my responsibility.

I began to realize that I had repaid Delores many times over for her taking extra punishment for me when I couldn't make the quota in the fields that Father had set. I was tired of letting my family be a door mat for Delores anytime she decided she wanted to step on us. I had let her use my husband and me for years.

He had said, "Enough is enough. It stops here." I decided to honor his wishes. We had done all we could to help her. Help was not what she wanted; she wanted someone to take all the responsibility for her and her family, while she put forth no effort at all. I believed she had given up on herself and considered herself unable to do anything.

She had insisted that someone wait on Carlos and herself, giving them anything they desired. I was tired of all that nonsense. I realized she had suffered for me when we were children. However, I felt like I had paid my debt to her long ago.

Chapter THIRTY-TWO

I WAS NOT told at the time that Mother had had a stroke after Elijah's funeral, that she could not eat or drink and had to use a feeding tube. A few weeks later, while trying to get me to send them money, Delores called me and told me that Mother was in the hospital. She'd had a stroke and was not expected to make it.

Instead of sending money, I flew down to see what was going on. I learned that Mother had been having strokes for nine years. I found that Delores had refused to help Rose Maria care for Mother, and that Rose Maria could not care for Mother and Aunt Lois properly alone. I found that Rose Maria would sit Mother in a recliner chair and go out, staying for hours, knowing that Delores would not leave her room to even check on her. Delores told me that she was there to watch Mother suffer and die, that it was payback time. I learned Rose Maria wanted the money to buy a lot of knickknacks, so she could have garage sales and sell them.

I started flying between California and Wichita to share the burden of Mother's care. I'd fly home to do payroll and to pay my bills. I hired another office girl because Georgie would do nothing except visit with the drivers and get in the mechanic's way. Frank wasn't any help. I paid him to work on his car and his parents' car. I flew back and forth to California and helped care for Mother. I did this until Mother's doctor wanted to take her feeding tube out and let her starve to death. Mother was hard to take care of, but she still had her mind and spirits.

Delores deliberately caused me trouble with Mother by telling her things that she knew would upset her. Especially when Rose Maria was out, Delores told Mother we could give her food and drink if we wanted to. She just wanted to mistreat her because she wanted to be ornery.

Mother would then try to throw herself out of the chair by leaning too far forward, saying, "I will crawl to the toilet and drink out of the toilet if you don't give me a drink of water."

Delores knew that if I gave Mother anything to eat or drink it would kill her. Anything she took by mouth went into her lungs. To feed her by mouth would have killed her. Delores did and said things to make Mother fight us. But she would not help us or bathe care for her in any way. Rose Maria finally agreed to move Mother to Wichita when the doctor wanted to starve her to death.

Delores' grandson, Carlos, stole eight hundred dollars, my phone card and my driver's license from my purse. Delores gave me back my driver's license and phone card, but not the money. At that time, Delores moved back to her daughter Judy's home in North Carolina.

I have received one letter with no return address from her since she left California. She said, "I hope you are proud of yourself. You messed up my future life. My plans were to live with you and George the rest of my life. I was forced to adopt Carlos out to Judy and Dickie. [Dickie is Judy's husband.] I had hoped you would leave the cab company to Carlos. Because of you, I have nothing I can call my own."

That was the last I heard from, Delores. I guess she is still mad at me.

Rose Maria and I made plans to move Mother to Wichita, Kansas. I called my husband and asked him if he would try to find a duplex and rent both sides of it, and to make sure that a wheelchair would go through the doors. Rose Maria would not live in George's mother's old house. We did not have decent furniture. It also had too many steps to get Mother in and out of in the house. George bought a duplex, instead of renting one. I would have liked to help him pick out the house, but it couldn't happen that way.

The last time I had gone home, I brought Audrie back to California with me. She seemed quiet and withdrawn. The only one she seemed to relate to was Mother, and Mother enjoyed her.

After I was at Mother's about a week, Rose Maria received a phone call. She talked for some time, and then she said that La Donna's mother was sitting there beside her. She said, "I want you to tell her what you just told me."

Rose Maria handed me the phone. The man on the other end of the line said, " I am one of four men who are supposed to come to Rose Maria's house." He gave me the address, and told me that he was to snatch Audrie from the alley where she played.

He then said, "You had no right to take her daughter away from her. We are supposed to get her tonight, but La Donna has not shown up. We are wondering where she is. I'm glad I called your sister. Rose Maria says Audrie is not La Donna's daughter."

I could not believe what I was hearing. I accused this man of trying to play some kind of a joke on us. I asked him who he was.

He said, "I am a school teacher in Phoenix, Arizona." He gave me my name and my husband's name; our address and phone number; and the name, address and phone number of my business. He told me the names of our sons and daughters, and their addresses and phone numbers; and the names and addresses of sisters and brothers, too. He told me what time my office girl made the deposit for my business every day.

This was kind of scary. I quit letting Audrie play outside. I was frightened that this man might be telling the truth. I felt I could take no chances. She could no longer play outside without supervision.

I assured this man that La Donna was not Audrie's mother, and that my daughter, La Donna, must be crazy. I explained that Audrie was born in 1990. At that time, La Donna had left her husband and three little children and no one even knew where she was. I think he believed me. I learned after that incident that La Donna did strange things on the Internet.

Audrie and I were to take Mother to Wichita by plane. Rose Maria was to drive a truck with their personal belongings and what furniture that we could get help to load. One of my nieces would assist her in the driving. I had never driven a large truck. Rose Maria had; she had driven trucks in the Army.

I needed Mother's hospital bed set up and ready for her when I got there. George sent Frank down to get Mother's bed. Frank came with a friend of his in a company vehicle. He said they wanted to stop at some casinos on the way back.

I said, "Oh, no you won't. I am sending Audrie back to Wichita with you."

After that phone call we had received from the supposed teacher, I was afraid to let Audrie play outside anymore. I thought this might be safer. I had to stay long enough to help Rose Maria pack and load the truck. I wouldn't be able to watch Audrie closely enough. I didn't want her to come up missing and never see her again, so I watched her carefully.

Frank had an accident on the way home. He rolled the van over about five times the police said. He totaled it and damaged Mother's bed. The hospital bed almost killed Frank's friend. Thank God that Audrie was in the front seat. Frank's friend was in the hospital for almost a year. We were responsible because it was a company vehicle, even though it was against company policy to have anyone not affiliated with the company riding in a company car. George did not know Frank was taking someone with him. This was against the law in our city. Our insurance finally got this lawsuit taken care of.

When I got ready to buy the plane tickets, the doctor told us that I would need a medical helicopter to take Mother any distance because she might die on the plane. We decided to take her by car. The doctor told us what to do in case she died on the way. Someone had to take care of Aunt Lois and Mother. We took the back seats out of the van, and put Mother's La-Z-Boy recliner in the back of the van. We asked Elijah's daughter to help us drive, and she was more than happy to do so.

I couldn't keep a continuous drip going in her feeding tube. I fed Mother with a syringe every 15 minutes. One night, we rented a room. We almost dropped Mother trying to get her out of the car. We made the trip kind of like "The Beverly Hillbillies." I believe my mother loved this excitement. It reminded Mother of early days and perked up her spirits. She watched the scenery and sometimes commented on it. She acted like I did when we first left Chicago when I was a child. She still had her mind and talked about her life in different places she had lived. Mother talked to me more on this trip than she had ever talked to me in my life.

George had things ready for us when we got to Wichita. He bought a duplex that was only a year old so we would have a decent place to care for Mother. We put Mother, Aunt Lois and Rose Maria on one side of the duplex, and we took the other side. I spent most of my time on Mother's side. Mother's grandchildren, great-grandchildren and great-great-grandchildren got to benefit from meeting Mother. Some of them were old enough to remember her, even if they really never knew their great-great-grandmother.

Mother thought I had bought a mansion for her. In her whole life, she had never had the pleasure of living in a house as nice as this one. She was so proud of the house that she bragged about it to everyone who came to the door. It pleased me that I could bring her this much joy in her last days. One of our neighbors was a doctor. He came to visit and listened to her talk when he could. He also perked up Rose Maria's and my spirits, too. We could ask the questions we needed to ask and get an honest answer from him. He gave me samples of my heart medicine when he could, and he kept check on my blood pressure. He gave us a lot of mental support. We felt better knowing he was just next door.

We gave George's mother's house to Teresa, George's daughter. She needed it the most. She had gotten another divorce and was having a hard time caring for her three wonderful children. She is a hard worker and tries hard to support her children, but unfortunately she has bad taste in men. This causes her a lot of trouble. I hope someday she will find a man she can stay with.

Chapter THIRTY-THREE

AS SOON AS I got Mother settled in, I wanted to see Audrie. Georgie said she was being punished and I could not see her. The next time I asked, my daughter said they had family plans. The next Sunday, I called when she did not bring her over as promised, and told her that if she were not delivered to my house within the hour, I would come and get her. Georgie did not bring her over. I went to their home and they were not there.

Georgie brought Audrie over about 9:30 on Sunday night. Audrie had to go to school the next morning, so I could not visit with her. Georgie said she was to ride the bus home from school the next day. This left me with no time at all to spend with Audrie. I was not happy at all. I talked to her for a few minutes and sent her to bed.

The next morning as I was driving Audrie to school, I asked her why she was not minding Georgie. She told me that she did mind Georgie but got angry when her mother expected her to let her little sisters get into her things. Yet Georgie would not let them get into her own things. Audrie was tired of getting into trouble because of the two younger girls. I laughed at her and told her that was what little sisters were for. She needed to put her things where they couldn't get them.

Then I asked her why she was refusing to mind Frank? Audrie stiffened up in the car seat, crossed her arms and got a look of stone on her face. She said, "I will not mind Frank; he does bad things to me."

I asked her what kind of bad things, and she would not answer. I asked her every kind of question I could think of, such as, "Are you mad because Frank makes you clean your room, or brush your teeth?" I asked every question I could think of like this. She just shook her head no, with the same stone look on her face.

When I entered the school parking lot I told her, "Honey, I can't help you if you do not tell me what is wrong."

She still did not say anything; she just started to cry. After I parked the car, I asked her if Frank was touching her in places he should not be touching her.

She moved her hands all over her breasts, and then she said, "This is what he does to me." She put her hands in her panties and said, "He puts his fingers in me down here." Then she said, "I let him do these things to keep the peace. But I will not put that thing in my mouth."

I held her as she cried. She said they had told her she could not tell me because it would just cause trouble. When I asked her who told her not to tell me, she would say no more, no matter what I asked her. I held her a few more minutes as she cried.

Then I walked her to the office to get a pass for her because she was now late. After Audrie left the office, I asked if I could speak to the counselor. I explained who I was and told her that I had guardianship of Audrie. She could find nothing in their system indicating this. I told her what Audrie had said to me and the school counselor called SRS. She told me to go get the guardianship papers I had on Audrie. She also said that since we had guardianship, Audrie should be legally living with us. I went home and got the guardianship papers. She told me not to send Audrie back to her mother's house.

I didn't talk to Audrie anymore until she spoke to a social worker. I didn't want to influence what she had to say. I believed someone had touched her, but I did not believe it was Frank. Audrie seemed to have too good a relationship with Frank for this to happen. I believed it was Frank's father, and Audrie was afraid of the man. This man had called Audrie a little whore and a prostitute when Audrie was only eight years old. I had told Georgiannia to keep him away from her.

I went to work. Georgie was our employee. At lunch, I told Georgie that I needed some clothes for Audrie. Since I always bought Georgie's lunch, we were in my car. Instead of driving to the restaurant, I drove toward Georgie's house.

Georgie said, "She does not need any clothes. Audrie is coming home this evening."

I did not want to say anything to Georgie until SRS had a chance to investigate. I told her that she, herself, had told me Audrie was having trouble minding them. I wanted to keep her a couple of weeks. That maybe I could find out what the problem was and be of some help.

When my daughter tried to argue, I told her, "Audrie is not going home at this time. I need some clothes for her to wear to school and I'm going to get them. I'm going to keep Audrie a few weeks." I proceeded on to Georgie's house.

As I continued to drive toward my daughter's house, my daughter said, "Frank has not touched that child. If anyone has, it was Timmy. She worships the ground he walks on. Timmy is like a god to Audrie. Besides, Audrie likes it; she asks for it. She flirts with Frank all the time. Anything that has happened to that child is her fault. What do you expect from a man when a child keeps asking for it. She is the one who needs to be punished for causing Frank to do these things to her."

Oh God, how I wanted to slap her in the face. I told her, " I didn't accuse anyone of doing anything to Audrie, now did I? So now what are you talking about?"

At this point, I knew in my heart that my daughter knew what was happening to Audrie. I couldn't prove it because I knew she would deny saying this to me. I got so upset that I ran into the curb and tore up the running board on my car. I felt like parking the car and beating the tar out of my daughter.

I got to Georgie's house and found a few clothes for Audrie. I walked through clothes knee-deep all the way to the children's room. There was moldy pizza sitting on the couch, and the sink was piled high with dirty dishes that had food dried on them. So, I didn't bother to get very many clothes. I figured I would just buy her what she needed.

I was confused about what Georgie had said, so I asked Audrie that afternoon when I got home from work where her mother was when Frank did these bad things to her.

Audrie said, "Sometimes she is at the store or over at Frank's parents' house. Sometimes she is cooking supper or taking a bath."

Then I asked Audrie, "Where in the house does he do these things to you?"

Audrie answered, "On the couch and in his bedroom. When we are outside, we get behind the car."

Later at the garage, I became even more confused when Frank said, as we were talking, "Audrie walked in the bathroom on me one time and wanted to touch my private parts, and I let her."

At this point, I was quite sure in my mind that Audrie was telling the truth. SRS called and wanted to talk to Audrie.

I told Audrie I was taking her to a woman called a social worker. She would need to tell the social worker the things she had told me. Audrie talked to several social workers after that. She said very little to the first social worker. Audrie did talk some to the second one.

The social worker said, "I need times and dates that Audrie can't give me."

Frank took a lie detector test and passed it. Frank was on heart blockers, and I don't believe he told them about that before he took the lie detector test.

We talked to our lawyer. She advised me against firing Georgie or Frank. She said, "They can sue you if you fire them."

Georgie quit two weeks later. Frank worked for eight months before he quit. At the same time, Audrie seemed to hate me and anything else that had the smell of authority to it. Georgie visited her every Sunday. She encouraged Audrie in her actions. I heard her tell Audrie that she did not have to listen to George or me, and there was nothing we could do about it. She told her that we had to keep her and take care of her, no matter what she did. Even if she killed one of us, the one left alive would have to pay for her monthly care. I also heard her encourage Audrie to run away. Georgie tried to make things as hard as she possibly could for us to raise Audrie.

This child hung on to every word her mother said. She tried hard to earn her mother's love. I learned more about what Frank had done to Audrie over the next year. The problem was that one day Audrie would tell me something and the next day she would deny it. I could not get her to tell a social worker or our lawyer what she had told me. When I mentioned these conversations to her later, she would deny having told me.

I took her to several counselors. All of them agreed that something had gone on between Frank and Audrie. I will never know what happened between them because she promised her mother, Georgiannia, she would not tell. Even after the entire ordeal the child went through, Audrie is loyal to her mother. I can understand this, where most people can't. Sometimes I wonder if this gene is inherited. But after what Georgie and Frank said, I have no doubt of Frank's guilt.

What I have learned about social workers up to this point is to stay the hell away from them. If you're not already having problems with your child, they will see to it that you start.

Audrie had made no progress in school since Georgie took her. Her reading level was at third grade, eighth month. So I put her in e-school through the board of education. She can now read on her own grade level. This year I gave her the choice of going back to regular school. She chose e-school. I pray that she does well. She will if we can keep her out of the chat rooms on her computer.

My sister, Vesta, who'd had cancer, had the opportunity to meet with Mother before she died. Vesta passed away in April 2003. Mother was aware of what had happened. She asked me to go to her funeral in her place and to give her grandchildren and great-grandchild her love.

Rose Maria, Audrie and I went to my sister's funeral. We did not feel welcome. We didn't go to the family gathering after the funeral. I did not drink and Audrie was a minor. Everyone else drank. We felt very much out of place and did not feel that we would be missed. Instead, we went home. It was a long drive after being up all day.

Rose Maria moved two of my half-sister Loretta's daughters from California into her side of the duplex. George and I were paying $2,600 a month for this duplex. We gave Rose Maria at least 200 a month for things she said Mother needed that she could not get. We bought groceries for Rose Maria. Yet she couldn't understand why we objected to her taking Loretta's girls to places like Kohl's and Penny's to buy their clothes.

Audrie helped care for Mother when I had to bathe her, change her diaper, feed her or just when Mother was being difficult. Mother seemed to enjoy Audrie. Audrie could do things with her that none of the rest of us could. They needed each other.

I was glad to have had the time I spent with Mother. The night before she passed away, we talked some about the past. She said Father would have killed her if she said or did anything about what he did to us girls.

Mother passed away in May 2003. As she was dying, she reached her arms out to hug me. I bent over her bed, and held her head and shoulders in my arms. She whispered, "I am sorry I was afraid to help you children. I love you."

And then she was gone. I believe that was when I finally truly forgave my mother for all the things she had done to me in my life. Mother lived for two years and eight months with us in Wichita. I believe that she enjoyed her time with me.

Six weeks after Mother's death, a semi-truck hit George's nephew head-on while he was on his motorcycle, killing him instantly. He had been on his way to a family reunion. Raymond often had gone water skiing with our children while they were growing up. Everyone missed Raymond.

After Vesta's, Mother's and Raymond's deaths, Audrie started exposing herself in public places when George and I were not around or not looking. She talked back and refused to do anything she was asked to do. She soon learned that she was stronger than I was. As time went by, Audrie began to behave a lot better. She does not talk back nearly as much now. I consider her to be a very good girl in every respect. Except, like all teenagers, she is lazy and will not clean her room.

After Mother's passing, Rose Maria wanted to move. Loretta's family, including her grandchildren and her daughter's boyfriend from California, her son, his wife and four children, wanted to move into the other half of our duplex.

I said, "No." Loretta's husband had been in and out of prison for selling and taking drugs. Her oldest daughter and boyfriend were on drugs. There would be at least 18 people in a three-bedroom apartment, most of whom took drugs, drank and fought. I didn't want to live in such an environment.

I told Rose Maria that I was sorry that we couldn't support the whole family. This made her angry and she became very insulting. She accused George and me of being selfish. She said, "You have plenty and should share what you have with the family."

What she didn't understand was that we had plenty for ourselves if the rest of the family quit holding out their hands. Another thing she didn't think about was that we worked hard for what we had, while the rest of them sat around, did nothing and drew welfare all their lives. Work was a foreign word to them.

Two months after Mother passed away, I told Rose Maria she needed to start helping us make the house payment. She had gotten a job and was saving money to go to Hawaii for a vacation. I tried to explain to her that I had been doing without my medicine for some time because I couldn't afford to buy it. She stood out in my driveway and screamed that it was not her responsibility to buy my medicine. I was ashamed; I'm sure the neighbors heard her.

But what the neighbors didn't know was that we had been supporting Rose Maria for the last few years. I believed it was my responsibility to see that Mother had what she needed during her last days. Rose Maria had power of attorney over Mother and Aunt Lois. In order to help Mother, we had to do what Rose Maria wanted us to do. Rose Maria moved out in the night. I have not heard from her since. I only know that she lives somewhere in Wichita and that she drives a city bus.

We later learned that Rose Maria got $800 a month in a retirement check from the military; Mother had gotten better than $600 a month Social Security and Lois had gotten $600 a month Social Security. In addition, Rose Maria got paid eight dollars an hour, 40 hours a week to care for Mother. She was also getting paid eight dollars an hour, 22 hours a week to care for Lois. She was getting paid a total of 62 hours a week, at eight dollars an hour, for doing what I was actually doing most of the time. She was bringing in a lot more money than we were.

George and I paid ourselves $10 an hour, and we helped every member of our family. Sometimes George would have to drive a cab at night after he had worked all day in the office just to be able to afford the things we needed to live. My family treated us like we were servants, put here for the sole purpose of caring for their needs, wants and desires. I no longer feel like it is my job to please everyone, and have to accept that, as a result, they think I'm a bad person.

George plays pool three times a week. When he doesn't play pool, he doesn't come home from work until late. When he does come home, he will not talk much to me. I have learned that he can't handle stress because of his diabetes and his heart condition. He avoids trouble at all cost. I am trying to understand and not get my feelings hurt.

We made a trip to New Jersey to pick up a motor home that George had purchased off of the internet. After we got back, George's body began to swell. When I commented to him about looking heavier, he said, "I am just gaining weight."

One night he put his foot on the bed while taking off his socks. I saw how swollen his feet were and I said, "We are calling the doctor in the morning."

George was hospitalized with congestive heart failure. The doctor said he'd had a heart attack earlier. I am sure, in my mind, that it was when that highway patrol stopped us on the way back from New Jersey.

George's heart is 85 percent blocked in four places. His veins are so restricted the doctors couldn't even get a one-millimeter camera through his veins. All they can do is give him blood thinners. George stayed six days in the hospital.

I have spoken of his faults, but if I had to stand in front of a mirror and count my faults, I promise you that, compared to me, George looks like an angel. He is still plugging along at the cab company, and trying to help Audrie understand the importance of her education. We are still taking care of Alice, George's Down syndrome sister. As I get older, it is getting harder and harder every day for me to care for her, but I am grateful for the blessings I have had, and for almost always being able to follow my heart, no matter how difficult.

THE END

EPILOGUE

I WROTE MY life story hoping I might be able to help someone else who is in the situation I was in. I hope to prevent someone from giving up, as I almost did a few times.

As a child, I started out as being someone's property. Then I went to having no rights at all. My father deliberately kept my siblings and me ignorant. We weren't allowed to talk to anyone other than each other. This way, we couldn't tell anyone what was happening in our household. We weren't allowed to go to school. We couldn't learn that Father was teaching us to do wrong things. We couldn't learn how other families lived. We were kept isolated from the rest of the world. We were taught to hate even each other. Work and sex were all we knew, and most of us were too young to understand either of these things. We just tried to survive each day.

As we grew older, Father abused us horribly – physically, mentally, emotionally and sexually. He also let other men abuse us sexually, emotionally and mentally. My mother and Aunt Joe stood by and watched him, without interfering in any way. We knew no other life. My sister, Vesta, felt she could tolerate no more and tried to run away. Father and his friends tracked her down and caught her. Father nearly killed her. He wanted to make sure none of us other girls would try to run away and get help. This little plan did not work. Delores and I found the courage.

But Jehovah God gave me a heart. Somehow, He wrote what is right and what is wrong in it. My father tried hard to change the way I felt about things. He shamed me; he made fun of me; he cursed me, calling me all kinds of filthy names; and he beat me and taught my brothers how to beat me. He even raped me and aborted the child he had impregnated me with. When my sister explained to me what Father had done, I felt cheated. I felt like I did when Father took my doll away from me. I realized this would have been a live doll to me, but my heart felt empty. My heart hurt.

But Father couldn't keep me from following my heart. Instead, he made me realize I had to do something about what he was doing. I had to stop him from hurting the younger girls. And I could not afford to make the mistake Vesta did and get caught. My sister, Delores, and I started plotting our get-away. We were careful not to let anyone know what we were up to.

I will try to identify the ten steps I took to get out of the life my parents had made for me. If you are one of the abused ones, you may have to take different steps, but take steps no matter what!

Step one was to make workable plans.

Around the last of April or first week of May in 1952, Delores and I left home, knowing full well it could mean our lives if we were caught. We thought we were going to find our mother in Chicago. This was my *second step* to freedom. I was probably about 11 years old at the time. My sister, Delores, was about 13 or 14.

When I finally got brave enough to go against my sister, Delores', wishes and talk to Mrs. Christian, our caseworker, it was my *third step* to freedom.

My *fourth step* to freedom was when I let Mrs. Bermingham into my heart. Mrs. Bermingham showed me another way of life. She showed me feelings of kindness, patience, gentleness and love, which enabled me to be able to show these qualities to my sister's three babies when they needed it so badly. Mrs. Bermingham encouraged me to continue to follow my heart. No one else had ever done this; instead, I got beaten because of the way I felt.

She taught me that the feelings I had were good. I shouldn't ever be ashamed of them, but be proud of them, and I should have confidence in myself. She taught me there really is a God, and that He didn't promise that life would be fair or easy; he only promised to provide a way out of our problems for us. It is our responsibility to find that way for ourselves. God will not point it out to us. Last, but not least, she taught me the joy of learning, and that I needed an education to succeed in life.

Even though my mother forced this step on me, I consider *step five* to be when I was married to Rex Carter. I thought I hated my mother-in-law, Wealthy; we just got off on the wrong foot. When she took a shower in front of me, and then asked me to demonstrate what she had taught me, she embarrassed me in a way I never got over. The truth is that Wealthy taught me many things I had to know in order for my children and me to survive. She made me grow up, which is another thing I had to do. She watched my children while I took a typing class that she paid for. She helped feed my children while I was with her son, Rex. I have many things to thank her for, but it is too late. She passed away in 1969.

Step six was when, with the help of a wonderful stranger, I left the city of Chicago. I like to think of him as one of God's special people. It was not easy, I made many mistakes, but I learned to live on my own, with my children, against all odds.

I believe that *step seven* was when I accepted the help of the state of Oregon. The state offered to help me get my GED and tried to further my education. I accepted their help. I earned my GED, but I didn't stop there. I continued to further my education. Did you know you learn something new every day that you live?

Step eight was when I did not give up in Pendleton, Oregon, when the state listened to an angry, jealous young woman try to ruin my life. With the help of the whole Jehovah's Witness congregation, I escaped her clutches. Jehovah was again in my corner. An older couple, Elda and Lon, were a great deal of help to me there. My children and I loved them dearly.

Step nine was when I had the nerve to put my son, Tommy, in his place and when I bought that house on Terry Way in Del City, Oklahoma. These two things were kind of intertwined because I would not have bought the house if Tommy had not gotten too big for his britches. For some reason, Rex did not follow me there. The last time I saw him was when I left Pendleton, Oregon. That was truly a blessing for me.

Step ten was when I married my present husband, George. We have been married for 34 years and have had few problems. He has made my life a whole lot better. We do not curse or fight with one another; we never have. I finally learned what it meant to love a man.

Compared to the rest of the world, most of my children didn't turn out too badly. I am proud of them, and I love each and every one of them.

Tommy is an inhalation therapist. He married a registered nurse named Veronica. She is a very good young woman, and I love her very much. They own their own home. Financially, they are doing great. They have two sons and three granddaughters.

Carol stopped taking illegal drugs and has straightened out her life. I am very proud of her for having the courage to do this. I know it was not easy for her on many occasions. She married a young man named Gregg, and they have been married for 30 years. His personality is a lot like mine. He has a good job and 20 years in the military. They have two children, Angelica and James. They have two granddaughters by Angelica and one by James. They own their own home. Carol is a licensed practical nurse.

Phillip married a girl named Margie; they had two children and five grandchildren. They are divorced and wasted their lives fighting. Phillip is dying from cirrhosis of the liver and hepatitis C. He has had a stroke, and had a brain tumor removed.

Vallerie married a scientist named Kurt. She is a licensed practical nurse. They own their own home. This is Vallerie's second marriage, and Kurt is her high school sweetheart. They had no children together, but he helped raise Vallerie's two children from her first marriage, Kenny and Megan. They are financially well off. Vallerie's first husband was an alcoholic and has passed away. Vallerie and Kurt have one grandchild by Megan and three step-grandchildren by Kenny, who we count as grandchildren too.

La Donna married a very nice young man. They had three children. La Donna walked away and left them when they were infants. She is now an apartment manager and an "internet whore." She has chosen a hard life for herself. I worry about someone hurting her because of her lifestyle. She is 42 years old. I can no longer control what she does.

Georgiannia married a man named Frank, and they haven't done so well for themselves. They live from day-to-day and depend on other people to feed and support their children. She is an accountant, but works very little and gets no help from, Frank. They have two daughters together. Georgiannia also has an illegitimate daughter, Audriannia, whom I have custody of.

Christopher is not married. He has been very wild and got into a lot of trouble with the police over minor things, like driving without a license and drinking, He has now straightened out his life and is about to get his driver's license back. He works two jobs, hanging sheet rock and dispatching for our cab company, to pay off the fines he owes the city.

Timmy is now married to a young lady named Misty. She has three children from a previous marriage, and they have two daughters together. They own their own home. Timmy is general manger of our company.

Teresa, George's daughter, has been married four times, but is not married now. She has three children, a good job and she owns her own home. (George gave her his mother's house because she was alone with three children.) She gets by on her own without help and is doing a good job raising her children.

It looks as though most of my children have finally grown up and are doing well with their children. I should have known they would do all right for themselves. It was bound to turn out well for most of them. I tried too hard to raise them to be good people. The job of raising them was not an easy one. I had too much interference from everywhere I turned, it seems, but I can now breathe easy. – they have their own good lives.

We had thought that now that our children have grown we could relax a bit (ha ha!), but we still have our granddaughter, Audriannia, and George's sister, Alice, who has lived with us since her mother passed away in 1975.

Today George and I own a business. I had the opportunity to take some accounting classes at a vocational technology school. I also took a computer class in Oklahoma City. I stayed with my sister, Vesta, while in Oklahoma City. Today, I am writing this book. Tomorrow, I will find something else interesting to do. I have learned to never give up.

I tried to give up several times, but I am thankful there was always someone there to lift me up and give me the chance to find the way out that Jehovah God had provided for me. I believe He always provides a way out; we just have to find it. He will not point it out to us. It is up to us to find the things He provides for our health and happiness.

I guess what I'm trying to say is that sometimes it can take a long time, and you may have to go through a lot of hardships. But if you don't stop trying, you will eventually get where you need and want to be. Listen to what your heart is telling you; it is most likely right, and you should always follow it.

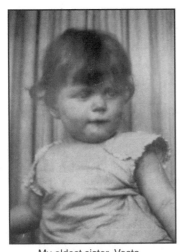

My oldest sister, Vesta –
about one year old.

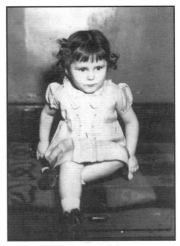

Me as a baby.

Back row, L-R: Delores, La Verne, Vesta; Front row, L-R: Orlaff, Orlando, Cathy,
Frances and Dennis. Grandmother took this picture after Susan's death.

I don't have any photos of my father, but this drawing shows how we viewed him – as some sort of evil monster.

This drawing shows how we were tied to bare bedsprings before being beaten by our father.

This drawing shows my sister, Delores, sitting in the coal bin in the basement when she was about five years old.

This drawing shows my father beating Delores on the front porch of our little house.

Me at age 15 – I was already married and had two children at the time this photo was taken.

My mother (L) and Aunt Marcella in Arizona, with Marcella's son, Ernie.

L-R: Bascom Carter (Rex's father); my son, Phillip, age one; my daughter, Carol, age two; Rex (the husband my mother sold me to); me at almost 17 years of age; my son, Tommy, age three.

Me with my son, Tommy, at the Lincoln Park Carousel in Chicago, July 1956. Tommy loved the merry-go-round.

Rex Carter playing with Phillip and Carol, March 1959.

My daughter, Vallerie, about age three, on a neighbor's tricycle at my sister Delores' house in Del City, Oklahoma.

La Donna (almost two) at the Lincoln Park Zoo in Chicago, just before we left.

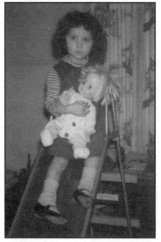

La Donna at about three years of age in Salem, Oregon – February 1967. It was not safe to let my children play outside because my husband, Rex, had found us. So I brought the slide inside the house; I didn't have much furniture anyway.

March 1967 – Here I am in Salem, Oregon, pretending to play the guitar. My children got quite a kick out of this.

L-R: La Donna, Vallerie, and Phillip at a Kingdom Hall gathering. (The woman standing behind Vallerie is a nurse; we called her Red.)

A Jehovah's Witness Assembly we attended in Eugene, Oregon.

A drawing of where we lived in Pendleton, Oregon.

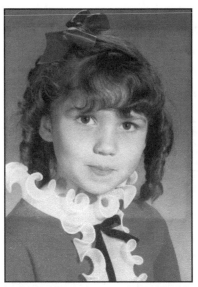

La Donna, four years old. She was really proud of her new dress.

My half-sister, Loretta Wilburn, in 1967.

My 1968 graduating class from nursing school in California. (I am sitting at the far left on the front row.) My children were so proud of me. At the celebration party afterward, I put on my first and only bathing suit. I was so embarrassed that I left the party.

My present husband, George, and our children. Seated, L-R: George Armbrust (age 45), our son, Timmy (9), and me (41). Standing, L-R: Our daughter, Georgiannia (11), and Christopher (10), the grandson we adopted.

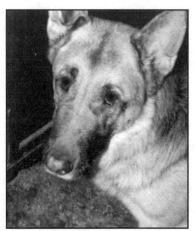

Our protection – his name is Rider.

My sister Delores' daughter, Debra. She was killed on a Dallas, Texas highway – shot in the head about 30 times and shot in the torso at least 60 times. She died at age 24, leaving behind a six-year-old son.

My mother (L) at age 79 and my Aunt Louise (67).

My brother, Elijah, who died from a heart attack in 1997 at age 50. He was an alcoholic who was never able to stop drinking.

This is Audriannia (Audrie), the grand-daughter I have custody of, at her kinder-garten graduation.

My mother at age 89 and Audrie, age 13. Audrie loved her great-grandmother and my mother loved her. Audrie was a big help when my mother was alive – helping to bathe, feed, toilet, and dress her.